CALLING NEW LEADERS

HOW LIVING YOUR CALLING WILL MAKE YOU AN INSPIRED LEADER OF THE MODERN WORLD

I0096312

"If you knew who walked beside you at all times, on the path that you have chosen, you could never experience fear or doubt again."
- Wayne W. Dyer

"Leadership is based on a spiritual quality - the power to inspire, the power to inspire others to follow."
- Vince Lombardi

CALLING NEW LEADERS

HOW LIVING YOUR CALLING WILL MAKE YOU AN INSPIRED LEADER OF THE MODERN WORLD

DR. L. CHRISTIAN DUPEROUZEL

CWP
Central West Publishing

Disclaimer
Every effort has been made by the publisher and author while preparing this book, however, no warranties are made regarding the accuracy and completeness of the content. The publisher and author disclaim without any limitation all warranties as well as any implied warranties about sales, along with fitness of the content for a particular purpose. Citation of any website and other information sources does not mean any endorsement from the publisher and author. For ascertaining the suitability of the contents contained herein for a particular lab or commercial use, consultation with the subject expert is needed. In addition, while using the information and methods contained herein, the practitioners and researchers need to be mindful for their own safety, along with the safety of others, including the professional parties and premises for whom they have professional responsibility. To the fullest extent of law, the publisher and author are not liable in all circumstances (special, incidental, and consequential) for any injury and/or damage to persons and property, along with any potential loss of profit and other commercial damages due to the use of any methods, products, guidelines, procedures contained in the material herein.

A catalogue record for this book is available from the National Library of Australia

NATIONAL LIBRARY OF AUSTRALIA

ISBN (print): 978-1-922617-57-6

CONTENTS

INTRODUCTION

When one looks out at the state of the modern world, it is hard to deny that we are living in perilous times. Across the domains that we occupy every day, there is evidence of systemic dysfunction that perpetuates itself at both the personal and communal levels. Whether it is in politics, religion, business, entertainment and social media, or the educational sphere in which I work, there exists a fundamental disconnect from the core dimensions of our humanity that impairs the effective and holistic functioning of not only these societal institutions, but also the flourishing of the people who move about within them. While there are a range of factors that contribute to the forms that this dysfunction takes, at the causal level I have observed two predominant problems that have worked to undermine our evolutionary progress, and will continue to have this effect until steps are taken to consciously grow beyond our current malaise. These foundational sources of dysfunction are:

1. The denial of spirituality, which separates us from each other and the nature of our vocational calling to life; and
2. The deficient practice of leadership that is ego-centred, and grounded on incomplete understandings of what the highest form of leadership entails.

As distinct as these two problems appear to be, they do share a common thread which is the indulgence of the false and superficial aspects of our being that lead us to live in a way that is out of alignment with the spiritual source of our true power. While it may be tempting to place the blame for this fractured and conflicted state on external factors such as political polarisation, the abuse of economic power or the culture wars, these are just tangible symptoms of a deeper seated disease that in their superficial treatment cease to yield meaningful insights and progress.

In order to bring about the change that we want to see in the world, we must courageously face the source of this disease in the human heart, as daunting as that may be. Dis-ease is something that we have all borne personally, and perpetuated in different forms and degrees, not because we are fundamentally bad people, but because we have become engrained in the habit of living unconsciously. Whether we are cognisant of it or not, this unconsciousness doesn't serve to facilitate our flourishing or that of the world, which is why we so often feel a gnawing sense of discontent with who we see in the mirror, and what we observe in the surrounding circumstances of our life. At our core, we yearn to reconcile with the truth of who we are, and play a purposeful role in restoring integrity to the world's functioning.

The good news is that each of us has been given life for just this reason, and just as we can freely make the choice to dwell in unconsciousness, so can we exercise the agency to elevate our being to the realm of consciousness where we can experience a richer form of life, and hold the space for an evolving world to reflect this prospering. It is my ardent belief that every person who is given life on this planet comes with a unique calling to serve the world and lead it towards an ever-expanding consciousness. What the intricacies of this calling are will vary from person to person, and they can never fully be known but by the agent that is called. Try as we might to characterise the terms on which another's commitment to spirit rests, we must possess the humility to realise that only their heart holds the answers to their life's questions. The best that we can do is nurture the connection that others have to spirit, and support the realisation of their calling by walking with them on their journey. This in essence is what this book is about.

Through its pages, I want to shine light on what I have come to understand about living one's calling, not just through the rigours of my research and anecdotal observation, but through the reflections and insights that have emerged during the process of connecting with my own calling and living it. As one of the respondents to my study emphasised with his narrative, *"your story is my story"*. In applying this wisdom to the domain of living our calling, there is much truth in it. While the details and context of our individual paths will differ, what remains is the essential humanness of our struggle to find ourselves and the depth of meaning which validates our life as one that was worth living.

The human spirit is the tie that binds. Its story is your story, as it is mine. In this intimate triangularity, there is no need for superfluous detail, only the life of the spirit as we come to know it through living this calling. What external forces such as religion, politics and popular culture have to say on the matter is largely inconsequential, as their workings often have the effect of confounding our natural inclinations which orient our lives towards the unfolding of our spiritual potential. Take for example the government initiatives that encourage vocational training for its citizens, yet pay little regard to the honouring of a spiritual calling in the decision that one makes to enter a particular field. In many ways, these programs are self-serving for those in power because they seek to promote an uptake of jobs for which there is a deficit in the economy, at the expense of ennobling individuals to align their soul with a pro-social role that resonates with them at this deep level.

When one is seeking to bring a calling or vocation to life, it is tempting to define those concepts in religious terms. If you were raised a Catholic as I was, you may have been conditioned to believe that only priests and nuns, who were thought to serve God directly, were endowed with a calling, and that everyone else went without experiencing their own abiding purpose to serve God's plan. Pursuant to this way of thinking, there are the vocational haves and have nots. As I have since come to learn, nothing could be further from the truth.

To be able to connect with our spirit and live our calling faithfully, we must become adept at blocking out the noise created by those worldly influences that would have us blindly conform to their dictates. Every day we are exposed to a multiplicity of messages about who we need to become if we are to make it in this world 'successfully', and in the void created by our lack of spiritual and self-knowledge, we readily adopt the substance of those messages and come to identify with them as the 'truth' of who we are. This is problematic because what we have labelled as true turns out to be more of a falsehood than a reality which accords to the natural order of life.[1]

In crafting this artificial and disempowering identity, we do great damage to our spirit by silencing it beneath the layers of these force-fed beliefs about how the world works and what our place is within it. Making us unreceptive to the voice of our calling in which our enduring purposes rest, what we settle for is a mundane existence either working a job to make ends meet, or pursuing a career to accumulate the material accoutrements which we have been conditioned to believe that we want from life.[2] I will address the distinctions between a job, career and a calling in more detail in Chapter two, but for now it is important to understand that the path of our calling is what leads to our flourishing at both the individual and societal levels. When exploring the manifestation of leadership virtues in Section two of the book, primary attention will be given to understanding their application at the individual level, but this shouldn't detract from the recognition of their presence and practical workings in the broader context of the world.

We find our life within an interconnected universal ecosystem of which each of us is an inextricable part. How we choose to live, and the consciousness that shapes the quality of interactions that we have with our environment, is no small thing, although it may appear to be when we look at the impacts of

---

[1] The validity of truth is not reliant on being labelled as such. Only that which is not of truth requires validation in the form of that label.
[2] This disconnect is one of the prime causes of the trend towards 'Quiet Quitting' where disengaged workers do only the bare minimum of tasks required of them by their employers, and the 'Great Resignation' that has seen record numbers of people leave their employment to partake in work that aligns more purposefully with who they truly are.

our life myopically. Part of evolving in the light of spirit is getting out of ourselves, or more accurately, becoming more than the limits of our ego would have us believe. While the ego tries to convince each of us that we are a remote island surrounded by a hostile sea that is indifferent to our existence, the intention of our spirit is for us to grow into the world in order to know it more fully. This is one of the central purposes that living our calling serves. As we live our calling in alignment with the promptings of our spirit, we not only perpetuate the presence of spirit in the world, but we come to relate to it more deeply, in the form that it takes in others, nature, and the places in which we serve.

Try as we might to find fulfilment in ourselves, that state of being spiritually nourished can't be attained as we remain isolated from the world. The world requires our unique gifts and virtuous expression as we go about the work of diligently fulfilling our given purpose/s, and we must reciprocate through our receptivity and active engagement, for the healing and evolution of the world is dependent on it. Were it not for this obligation to serve the source of our calling faithfully, we never would have been given life in the first place. Yet, here you are, and here I am being given this space to hold together. I don't know how it is that you came across this book to read its pages, but I am most grateful for your availability to what it has to offer.

This is the book that I feel called to write. One that combines two of my great interests and passions, being the living of one's calling and the practice of leadership. As early as 2010, I felt myself to be possessed with the idea of understanding how the living of one's calling shapes leadership behaviour, and pursuing a PhD that explored the topic. By that time, I had encountered a seminal turning point in my life that clarified for me the vocational direction that it was going to take. For so long, I had considered writing as a necessity, not in a vocational sense, but as something of a task that was required to succeed in the academic and professional domains. This was especially the case when I was studying law, being a discipline that emphasises the importance of the effective use of language and written communication. To say that I derived pleasure from its practice would be a stretch, but what I did enjoy was the challenge of putting my thoughts to paper and structuring them coherently in a way that would convince a reader of the validity of my perspectives.

In this sense, I valued the connective quality of writing and the promise that it held as a vehicle for in-formation. But what for me was missing from this experience of writing was a meaningful sense of creative self-expression.[3] Who I was, or understood myself to be at the time, did not have the scope to reveal itself through what I was writing, and this left me wanting more. By that stage, I was open to further exploring this natural inclination to write, as for some time I had been engaging in the practice of personal development, but what I had yet to connect with was my calling to the art, and the depth of yearning that my spirit had to speak its truths. That changed early on a May morning in 2008 when I received the inner call that is the closest thing I have ever experienced to a 'Road to Damascus' moment. Instead of trying to recount what I remember of the encounter and risk distorting the details, I have included the relevant excerpt from my journal here to do the experience justice:

> *"Wake up!" My eyes opened and I was staring at the white ceiling of my bedroom fully awake. I felt very strange. My body was light, like another pillow on the mattress. My mind was a still pond that knew neither thought nor drowsiness. I turned my head to the right and I observed my alarm clock. 3:00 is what it read.*
>
> *What was that voice? I sat up and looked around the dark room that was illuminated only by the soft light of the streetlamps outside. Nobody was there. Somebody on the street? Surely not. I turned to look outside the window. Not a sound. No movement of wind, no cars and nobody in sight.*
>
> *'Is this a dream?' is the question that I posed to myself. But the 'I' of my essential being already knew the answer. Feeling myself as one with the pulse of the moment, I was reassured that it was real. Beautiful and peaceful, the silence carried a reverent power. It was then that I knew I was not alone. "Go. Your work awaits you." I knew what I had to do. After putting on a jumper and pants, I went into the study and turned on the computer.*
>
> *For the next three hours, I expressed the promptings of my spirit. I was not in charge. How I felt was like a pen with a heartbeat. What moved through me was effortless, yet purposeful. Much needed to be spoken. This I allowed to the best of my ability. I was humbled by the experience. Having received its hand on my heart, I knew that grace had touched me. But I stopped not to ponder, for this was only the beginning.*

Since that time, I have written a lot, both formally and informally, and the effort expended in this task has been incredibly formative in moulding the voice that speaks to you in these pages. The more that I have written and come to trust in its process that is so clearly aligned with the call of my heart, the greater is the resonance I feel with the leading quote for this book. When

---

[3] I strongly suspect that a good number of lawyers have felt this way about the written component of their work, which perhaps explains why a notable cadre of former lawyers have carved out successful careers as authors; John Grisham and Erle Henry Gardner (of Perry Mason fame) being foremost among them.

I first came across the book from Wayne Dyer that contained this jewel, it didn't have the same power because I hadn't yet claimed the path that my spirit had chosen for my life. Only after I came to reconcile my being with the source of truth from which Dyer spoke, did I recognise its wisdom, and find the strength and conviction to never look back.

By honouring this calling to write, the foundation was laid for both the exploration and expression of the idea which animates this book. In many ways, I feel that after that morning of being receptive to the call of my spirit, I became more of a leader that I ever was previously. For much of my childhood and even moving into young adulthood, the behaviour that I exhibited was symptomatic of a follower, and even though in my personal life I had demonstrated some characteristics of being able to lead myself, as it pertained to my relationship with others and the external world, I was too conceited, too much of a people pleaser who was overly concerned about how I presented myself to others and was perceived by them. The role that I was playing was that of the 'good boy/guy' in a pseudo sense, because I wasn't really manifesting that goodness from a deep spiritual place, but from the shallow ego identity that I operated from. In this way, I was kind of like some of the churchgoers from my childhood, who used to present at mass as pious and faithful members of the congregation, while outside of the four walls of the church there were things that they engaged in which chipped away at the façade which they had sought to erect for the world.

At the time, I didn't really think about it in terms of building and preserving a social reputation, but in effect that was what I was doing. I was one of those people who concerned themselves more with reputation (what others think of me being a definition of self) than with character (the inner fabric of who one authentically is, the dimensions of which I will cover throughout the pages of this book). Having this distorted focus proved to be a significant barrier to the embodiment of leadership, as what I would later come to learn is that the highest form of leadership centres around the character of the person leading. This is not to say that reputation is unimportant, it is just that it is secondarily reliant on having high character. In other words, if one possesses high character, then their reputation to those people who encounter them will take care of itself.

In many ways, this book is about the dis-covering of character, but not in terms of what character is traditionally understood to mean. I think that when most of us hear the word 'character', we think about someone who is operating in alignment with a sound moral framework or putting practice to their values, but how I have come to understand the word is quite different from this. Character, for me, is something that is embodied by a person who is connected to their spirit, and through living in alignment with it, manifests its core virtues and associated behaviours in the wider world. These fruits of faithfulness to the life-giving dimension of our being which calls us will be discussed in the second section of the book, with each chapter representing a core theme that was highlighted by my research.

In the first section which precedes the exploration of these core themes, I want to lay the foundations for understanding the features of a lived calling in more depth (Chapter two) and how it contributes to the conscious practice of leadership (Chapter three). To facilitate this understanding, it is necessary to pre-emptively orient our attention towards the two facets of self from which we live and create the conditions of the world that we see. Chapter one will thus examine the spiritual source of our calling, from which we live consciously, and the artificial ego identity, which is the constraining and corrupting source of unconsciousness in our lives.

The third section of the book will take us into some different territory, and illuminate some of the more interesting findings from my research work. The journey of living one's calling and demonstrating conscious leadership, it turns out has its fair share of enabling factors and barriers. Chapter nine will bring your attention to these phenomena which hopefully serves you in navigating the nonlinear twists and turns of this authentic path. Chapter ten concerns itself with the pivotal moments along the journey that can serve as forks in the road which bring us more fully into alignment with our calling. In the last chapter of the book, I will present an amalgam of advice and additional commentary that can help launch you towards the practical implementation of the central ideas contained in the book.

At this early juncture, you might be tempted to ask what you have to gain from reading a book such as this. To this, my response would be a significant amount, particularly if your aspiration is to connect with your calling and/or cultivate a transformative leadership capacity. Whatever your age, occupation or current station in life, this book will have something useful to offer you. The evidence of this emerges from my speaking and consulting work, during which it has become clear to me that the framework presented herein has great potential to inform what the desired future of work will look like. Seeing also the inherent potential that this framework offers, leadership development personnel and human resources professionals have expressed a strong interest in its themes, which challenge some of the conventional and outdated ways of thinking about human motivation and bringing forth the best out of others.

Of the numerous books that I have read and come across for my research, none cover the same ground as *Calling New Leaders*, which uniquely blends the three major themes of:

- Living one's calling or vocation in life;
- Demonstrating a transcendent form of leadership (conscious leadership) in this process; and
- Identifying the qualities of the human spirit, and explaining how these virtues are enacted along the lived calling/conscious leadership journey.

While there are a number of works that cover elements of these themes in their pages, there is yet to be a book which brings together these themes holistically to illustrate the intricate relationship that exists between a lived calling and leadership. Not only does this work serve this purpose for the reader, but it does so within the context of a universal spirituality, and with reference to a recent major research project conducted by the author on the subject matter. Another important point of difference between *Calling New Leaders* and other works which cover elements of its themes in their pages, is that these other works explore the living of one's calling and how that might relate to leadership from a bounded religious standpoint. The effect of this is that their exploration of these themes are often narrow and devoid of the depth of insight that comes when these themes are looked at through the neutral and spacious lens of a universal spirituality.

What I hope will come across in these pages are the rich lessons that I have learned and earned through the winding and often difficult path that I have taken to live my calling. To this end, what I recount in these pages is not the vain or naïve tale of someone who hasn't walked their talk, or shied away from asking the hard questions of life. One of the personal maxims that I ascribe to in my life is *'you can't have the gold without the road'*. The 'gold' here does not represent the symbols of worldly success which many people have come to idolise, but the rich inner life that comes through the challenging process of connecting with our spirit, and diligently working to embody the fullness of that authentic self. While some people may see the strenuous road that they have taken as a barrier to the actualisation of their being, I have experienced it as an enabler of this fundamental human aim. There is still so far to travel and I am convinced that the journey will never end, but I am most grateful for the grind that got me here, to this point where I can share these words with you. *"If you are irritated by every rub, how will you ever become polished"*, said Persian sage Rumi. Fortified by the presence of spirit and the calling that is mine to live, I will not only endure but prosper, as will you when you make the commitment to venture down this most glorious of roads. May you be inspired by the pages that follow to evolve into a conscious leader that the modern world needs to transcend the limitations of its present unconsciousness.

SECTION ONE: THE FOUNDATIONS

CHAPTER 1: The One Who Calls and the One Who Corrupts

Before we can really understand the characteristics that define a calling, we need to explore the nature of the one who calls. This 'caller', which invites us to be in unity with it as we go about the daily task of living, goes by many names, according to the respondents[4] in my study. When asked what the source of their calling was, a good number of respondents cited God, the universal life force, Logos, the heart or soul, or a higher power/presence, while others spoke of their calling as emanating from an inner spirit that is connected to and pervades all forms of life.[5] Regardless of the terminology that was used to identify the source of their calling, what became clear from the way that these people talked about their relationship with this life energy and the nature of its workings as they had experienced them, was that they were attempting to characterise the same thing.

As Lao Tzu, the author of the *Tao Te Ching* teaches us, the Tao that can be named is not the eternal Tao. This Tao that he writes about, which is an alternate name that can be given to this life force, encompasses all that is and orchestrates the path of being in the world. To try and distil such an all-pervading presence into a word or phrase will always be problematic, for the instruments of language that we have devised to convey meaning are incapable of capturing the essence and totality of this life force. As one of my respondents posed in a question to me, *"how can you adequately describe the taste of an apple?"*, or Alan Watts posited when he said that *"you can't get wet from the word 'water'"*, what we choose to label something does not embody the essence of its being. We only really encounter this essence and come to know it as we are relating to it through our experience of life, whether that is actually eating the apple or wading through the ocean. The presence of these labels, while useful for the purpose of distinguishing one thing from another and marking their practical utility in the world, have their limits and we would do well to humbly acknowledge this if our intention is to come to know this eternal source of life in its wholeness.

What we think that we know about the world often fails to deliver genuine insight because the substance of that thinking is not experientially grounded. Instead reflecting the shallow exterior conditioning of our minds that we have uncritically accepted as being representative of reality, this presents a

---

[4] The respondents were the individuals who I interviewed for the research project on which this book is based.
[5] This sentiment was eloquently conveyed in the following quotation, *"I'm one of one. I am everything. I am part of everything because it is a part of me."*

significant barrier to our spiritual growth and the knowing which that facilitates. By possessing a mental model of the world that needs to be defended in order for us to believe that we are right, we prove to be incapable of opening ourselves up in the way that authentic learning requires. As I will discuss in Chapter five, the human spirit has an actualising quality to it which prompts us to continuously engage with and learn from life in order to know it more fully, and to follow this natural inclination we cannot be encumbered by a personal agenda that endeavours to make the world into an image that is palatable to our ego, or the tribes with which it identifies.

We see this kind of ego-oriented perception at work in religious circles where, for example, God can be believed to be vengeful towards those who disobey 'him' and thus should be feared, or he is disapproving of certain groups of people in society i.e. members of the gay community or 'infidels'. As much as the religious followers who subscribe to these beliefs would try to convince you that they are reflective of a divine and objective truth, in reality the substance of these beliefs has been conceived by the religious institutions themselves in the form of doctrine, and these individuals are perpetuating them because it strengthens their sense of identity as a member of that religious group. So while they may have taken steps to understand this doctrine and its accompanying rituals at the intellectual level, at the deeper level of their being they are not really engaging with the life of the spirit. Here, they may know about God as that entity is conceptualised in their holy book, and be able to recite passages of it by heart, but do they really know God as a co-creative force who walks with them on the path of their calling? I highly doubt that, if their ideological proclamations are a sign to go by. In many ways these institutionalised religious dogmas act like a barrier to our ability to align ourselves with the spiritual source of our calling, but until we can consciously distance ourselves from the dependence that we have on them as defining features of our piousness, we will know no better way to an inspired life.

In a similar vein, to know about this eternal source of life is quite a different thing from knowing it intimately. We can read about meditation techniques on the internet or talk to others about their journey to peace and forgiveness, and these are good ways of learning something new to expand our horizons, but they are not a substitute for the practices that when engaged in bring us into union with our spiritual source and the calling/s which emanate from it. In this age of pseudo spirituality where people are more concerned with looking the part than evolving to walk their clichéd talk, this is something that we need to be mindful of.

The human ego is a cunning influence that is adept at using our natural inclination to virtue in the service of its own ends. We see this at work in the performative virtue signalling on social media platforms where those posting want to be seen to be good by standing on the right side of the contentious issues of the day, despite these faux acts of solidarity doing nothing to make a real difference in alleviating the problems that they profess to care so much about. This is but one of many examples of how the ego's workings infect our daily movements, and act to sabotage our efforts to live consciously in the service of our calling.

Author Ryan Holiday was indeed onto something when he titled his book, *Ego is the Enemy*. This enemy, along with the spiritual source of our calling that I advocate for you to align yourself with, will be the focus of this chapter. In every moment of our lives we have a fundamental choice to make, and that choice centres around the consciousness from which we think, act and become. Each of us is a creative agent who is continually shaping the world through our faithfulness to either spirit or ego. What we choose to be a conduit for will not only come to characterise the condition of our life, but it will also play an impactful role in the lives that others lead and the workings of the wider world. The consciousness from which I live will sculpt the lessons that I teach to my children and students, not only in the spoken form, but more importantly through my actions. If I allow myself to live unconsciously from the ego, then I implicitly give these vital members of the next generation, who are pregnant with this leadership potential, permission to do the same.

One of the most important leadership lessons that I have to impart is that we are always leading by example, whether that example expresses the fruits of virtue or the foibles of vice. Some people won't like or can't handle the weightiness of this statement because it imposes a significant responsibility on each of us that cannot be abdicated, and even if we try to remain ignorant to its reality, the effects that is has are immutable. In this sense, it is a form of universal law that is perpetually in operation regardless of how we feel about it. Given its application to our lives and leadership, we would be wise to eschew the more comfortable roles of denier or victim that, to paraphrase a quote from Nelson Mandela, allow the enemy (the ego) to determine the grounds for battle. While I don't see life and leadership as a battle against anything other than the corrupting pull of this ego self, I do see them as presenting a challenging set of circumstances that can bring forth the best qualities of our humanity when they are faced in the right way. Righteousness, in this sense, emerges from our alignment with spiritual consciousness that defines both life and leadership in their purest forms.

The old Cherokee tale of the two wolves describes the inner conflict that we experience as human beings in a unique way. *One evening an old Cherokee Indian told his grandson about a battle that goes on inside people. He said, 'My son, the battle is between two 'wolves' inside us all. One is Evil. It is anger, envy, jealousy, sorrow, regret, greed, arrogance, self-pity, guilt, resentment, inferiority, lies, false pride, superiority, and ego. The other is good. It is joy, peace, love, hope, serenity, humility, kindness, benevolence, empathy, generosity, truth, compassion and faith.' The grandson thought about it for a minute and then asked his grandfather: 'Which wolf wins?' The old Cherokee simply replied, 'The one you feed.'*

The evil wolf that the old Cherokee Indian describes is our ego identity, and the good wolf is the spirit that is the essence of our being. While it is a simple story, it holds a lot of wisdom that is pertinent to this work, which I will explore in more granular detail as we make our way through the chapters of the book. In every moment, with every thought, intention and action, we feed one of these wolves within ourselves, and as we feed that wolf, its appetite will grow to dictate a way of being in the world, which explains the consistency of consciousness that people exhibit with their behaviour. Those individuals who choose to habitually feed the wolf of their ego grow more egocentric and distant in their relationship with spirit, while those who choose to nourish their spirit in the present moments of their lives will strengthen their connection to it, and cultivate more of a conscious awareness of the workings of their ego that will allow them to stave off its attempts to co-opt their thoughts and behaviour.

This doesn't mean however that they will do this perfectly all of the time, and perfection isn't the goal here. Individuals who have nurtured a deep relationship with spirit can still succumb to ego in moments of vulnerability or impulsiveness, and people who identify strongly with ego are capable of acting in ways that give voice to their spirit by giving generously to others or demonstrating courage in the face of testing circumstances, for example. This is why it is problematic to label people as either good or bad, principled or immoral because each of us is a multi-dimensional being who has the propensity to feed either of the wolves who live within us at different moments in time. Ella Wheeler Wilcox recognised this dichotomy in her poem 'Two Kinds of People' when she puts forward that *"it's well understood that the good are half bad and the bad are half good"*.

While I am well aware of the dangers of binary thinking that can be over simplistic and narrow in their real word application, the characterisations of spirit and ego that are to follow carry practical weight because their presence and workings are readily observable in the form that a person or group's behaviour and state of being takes. I don't know whether it is because of the research that I have done into this, or the expansion of awareness that I have experienced through taking my own journey of conscious growth, but I am very sensitive to the movements of spirit and ego in the world. I suspect that both of these factors have had a part to play, and will contribute to informing the substance of this book. Another one of my hopes for this work is that you too will become attuned to their presence, particularly in yourself, which will empower you in your efforts to evolve and make the contribution that is uniquely yours to make. Let us now start our exploration of spirit and ego, and we will turn first to the eternal spirit that is our essential source of being.

The Spirit: The one who calls

You are much more than all of the worldly things that you value, and have identified with to this point in your life.

Each of us is infinitely more than we think that we are, and our limited thinking about ourselves and the world greatly inhibits our understanding the truth of who we are, and the relationship that we have to all that life encompasses. If I were to ask you who you are, you would likely respond by describing in some form the various roles that you occupy in your daily life, and the other things that you identify with or attach yourself to. You might say that you are a mother, father, sister, brother; that you work as an architect, banker, chef or school teacher; are a die-hard football or basketball fan of a particular team; or a member of a particular religious or cultural group. While these ways of identifying ourselves are not necessarily wrong because we have evidence of their reality in the physical world, they are however superficial, transient and incomplete because they do not touch the spiritual heart of life within each of us that is always present and impervious to death in a way that the corporeal aspects of our lives are not.

While our physical body will age with time and take on a very difference appearance than when we were young, the silent witness to this process, our spirit, has never aged because its existence transcends the changeable nature of the physical world. This is why it is so easy to be mystified by the limitations of our physical body as we age because within ourselves we still feel like we did earlier on in our lives. We can similarly become disordered when we come to confuse our thoughts as an expression of who we really are. Like our bodies are continually changing their form, so are our thoughts about ourselves and the world. As it concerns our thoughts about who we are, these can seem so real that we easily mistake them for the truth. Think about some of the things that you used to believe about yourself in the past, say ten to fifteen years ago, and I am willing to bet that you don't think the same way about yourself now because you have grown to see the illusory nature

17

of these prior beliefs. When I was in my early twenties, I subscribed to the notion of body beautiful and held the belief that my value as a person was primarily determined by how I looked in the mirror. It was only as I evolved through doing my own personal work that I came to realise that in subscribing to this belief, I had unconsciously allowed myself to be conditioned by this external perspective that beautiful is better. When I achieved this clarity, it was extremely liberating because I came to identify more closely with the spiritual bedrock of my life, and loosened my attachment to these false beliefs about myself that we are all exposed to in some form, and perpetuate in our own lives.

The metaphor of building your life on a solid foundation of rock rather than the shifting granules of sand has resonated with me so much more strongly since I have stepped onto the path to living my calling. Through travelling that path, I have come to connect with who I am as an extension of spirit, and learnt to not so closely identify with the myriad of things in the physical world that I had previously been conditioned to accept as defining features of who I am. While I may currently work as a lecturer at a fine academic institution, I know that neither the role that I occupy, nor the regard with which my employer is held, touch at the heart of my spiritual identity. This foundational dimension to my life was present before I took up the role, and it will not be diminished once I move on to something different. The same goes with the university qualifications that I have achieved over the years. While they constitute verifiable evidence of my growth in worldly knowledge, they don't bear witness to a deeper evolution of my spirit and the impacts that its wisdom has had on the quality of my life. Even if I didn't have these qualifications, I would still hold a fundamental worth and dignity as a human being that is unalienable. The same could be said for the income that I earn, or the number of social media followers that I have or don't have. None of it matters in absolute terms, although we will convince ourselves that it does if our relationship with life is artificial and ego-based.

Just as these facets of my worldly existence do not genuinely define me, so don't the physical conditions of your life concretely define you. If you had spent thirty years of your life working in a particular profession and were one day made redundant, that would not bring an end to your existence. It may bring an end to your time in that profession, but not to much else. If you were once married to somebody and then separated from them, you would no longer be that person's wife or husband, but life beyond that role or label would go on. This same type of thinking goes for religious affiliations also, where what we might come to understand about ourselves through a religious order doesn't ultimately define who we are. Hopefully, it plays some part in illuminating the core dimensions of our humanity, but we don't have to become dependent on religion for this aligning, given that a vast number of people have come to connect with their spiritual life vein in the absence of religion.[6]

In the same way that we often come to understand what we want in life through coming into contact with that which doesn't resonate with us, the journey to knowing ourselves at the deep spiritual level is facilitated by a gradual learning of who we are not in real terms. While these learnings can be quite painful at the time that we experience the events that convey them, they serve a very valuable purpose if we are open to receiving them. The challenge with this is to move beyond the fixation on our suffering to perceive the lessons that this egocentric act of indulgence obscures.

Maybe a romantic relationship that you were involved in broke down because your partner perceived you as being needy and suffocating. If this perception had a basis in reality, it likely reflected your erroneous belief that who you were was in some way defined by that relationship. By thinking in this way, you could not stand the thought of being without this other person as that would have equated to a diminution of your being, which was a proposition that was unpalatable to your ego. But was this not a deluded perspective? You may have voluntarily invested so much of yourself in that relationship, but that did not mean that you *became* the relationship. You were likely a more self-reliant and adaptable version of yourself before entering it, and you will have to demonstrate these qualities again now that the relationship has come to an end. This presents a fertile opportunity for both growth and discovery. In the space created by the void that the other person has left, you can re-connect to who you essentially are. If you are open and honest with yourself in this process, you will come to understand that you do not need love from an external source, for you already are love, which is a defining feature of your spirit. As you move forward from that recognition with a conscious connection to your spiritual source, your capacity to love and be loved in a relationship is transformed. Through the unburdening of your previous baggage, you can relate to significant others with freedom and generosity in your future, and allow them the same dignity and autonomy as they relate to you.

---

[6] Ultimately, the life of the spirit is nested at the heart of all of the World's Great Religions, which is why they uniformly advocate for the embodiment of virtue, and this being the process of returning to oneness with our creator. Therefore, it is possible to have spirituality without religion, but because of the centrality of spirituality to religion, it is impossible to have the latter without the former. In making this claim however, I don't seek to diminish the role of religion in people's lives, particularly when it is faithfully practiced to manifest the virtues of the human spirit, which is the same purpose that this work is striving to affect.

These types of 'failures' hold great potential for transformation because they invoke humility, which is a virtue of the spirit that I will discuss in more depth in Chapter six. Thus, as we practice this quality, we live in alignment with our spiritual nature, from which we can embody its other virtues if we choose to hold the space for revelation and remain conscious. As much as we might feel compelled to jump straight into another dysfunctional relationship in order to feel complete, we can make a better choice and validate ourselves under the light of truth that has been our blessing to encounter. This in essence is what I did when I literally got off the treadmill of defining myself in terms of a beautiful body, to look deeper within and connect with my true source of being. Once I did this, I took a step away from my unconscious identification with the ego, and moved towards a more authentic relationship with my spirit. Feeling to me like the process of a snake that sheds a layer of skin which is no longer capable of housing its being, it is a progression that I have since endeavoured to consistently replicate on my life journey.

To adapt one of Shakespeare's most famous sayings, to evolve or not to evolve, that is the question! While some people may be willing to occupy that dead skin and be defined by what it represents to the world, I believe that each of us is called to realise so much more. Our spiritual nature has an actualising quality to it, and it is continually prompting us to grow and improve, not only ourselves but also the state of the world. This became clear as I was interviewing respondents for my doctoral study who were living their calling in alignment with their spirit. Consistently, these individuals spoke of this inner drive that they felt to evolve into their fullness, and bring that to bear on the functioning of the world, not in an egotistical sense, but as a loving act that benefited both themselves and the rest of humanity.

If you were to look at Abraham Maslow's hierarchy of needs, you would see that this spiritual impulse to actualise sits upon the top of the pyramid, above both our psychological needs and our basic needs. Encapsulating our essential need for spiritual fulfilment through personal growth and renewal, and the creative expression of our natural talents, we find these elements being present in individuals who are living their calling. Who they were born to be, they must be, even if this takes a lifetime of discovery and work. The journey to living our most authentic life is not easy by any stretch, but it is simple in the sense that it only requires us to be who we were created to be. Therefore, there are no 'secrets' to the spiritual life, as some books on spirituality try to claim for their authors. Everything that is required to manifest the highest form of our life will be revealed by our spirit as we venture down the path of living our calling, but before we can glimpse this inner bounty of rich resources, we first have to come to trust ourselves as an extension of its being, and have the courage and openness, not to walk to the beat of our ego's drum, but to the heartbeat of life itself. As French novelist Antoine de Saint-Exupery so beautifully surmised on this point, *"It is only with the heart that one can see rightly; what is essential is invisible to the eye."*

The prospect of encountering death has a way of bringing sharply before our eyes what is paramount to living this highest form of life. In her book, *The Top Five Regrets of the Dying*, Australian palliative care Nurse Bronnie Ware relays that the most commonly cited regret that she heard from the patients that she cared for was that they didn't have the courage to live a life that was true to who they were. Having chosen instead to live a life that others expected of them, the tragedy of what these people had to confront was that they had not truly lived by eschewing their calling for the empty validation that the ego seeks to gain by trying to get others approval or make them happy.

While we might prefer it if life were easier and more accommodating to our individual will, its quality of being is indifferent to this egocentric desire that so many of us have to create a world that is palatable to our sensibilities and thus enables our comfort. The spirit of life just is in its fullness and flow, and it doesn't conform to our bounded expectations that would try to diminish it or stifle its movements. Some people believe that life is a burden because they are addicted to the struggle or enjoy playing the victim a little too much, and by characterising life in this way they greatly diminish their ability to meaningfully engage with it. Rather than embracing life for what it is and aligning their presence with the nature of its being, they persist in resisting its movements and the rich learnings that it benevolently seeks to impart.

As one of my respondents so insightfully commented on this point, *"life does not happen to us, it happens for us"*. Being a conclusion that this amazing woman came to after overcoming a near fatal bout of cancer and having her life turned upside down during the time of her illness, it was clear as I was speaking to her that her struggle had facilitated her surrender, and brought her to a place where she could serenely live in alignment with her spirit. While many people in her position would have adopted a victim's perspective in response to what had happened, she assumed an alternate position of power and responsibility for the learnings that her soul's journey had facilitated. On this, she posited that *"things have happened for me, and at a deep level, why do these things happen to me and not to the next person? Because that person has different lessons or different learning."*

Life happens for us because the spirit, by its nature, is generous and loving. Wanting us to learn from our experiences so that we can grow into the best

21

version of ourselves, and express its virtues in the world through this flourishing, it prompts us to reveal our essence through life's trials, tribulations and awe inspiring moments of beauty and joy. By responding to these prompts with an open heart and teachable mind, the life which we create can be extraordinary in reflecting the potential of which human beings who live in alignment with the spirit are capable. Late Irish actor and singer Richard Harris touched upon the benevolent presence of spirit in his beautiful poem 'There Are Too Many Saviors on My Cross' when he mused that, *'I am not in heaven, I am here, hear me. I am in you, feel me. I am of you, be me. I am with you, see me. I am for you, need me. I am all mankind; only through kindness will you reach me''*. As an advocate for the wisdom of surrendering to our spirit, he was without doubt someone who had connected with his calling in a very profound way.

To connect with our spirit in the present moment, we must become as it is with our thoughts, words and actions. Being just to others and rendering genuine service both affect this integral alignment, as does demonstrating gratitude which brings together through that which is given, the one who gives and the one who receives. To use Harris' example of kindness, when we treat others well, the world responds in kind because through these actions we enter into unity with the spirit of others whose lives have emerged from the same source of being that has birthed ours. In affecting this integral alignment with our spiritual source, we contribute to the creation of heaven on earth. One person at a time, one moment at a time, we can move towards this transformation of worldly conditions, and while our journey will be long and seem impossible at times, this in no way diminishes the worthiness of evolving to meet that aim.

What I learned in my youth about the second coming, I now know is not about a saviour coming back through time to rescue us from sin. Instead, it is about each of us awakening to the consciousness of who we are, which through our conditioned unconsciousness we have forgotten ourselves to be. The second coming is about reconnection to our spirit and the subsequent manifestation of the fruits of virtue that the religious prophets and other enlightened beings embodied with the fullness of their being. It is therefore not a passive act on our part, from which we are excused of the responsibility of participation. Whatever salvation that we hope to find, will come from our own hands, as we walk in the company of God and our truth seeking neighbours.

Any form of reconciliation requires collaborative effort, whether we are aligning our energies with the human spirit at the personal level, or joining others to affect positive change at the societal level. Both journeys trace a path back to wholeness in different forms. Why the personal journey to re-integration is so significant is because it leads us to bring the wholeness that we find within to the workings of the wider world. So unwavering is the solidarity and compassion of the human spirit that it can't help but serve those in the world who have dampened it though their unconsciousness.

How we allow this solidarity and compassion to guide our actions in remaking the world in the image of spirit is by first forgiving our own unconsciousness. As difficult as this step can be, we can't affect the process of healing without it. What is manifested without, must first be manifested within, and we can't give to the world what we refuse to give to ourselves, whether that is love, acceptance, forgiveness or any of the other fruits of virtue. I know this to be true because of the inside out transformation that I have had to undergo in my own life.

Whilst I don't profess to know the unconsciousness that you have manifested in your own life, what I can say is that whatever you or I have done in unconsciousness is nothing to lose our lives feeling guilt or self-recrimination for, if we take full responsibility for having brought it into being and commit our lives to bringing the light that we have found to the dark corners of the world. Only as we do this do we honour the learnings that our unconsciousness has taught us about ourselves and the bridging function that we are to occupy to make the world a more fertile place for consciousness to flourish.

To blame the world for our unconsciousness only enables it to exert more control over our lives. Being a temptation of the disavowed life, it is not one that the purposeful and inspired agent of transformation would succumb to. By taking responsibility for our evolution and that of our world, we interrupt the conditioned habits of ego that disempower us spiritually and halt our march to progress. When I think of what it means to embody this shift and move from disempowerment to a locus of power, my mind turns to the example of activist Rosa Parks who played a significant role in the civil rights movement when she refused to relinquish her bus seat to a white passenger in defiance of the racial segregation laws that existed at the time.

Explaining in her autobiography the basis of her decision not to vacate her seat on that fateful day, she writes that, *"I was not tired physically, or no more tired than I usually was at the end of a working day…No, the only tired I was, was tired of giving in."* With her weary spirit that had experienced enough of the systemic oppression that sought to diminish her being, Parks could no longer tolerate being complicit in this subjugation of her essential rights as a human being. Taking it upon herself to make a stand for her spirit, and her people, she courageously shone light on the abomination of racial segregation and inequality, even though it would come at a great personal cost to herself and her family. Where others would have looked out at the world and impotently blamed others for the conditions that they found themselves in, Parks knew better than to engage in this futile exercise. Choosing instead to engage her spirit and speak her truth in service of a cause that she knew to be right, she transcended the falsity of the social conditioning that sought to invalidate her fundamental worth. Becoming a transformative figure in this process, her example is a powerful one to those who endeavour to lead more spiritually attuned lives.

Small acts can make a big difference, not just in our own lives but also in the life of the world. An act of kindness or caring inquiry can save a person's life. Cultivating the habit of meditation or prayer can evoke a sense of peace and gratitude that change one's relationship with the world. By earnestly reflecting on our behaviour, we create the space for vice to be replaced by virtue. While none of these actions are grand by any measure of what society values, they are however profoundly significant in stimulating a depth to life in which consciousness can expand.

The life of the spirit is a life of connection to the moments that comprise it. Being the only medium through which we can receive wisdom and bring that to bear on the world, our challenge is to engage with the world fully and be open and vulnerable in this process. In each moment, it is all too easy to play out familiar but inauthentic patterns of relating to the world that fortify the shell of unconsciousness which separates us from new life. By living in this closed manner, we stifle the potential for rebirth that the spirit wants to affect in us. Now is as good a time as any to bridge the divide and make ourselves receptive to the truth that underlies our existence. With what will be revealed, we have nothing to fear or lose, despite the ego's protestations to the contrary. As I have expressed above, trust that your connection to the source of consciousness is irrevocable. Whether you are aware of it or not, it is there, and how you have chosen to define that relationship in your mind does not diminish its existence in any way.

For millennia, human beings have written about, spoken about, sung about and created other art about the life of the spirit, and the inspired essence of what has emerged has been remarkably consistent in reflecting the substance of what this spirit embodies. You are not so untethered as to be unable to write your own love song as millions of others have done before you. But to bring this song to life in the world, you will first need to find your voice, or your calling, which is what this book will assist you in unearthing.

In this section on spirit, I don't want to pre-empt too much of what is to come in Section two which more deeply explores the qualities of its character that manifest in leadership when one is faithfully living their calling, so with this I will shift our focus to the ego, which we must understand in a conscious light if we are to successfully resist its corrupting influence in our lives. In *The Art of War*, Chinese military strategist and philosopher Sun Tzu, instructs us on the point by writing that, *"If you know the enemy and know yourself, you need not fear the result of a hundred battles"*. By knowing ourselves as both a manifestation and source of spirit, and the enemy as the ego which I will now characterise, we can discern a path to victory in an evolving world that is calling for new leaders to give voice to their innate virtues so that we may consciously and collectively meet the rigours and emerging challenges of contemporary life.

The Ego: The one who corrupts

To live from the ego is to have an unstable identity that at best can be believed in, but can never be known to be true.

For all of the visibly serious problems that we are encountering in the world today, such as climate change, energy security and the rise of extremist ideologies, there is a less conspicuous challenge that each of us is facing in our daily lives, and that is to evolve our consciousness beyond the level of ego. Before I proceed to describe the different ways in which ego manifests itself in our lives, it is important that I define what I mean by ego for the purposes of this work. Ego is the false self that we believe ourselves to be, but are not, to the extent that these beliefs are not reflective of our spiritual identity. Not everything that we believe about who we are is real, and while these beliefs may appear to be real by virtue of us holding them, this doesn't constitute the basis of their legitimacy. As an example, I might hold the belief that I am a very important person because of the work that I do and the amount of money that I am remunerated with, but neither of these two things ultimately define who I am. At best, they describe what I do and what I get paid for doing what I do, but to define myself by them would be to set myself up for a tense life of status consciousness and the insecurity that inevitably flows from that superficial means of identification.

Were I to be moved on from this role, then pursuant to this distorted belief that I am what I do and earn, I would literally cease to be. Clearly, this is a ludicrous proposition, and one which reality would prove to be false once I continued to enjoy an existence post-role, but it is amazing how much of our identities are based on these distorted mental constructions. Whether they are self-created, like my earlier example of my worth being defined by how attractive my body appeared, or influenced by the external conditioning of our childhood or the social/cultural context in which we were raised, these erroneous beliefs create a harmful divide between who we really are and who we present to the world as in order to find a place in it.

In the previous section of this chapter, I expressed that who we really are at the essential level is an embodiment of spirit. This understanding does not come to those of us who are so steeped in ego consciousness that they can't see beyond it to realise that there are deeper levels to their being than the world will give them credit for. In the eyes of the broader population who ascribe to the doctrine of the ego in defining themselves, our reputation precedes us, and we will be judged on the label that is our name, what we look like, the work that we do, the car that we drive and the suburb in which we live, our country of origin, the cultural practices that we engage in, the branch of religion that we belong to, how many social media followers that we have, and the list goes on and on.

In terms of what really matters in life and who we fundamentally are, these things are illusory. While they do form a part of the narrative that tells the story of our physical existence on this planet, they don't touch at the spiritual heart of our eternal nature which can't be classified or contained by the limits of form. When we fail to appreciate the disconnect that emerges through these artificial means of ego identification, we invite much emptiness and suffering into our lives. While we may prove capable of revelling in pleasures and feeling the fleeting satisfaction that these experiences may produce, at our depths we will remain unfulfilled and diminished in our capacity to experience a lasting sense of joy that is not dependent on life playing out in a way that is acceptable to this false self. A mantra that I have created to anchor this truth within myself is *'pleasure is not joy, as satisfaction is not fulfilment'*. When we live from the ego and indulge its hedonistic desires, we will gravitate towards the pleasures of the world that stimulate our bodily senses, which may take the form of food, drugs, alcohol, sex, gaming, gambling, amongst other things. At best, these indulgences will produce a feeling of satisfaction that goes just as quickly as it arrives (think of the fleetingness of satiation after an extravagant meal or the brief ecstasy of an orgasm), and what we are left with is the same void of craving that motivated us to move towards those external forms of stimulation in the first place. This describes well a key aspect of the cycle of addiction which many people find becoming trapped in when they invest themselves so heavily in their ego identity.

Joy, on the other hand, requires more of a person to be engaged with the world than just their physical senses. As this emotion is roused by their spiritual heart, a more enduring state is evoked to permeate their being. With authentic giving for example, where a person gives to another without expecting any form of reciprocal benefit to flow to them, the servant is giving from their spirit and of its virtues to that other person and the world, and while this might make them feel good in the moment, it also leads them to experience a deeper level of fulfilment that nourishes their soul and fortifies their connection to life. While life's normal challenges are inescapable and still impact these individuals who live in alignment with their spirit, these slings and arrows are made more bearable through their inspired and joy filled approach to living, and the sense of fulfilment which accompanies that buffers them from the adverse impacts of these hollowing events. By having this glass half full outlook, which is how some of my respondents described their way of seeing the world, what these people focus upon is the abundance of good things in their lives that they are grateful for, and which stoke the fire of their inner joy and contentment.

Each of us has encountered people in our lives who have faced the tests of the world gracefully, with an even keeled serenity, which indicates that they are living their lives from the foundational realm of spirit, out of which both joy and fulfilment spring. Unlike the ego centred amongst us, who resist so mightily against the forces that threaten to take them away from the objects of their pleasure and superficial desire, these spiritually centred individuals are not so dependent on these objects, and are thus more capable of practicing surrender to those forces which are beyond their ability to control. In this, they are liberated and empowered to revel in life's depths and find a footing that gives genuine purpose and meaning to their lives.

Here, I invite you to reflect honestly about your own life and how you have come to define yourself. Is the strength of your identity dependent, among other things, on the title that you hold at work, how much money that you have in the bank or what you social circle looks like to outsiders? If so, you have allowed the ego to direct your life and to define the standard of 'success' that you are hoping to reach, and this has you standing on fragile ground. None of these symbols of social status, as impressive as the world finds them, bring us true joy or lasting fulfilment, and perhaps you have come to realise this already, at the subconscious level of your mind, or through the muted feelings that you have felt in response to the simple pleasures of life. If you have experienced this intuitive inkling, why do you then persist in identifying with those things so closely? Is it because you fear not knowing who you are in the absence of those things, or you don't believe that there is a richer form of life available to you underneath that superficiality? I concede that these are difficult and confronting questions to answer, but if our goal is to know ourselves as Socrates implored us to do, then we have to ask these honest questions and cease to indulge the false side of ourselves that promises much but delivers little of substance and meaning.

For one to connect to their calling, their true purpose, they need to peel back those layers of their personality that have been built on the constructions of the ego. Like an onion, we each have many layers to our being that form at different stages of our lives, and consist of the beliefs, values and conditioning of the environments that we have inhabited. This makes us complex beings who are difficult to understand, even to ourselves. Making this endeavour to know ourselves even more problematic is the enmeshment that we have with the characterising features of these layers that leads us to mistake who we are at our core with these surface layers of self that the world relates to and validates. Being deficient in self and spiritual awareness as we live in the ego's shadow, it is easy to see how we lose the perspective to discern that there is still work to do in peeling back the layers of self that obscure the spiritual basis of our lives, and all of life.

Our over-identification with these layers of personhood helps to explain our preoccupation with role playing in the world. What we like to think of as an exercise that is reserved for children, we adults have become masters at. When my daughter Eloise was young, she, like other little girls her age, wanted to be her favourite heroine and princess characters. Each day, she would desire to be someone different and go into her dress up box to put on a new costume and get into character by acting out the famous scenes from their movies. One day, it might have been Anna or Elsa from *Frozen*, and on another, the brave Rapunzel or Ariel from *The Little Mermaid*. On some occasions the transformation would be so swift that it was difficult to keep up with who she was playing. As I was observing one of these transformations unfold, it occurred to me that we adults who are not grounded in our true spiritual identity are not all that different from children who engage in this act of role playing. When we do not know who we essentially are, we fill that void by taking on an inauthentic personality or characteristics that serve an ego oriented purpose in our lives. An example of this could be the over friendliness that a person demonstrates, which can often seek to mask feelings of inadequacy or a need to be liked and approved of by other people.

This unnatural state of being also has an adaptive quality to it that allows one to present 'themselves' safely to different people in different social contexts. Being like the chameleon that changes the colour of its scales in order to blend in with its environment and avoid the dangerous attention of predators, these untethered individuals have similarly taken on different personas as a means of navigating a world that they unconsciously fear or feel ill equipped to handle. While demonstrating this form of adaptability may be seen to be a positive trait, I do not believe that it evidences an integrated form of being from which one can live their calling with strength and commitment. This is because it is a superficial form of adaptability that is not anchored in an awareness of who we are independent of these roles that we play.

For my young daughter, and other children, who have much to learn about who they are and the path that is uniquely theirs to walk, it is completely understandable that they would try to find themselves in the TV and movie characters that they identify with. We have all been there at some point during the early stages of our lives, and reflecting on these experiences, we can see how those identifications may have clarified our understanding of who we wanted to be in this world, or what our destiny was to become in the ensuing years.

If we can move into adulthood with this introspective understanding of who we are becoming spiritually, then we can take the conscious step of letting go of these superficial identifications that have defined our past selves, to allow this authentic self the inner space to more fully emerge. Being a natural consequence of partaking in intentional growth and maturation, this ascension to the higher realms of human unfolding won't be able to be affected if we are unconsciously preoccupied with playing these artificial roles for the world to see. When we engage in these acts of hiding, the truth of who we are remains obscured, and this presents a significant encumbrance to relating to others and the world from the reality of who we are.

Try as we might to know the world intimately, we will never succeed in this endeavour if our understanding of ourselves is superficial and grounded in ego consciousness. So limited is the perspicacity of this false self that it can't help but distort the reality that it gazes upon. Here, think of the CEO who is intent on playing the role of hero in his company's story. Believing that the company cannot survive without his presence, he detrimentally attempts to seize control of its operational processes through micromanagement, despite the clear negative effects that this is having on the morale and effort of the people who work under him. Embodying also this warped sense of identity, and thus reality, is the diva with a princess complex who is convinced that other people dislike her out of jealousy, when the real cause of their distain is her pompous behaviour and transparent self-consumption.

While these may be extreme examples that I have used, there are a multitude of subtler ways in which our alignment with ego brings us out of alignment with the natural state of our world. When we have ego based thoughts such

29

as a competitive dislike for somebody who we want to best, this produces an internal state of discord that interferes with our spirit's harmonious character. If being free of these ego oriented thoughts makes our mind like the calm still surface of a pond, then introducing them into this medium of consciousness would be like throwing a large stone into that body of water. Creating a cascading ripple effect that has disrupted the equilibrium of that body, the ensuing disturbance also presents a double barrier to being able to clearly see one's reflection on its surface and peer into its depths.

This explains why we so often struggle to access the inner wisdom and other virtues that we possess, and live in accordance with their promptings. By living in a way where these surface level disturbances become routinely indulged, the effect on our conditioning is for it to represent a disoriented state of affairs through which we are susceptible to believing that our role in life is to be found and lived out in the milieu of this chaos and drama. This role though, when conceived amidst this unrelenting storm of ego driven activity, won't be reflective of our deeper spiritual calling that the storm shrouds, and the redeeming purpose that it has to heal all misconceptions that we have of reality.

While the ego wants to revel in the drama filled mess that is has created in our minds, the spirit wants to cut through this polluting clutter so that we may reconnect and relate to the pure consciousness of the world that finds life in all things. This is why the space created by deep spiritual practice is so valuable. Stemming the unforgiving current of fallacious and nonsensical thoughts, what emerges from the mind is the conscious realisation that the roles which we play in life do not define us. Being like different sets of clothes that we adorn and remove depending on whether we are going to the office, a family function or place of worship, they fall short in being able to define us in an absolute sense. While the ego would try to convince us that we are the appearances that we project to the world, our spirit in its wisdom is not fooled by this shallow appraisal of our worth. Being aware of appearances without giving them the weight of a characterisation, this goes a way to explaining the spirit's reluctance to engage in judgement, particularly on the basis of what can only be seen with the visual sense, but not known in its interiority.

With this I ask, who or what can be judged rightly, that cannot be seen at all? So blind and confined is the ego that it does not know what it cannot see, and yet it so readily gives voice to its righteous opinions about how the world works. Blustering about these perceived realities to protect itself from the revelation of its falsehood, it makes an ignorant fool of the person who would speak its untruths. Often it is the case that ego oriented individuals would prefer not to be acquainted with the truth of a given situation if that were to diminish the identity that they have built up for themselves in their mind. Needing the world to accord with the distorted picture that they have painted with their unconsciousness, they are masters of denial who have learned to play the inauthentic roles of life to a tee. Inevitably, how they present to the world in one area of their life is how they will also present to the world in the other areas, with a stranger's mask on.

This might seem like a harsh and overarching statement to make, but from what I have observed in others and in myself, it is invariably true. One doesn't wear half a mask in any given moment, and they are either consciously bringing the spirit to bear on the life of the world, or relating to it from the shadows of unconsciousness. In this, we can't not make a choice that reflects the intention to either be a bearer of life or a dealer of death. Where the former consequence is manifested through presence, the latter is brought about by a separating movement away from integrity or wholeness. If you are unaware of your ego orientated way of relating to the world, as we are prone to be when we live unconsciously, look at the outcomes that your thoughts, words and actions produce, for guidance on this point. As it concerns the individuals with whom you relate, do you tend to silence them, break them down, lead them astray or divide them from a broader group of people? Or what about the effects that you have on the objects of this world. Is your inclination to destroy or denigrate nature or what others possess, or manipulate the use of resources to bring about a result that serves you, but detracts from the fulfilment of a greater good?

If you look at the impacts of some of the most infamous leaders in world history, you will see in their wake a path of destruction that testified to their egocentric nature. Joseph Stalin, Adolf Hitler, Saddam Hussein, Mao Zedong and Pol Pot were directly responsible for torturing and killing millions of people. Muammar Gaddafi quashed the prosperity of the Libyan nation and silenced his political dissenters by making their opposition illegal. Slobodan Milosevic played a significant role in the Yugoslav conflicts of the 1990's that would subsequently break apart that country. Months after writing this, Russian president and authoritarian strongman Vladimir Putin launched an unprovoked war against Ukraine that has put the stability of Europe and the larger world in jeopardy.

These examples present a consistent pattern of divisiveness that is related to another penchant of the ego, which is to participate in zero sum games. For the ego driven agent to win or get ahead, others have to lose, or be reduced to a means of their advancement. This explains why individuals who are steeped in ego consciousness are prone to mistreat others by exploiting and manipulating them for purposes that are self-serving. To them, there is never enough of the 'good things' in life to go around, and for others to enjoy prosperity in any form means that there is less of that prosperity that is available to flow to them. Underlying this mentality is a deficit of spirit that breeds a fear of lack and missing out which produces a tremendous amount of anxiety and grief that pervade every aspect of how these individuals live their lives.

We all know people who struggle to be genuinely happy for others when good things happen to them. In most, if not all, of these cases, the phenomenon that I have described above is at work. Despite the close nature of the relationship that may exist between the two individuals, and the willingness of the person who has prospered to share of their gains with their friend or family member, the other party to this relationship won't be able to get past their perceived deprivation of not receiving what the other person has. By adopting a victim mentality in response to these circumstances, they will fortify their entitled ego orientation and become more motivated to out possess this other person in the future, if that means that within themselves they will feel superior in comparison to that other.

While this might feel like a sustaining victory for these people, over the long haul these types of battles prove to be deleterious to their being. If the ego were to have its way, this oppressive game of needing to one up others would never end. Being irresistible in its habit of looking out into the world for a point of comparison that elevates its perceived standing in it, there is never a shortage of others to point to who have less of what it values than the agent who chooses its company. With these comparisons producing a sense of supremacy that brings a temporary satisfaction and strengthening of their worldly identity, the fall comes with the fading of these feelings which don't last for very long. The reason for this is that amongst the other points of comparison that are encountered in the world are those who invariably possess more than the ego aligned agent, who in the company of these more affluent individuals will feel deficient and insecure because of their relative material shortcomings. Equating their self-worth to what they have which doesn't measure up to what these other individuals possess, they are easily diminished in their own estimation, and in the eyes of the world that will reflect how they perceive themselves.

With this relentless ebb and flow of their strengthened and diminished sense of identity, life takes its toll on the ego aligned agent, as peace and fulfilment become exceedingly difficult to find amidst the externalities of the physical world to which they have ceded control for how they will be defined. Try as we might to thrive in the world, we won't prove capable of achieving this end if we don't live our lives with an internal locus of control that puts us at the centre of our experience of life, in terms of autonomously exercising our decision making ability and interpreting the events in our lives from an empowered perspective. As it pertains to the narrative that we construct about our lives which will orient the path that we will take into the future, the one that is crafted by the agent with an internal locus of control is most aligned with the character of the human spirit and the intention of our creator to endow us with the abilities to exercise free will and self-determination.

Contrary to what the ego puts forward, one does not have to come at the expense of the other. We can affect win-win outcomes where interests align and prosperity is shared amongst individuals and nations. When we evolve to recognise that others are spiritually an extension of ourselves, and that the future of humanity is forged on common ground, it becomes clear that there is no viable alternative to us collaborating in order to get what we need and want from life. What benefits one benefits all, and we would be wise not to deprive others of what we look for ourselves, being the essential things that are required in order to lead a good life. To greedily and unjustifiably take these things away from others so that we can be further 'enriched' for the sake of keeping up with the Joneses, not only reduces the quality of their lives, but also more broadly it diminishes the security and sovereignty of our own. When poverty is widespread across a population, for example, this not only makes life miserable for those who can't afford to make ends meet, but it also produces a more perilous societal landscape for those who are not without to navigate. Add to this the various fears of violence, theft, terrorism and the effects of substance abuse, among others, that contaminate the minds of this society's privileged members by arousing their suspicions and anxieties, and it becomes evident how we all lose out by allowing such inequitable conditions to materialise.

For all of the superficial quick fix solutions that have been proposed by governments and other instrumentalities over the years to rectify these problems, not many have worked to affect sustained and meaningful change to the dysfunctional behaviour that has led them to occur. This is because ultimately, external mechanisms cannot reconcile any deficits in consciousness that are innate to the members of a given population. As well intentioned as politicians may be in believing that changes to the law, sound policy making and well-funded community programs have the power to drive social progress, the impact of these initiatives will be limited if at the individual level the members of these communities don't endeavour to evolve out of ego consciousness towards a spirit centred life that gives a voice to their calling. This inner work and journey is the true essence of what leadership is. Before one can lead others in the world, they first have to lead themselves out of the shadows of unconsciousness. Only then can they become a beacon of light that is capable of illuminating the path to a brighter tomorrow.

In Chapter three, I will expand on this idea that our innate leadership capacity is intimately connected to the manifestation of our calling/s and the virtues of spirit that we have been given life to express, but before we go there, it is necessary to outline the core qualities of a calling that add to our understanding of the spirit as the caller in our lives. It is my hope that in the body of this next chapter you will come across some insights that will assist you in determining whether you are currently living your calling, or enlighten your path towards that future direction.

CHAPTER 2: The Anatomy of a Calling

"Racing has been a part of my life since I was eight and it is literally an extension of my life and my body. It's really odd, but I feel it. I guess that's why I'm good at what I do, because I don't just drive with my head, I feel it in my heart, I feel it in my chest, I feel it in my abs, I feel it in my butt, I feel it in my neck, I feel everything. That's why I love it, because there is nothing else that I do that feeds all that and I can get those feelings from." ~ Lewis Hamilton, seven-time Formula One World Champion.

What have you been put on this earth to do and become? In what domain/s do you feel most alive and find an outlet for the authentic expression of who you really are? How do you want to make an impact and leave a legacy that is worth being remembered for? What brings joy, fulfilment and meaning to your life?

If our intention is to ascend to the highest levels of human functioning and flourishing, we can't avoid asking these important questions of life. In the answers that emerge from the depths of our spirit, we find, or should I say uncover, our abiding purpose for being. This purpose, we will describe as our calling or vocation, which is derived from the Latin word *"vocare"*, meaning *"to call"*, and *"vox"*, which translates as *"voice"*. While a calling has many more dimensions to it, which I will describe throughout this chapter, at its heart lies this purpose that gives direction and meaning to our lives, and brings us into union with the world and the need that it has for what our unique and authentic being has to offer. Were it not for this need being present in the life of the world, we would never have been born in the first place, and yet here we find ourselves despite the miraculous and near impossible odds of each of our lives taking the form that it has.

When you think about it, each of us embodies a non-replicable composite of genetic material that has been inherited from generations of our ancestors, who amongst the billions of people to have lived on the planet, had to come together at precise moments in time and place in order to eventually produce the offspring that kept alive your chance of successfully entering the world. And all amidst the perilous threats of war, disease, famine and the like. Despite these formidable obstacles, and perhaps because of them, you and I made it. Quite clearly, resilience is etched into the physical and spiritual DNA of the human species, otherwise we would have died out like the dinosaurs did millions of years ago.

That we have this opportunity at life is no accident, and to do this blessing justice, we should not waste it by living shallow and hedonistic lives that are disconnected from the spiritual source of our being. American philosopher

Henry David Thoreau once lamented that the mass of men lead lives of quiet desperation, and go to the grave with their song still in them. This song that he writes about is our calling that is sung by the voice of our spirit. Whether you are presently aware of it or not, you have a song to sing and a voice within you that is yearning to sing it. Perhaps in your most introspective moments you have acknowledged this and allowed your spirit to speak to you, so that you know it is there. By you already having a conscious recognition of this presence of spirit within, a strong foundation exists for you to strengthen that relationship and cultivate trust in your spirit so that it can guide your path into the future.

In the absence of you having this spiritual awareness, there will be more work for us to do before you can come to the realisation that you have a calling to live. That work will involve cutting through the self-serving beliefs of the ego that have until now prevented you from enjoying a more intentional and fulfilling life. With this, it is important to understand that the ego doesn't want you to be receptive to the spiritual voice of your calling, for as you listen to that call and allow yourself to be guided by it, the ego loses the power to control your life. This is why it tempts us to trivial distraction that has us running away from the lives that we were born to live like hamsters on a wheel. The outcome of living in such an evasive way is as Thoreau described: a life of quiet desperation, which if they were honest could be attested to by those poor souls who have lost themselves in the hustle and bustle of the societal rat race that has them consign their faulty ladder of 'success' to structures that their spiritual heart has no compelling reason to scale.

For portions of my life I had my ladder up against the wrong wall, so I can speak to the internal emptiness that is experienced when we deny the voice of our calling. In my early twenties, I worked as a deckhand on the family fishing boat for three years, but this was a role that I had reflexively entered into to earn a living. I had no passion for the work and I mainly went into it because I thought that it would be easy and provide security. While I did like aspects of the work such as its physicality and being out in nature on a daily basis, as a whole it didn't provide me with a feeling that what I was doing mattered in the grand scheme of things. Perhaps to someone else who had a calling to crayfishing, they would have experienced a deeper meaning to their work, but for me this was not present. In writing this now, I can see how this meaning and fulfilment was not present at that time because I was not present in the company of my spirit.

In so many ways, I was immature and walled off at that stage of my journey, and not having a solid understanding of who I was or what I wanted to do with my life prevented me from really engaging with the work and giving of myself to it. In this respect, it was like being part of a one-sided relationship where I was taking what I wanted from the other person and not reciprocating by withholding what they needed from me. Just as this would produce an unsatisfying and dysfunctional union that was destined to end at some point, so was my time in this job on borrowed time because I had not previously done the challenging work of discerning what my authentic gifts were and figuring out whether they were aligned with what this role required of me.

One can't give of what they don't have, or are blinded to within themselves. We therefore need to open our eyes and look inward to find the natural talents and inclinations that we were born into the world with. This will begin the process of reconnecting to our spirit, from which these giftings and powerful instincts can emerge forth. As doubtful as your conditioned mind may be that this search will bear fruit, your heart holds no such doubts or fears of a transformative outcome being affected through your spiritual inquiry. Having waited on your receptivity to its promptings with infinite patience, its commitment to your unfolding is resolute.

Although you may waver in taking the initial steps away from the ego centred life that you have become used to, take comfort in knowing that you have nothing of true value to lose and a tremendous amount to gain by aligning with your calling. Promising an abundance of blessings that your ego cannot deliver, the spirit's offerings are worth more than money can buy. If you were to ask someone who has found their calling whether they could imagine themselves doing anything else with their life, they would respond in the negative. Such are the intrinsic and extrinsic rewards that flow into our lives when we have the courage to venture into the unchartered waters of our true selves.

Attesting to the tangible benefits that flow from living a calling are a collection of academic research studies which not only evidence that living one's calling promotes and sustains meaning in life[7], but that other positive effects include greater work and life satisfaction[8], increased well-being with reduced

---

[7] Bunderson, J. S., & Thompson, J. (2009). *The call of the wild: Zookeepers, callings, and the double-edged sword of deeply meaningful work.* Administrative Science Quarterly, 54(1), 32-57.; Duffy, R. D., & Sedlacek, W. E. (2010). *The salience of a career calling among college students: Exploring group differences and links to religiousness, life meaning, and life satisfaction.* The Career Development Quarterly, 59(1), 27-41.

[8] Wrzesniewski, A., McCauley, C., Rozin, P., & Schwartz, B. (1997). *Jobs, careers, and callings: People's relations to their work.* Journal of Research in Personality, 31(1), 21-33.; Duffy R., Bott, E., Allan, B., Torrey, C., & Dik, B. (2012). *Perceiving a calling, living a*

incidents of stress and depression[9], experiences of inspiration[10], clarity of self-concept[11], more engaged and adaptive professional development[12], stronger work commitment and task involvement[13] and enhanced organisational effectiveness and productivity.[14] Several studies have also shown the importance of actually *living* a calling to increased life satisfaction (as opposed to merely perceiving the presence of a calling).[15]

As dark as the world can seem at times, it is illuminated by those bold men and women who have seen the light and realised that it shines within each of us. Throughout the course of human history, it has always been this way. These leaders, or beacons of hope, have drawn upon the energy of their

calling, and job satisfaction: Testing a moderated, multiple mediator model. Journal of Counseling Psychology, 59(1), 50-59.

[9] Treadgold, R. (1999). *Transcendent vocations: Their relationship to stress, depression, and clarity of self-concept.* The Journal of Humanistic Psychology, 39(1), 81-105.; Peterson, U., Demerouti, E., Bergstrom, G., Samuelsson, M., Asberg, M., & Nygren, A. (2008). *Burnout and physical and mental health among Swedish healthcare workers.* Journal of Advanced Nursing, 62, 84-95.

[10] O'Grady, K. (2011). *The role of inspiration in organizational life.* Journal of Management, Spirituality & Religion, 8(3), 257-272.; O'Grady, K., & Richards P. S. (2011). *The role of inspiration in scientific scholarship and discovery: Views of theistic scientists.* EXPLORE: The Journal of Science and Healing, 7(6), 354-362.

[11] Duffy, R., & Sedlacek, W. (2007). *The presence of and search for a calling: Connections to career development.* Journal of Vocational Behavior, 70(3), 590-601.

[12] Constantine, M., Miville, M., Warren, A., Gainor, K., & Lewis-Coles, M. (2006). *Religion, spirituality, and career development in African American college students: A qualitative inquiry.* The Career Development Quarterly, 54(3), 227-241.; Domene, J., Dik, B., & Duffy R. (2012). *Calling and career outcome expectations: The mediating role of self-efficacy.* Journal of Career Assessment, 20(3), 281-292.

[13] Serow, R., Eaker, D., & Ciechalski, J. (1992). *Calling, service and legitimacy: Professional orientations and career commitment among prospective teachers.* Journal of Research and Development in Education, 25(3), 136-141.; Jia, Y., Hou, Z., & Wang, D. (2021). *Calling and career commitment among Chinese college students: Career locus of control as a moderator.* International Journal for Educational and Vocational Guidance, 21(1), 211-230.

[14] Fry, L., & Slocum Jr, J. (2008). *Maximizing the triple bottom line through spiritual leadership.* Organizational Dynamics, 37(1), 86-96.; Jeon, K., Passmore, D., Lee, C., & Hunsaker, W. (2013). *Spiritual leadership: A validation study in a Korean context.* Journal of Management, Spirituality & Religion, 10(4), 342-357.

[15] Duffy, R., Allan, B., & Bott, E. (2012). *Calling and life satisfaction among undergraduate students: Investigating mediators and moderators.* Journal of Happiness Studies, 13(3), 469-479.; Duffy, R. D., Allan, B. A., Autin, K. L., & Bott, E. M. (2013). *Calling and life satisfaction: It's not about having it, it's about living it.* Journal of Counseling Psychology, 60, 42-52.; Allan, B. A., Tebbe, E. T., Duffy, R. D., & Autin, K. L. (2015). *Living a calling, life satisfaction, and workplace climate among an LGB population.* The Career Development Quarterly, 63, 306-319.

inspiration, creativity and conviction to bring humanity out of the shadows of its own unconsciousness to envision the higher potential of which we are capable of fulfilling. Whether these extraordinary people were well-known or not, what separated them from the masses of people who were living ordinary lives as unquestioning followers of the status quo, was that they were determined to become all that they were capable of being so that they did not go to their graves with their music still in them.

To have a calling is to recognise intrinsically that whatever it is, it is something that you absolutely must do. Another way of saying this is that you cannot not follow your calling once you connect with it within yourself, which is how a number of respondents described their feelings towards living their particular vocation. One of these respondents, who is a brilliant and very accomplished chef and restauranteur, articulated on this point that he feels positively addicted to his purpose, in the sense that the more that he engages with it, the more intense is the impulse that he feels within to immerse himself in its workings. This can turn into a problem of course if one's passion for their work is not seen as a part of a broader calling that one has to their family, for example, or the self-care practices that are necessary to support sustained engagement in that calling over the long term.

Once we have seen the light, the prospect of returning to the darkness, where we resided in unconsciousness, becomes unpalatable to our higher self. To do so would feel like we are backsliding with our lives, which even to those who are not living their calling, would appear to be an unattractive path to take. As comfortable and familiar as that darkness may have been to our base ego self, when we have awakened to the presence of our spirit within, our very being enlarges, and what once housed our conception of who we were, now becomes a restrictive and even painful place to reside. If one were to have size eleven feet, they wouldn't think to wear size seven shoes, despite those shoes having fitted very well at a previous point in time. To unwisely persist in wearing those size seven's in the present, suffering, in the form of blisters and muscular cramping, would be invited to diminish their experience of life in unwanted ways.

What we desire and expect from life changes as we evolve, and when we connect with our calling, we begin to experience the most significant in-life transformation that a human being is capable of achieving. Being like a near-death experience that opens one's eyes to what really matters in life, when we come to face our calling, we effectively turn our back on what we thought that we wanted from life from an ego based perspective. Through having our life purpose revealed to us, we become disillusioned, which sounds like a bad thing to the ego, but is a blessing to those who seek to be liberated from the confines of falsehood. Disillusionment is the breaking down of that which is not real to bring truth to the surface of our conscious awareness, which frees us to act independently of conditioned norms of behaviour that don't resonate with what we now know in the light of truth makes for a meaningful life. Duty is joy, as is doing good deeds for others, and guided by these virtues we can make a real difference to the quality that life takes in the world. When we are living our calling, we do this by infusing the essence of who we are into our work, in ways that others are not capable of when they are merely working for themselves in a job or career. With this, it is important to understand what differentiates a calling from these other two modes of participating in work.

A job is something that we do to get by in the world, to pay the bills, buy necessities and to enjoy some pleasures in life outside of our work. Seen merely as a means to these ends where the person in the job is effectively disengaged from the work they have been tasked with performing, a job falls far short in its ability to deliver a meaningful experience of work. In terms of fulfilling our other higher order needs as human beings, working in a job is a woefully inadequate means of achieving that end, and it most certainly won't allow us to scale the heights of Maslow's pyramid and self-actualise if that is our intention. I say this not to denigrate jobs as their utility is evident at different stages of our lives. My entrée into the world of work on the fishing boat was one such example in my life.

While being different in its character from a job, a career is similarly limited in its ability to deliver a spiritually fulfilling experience of work. This is because the motivations that are associated with it are often ego based, and they neglect to factor in the meaningfulness of work as a primary determinant in deciding what career to pursue. A person who is intent on forging a career will base their decisions on external considerations that will best allow them to increase their social standing over the medium to long term of their working lives. The types of things that they will be concerned about will include where they can make the most money or enjoy a greater number of perks, how long it will take them to advance up the promotional ladder, and the perceived status that their career endows them with relative to other lines of work.

While a career can and often does bring a person into alignment with their natural aptitudes and passion for a line of work, the self-centric way in which it is pursued can affect a divide between participating in the work itself and the fulfilment of the deeper social and spiritual purposes that one might subconsciously long to realise through their involvement in it. When one sees their work as a career, thoughts of how they can contribute to the common good of the world or the strengthening of communities, for example, are only secondary drivers of how one's work is carried out, if these higher aims are even contemplated at all.

Contrast this to a calling, where the higher virtues of spirit drive how one fulfils their overarching purpose, engages with the world on a daily basis, and aligns their being with the life of their work. In this, a calling is all encompassing, and there is no divide that exists between who a person is at their core and the function that their work allows them to serve in the world. This produces an integrity that is just not present when one is involved in either a job or a career. While a career promises to satisfy more of the needs identified by Maslow than a job can, it still doesn't bring us into union with the yearnings of our spirit to live a life that nourishes more than just the physical, emotional and psychological dimensions of our being.

Who we are is not limited to the physical body, our emotional expressions or the mental constructions that we have of ourselves, and we can only understand this as we stand outside the concentric circles that represent each of these elements. From this broader perspective, we can see that there is more of ourselves that needs to be considered and given a voice through the sacred work that we have been called to do. When I refer to 'work' in this context, it has a wider application than you may previously have considered. Raising children in the home is most certainly work for which a calling can be felt, as is volunteering to assist others, even if this does not involve monetary compensation.

Not only does our calling encompass our work in the world, but it also comprises the inner work that shapes how we will go about performing this worldly work. I think that when most of us think about living our calling, we limit it to the domain of what might traditionally be thought of as service to others, which is the realm in which we do, but our calling also extends to who we have been given life to become. Quite simply, we have been given life to be as spirit is, or to say it another way, to embody the character of our creator, that some call God, in our being. This explains why the life of virtue has been held up as the ultimate human aim over the course of recorded history. Even the ancient Egyptians honoured the concepts of truth, balance, order, harmony, law, morality, and justice through the Goddess Maat, who was believed to personify these virtues.

To live our calling is to consciously evolve towards that life of virtue. Inherent in this task is the duty to develop ourselves and others. The word 'develop' is an interesting one from an etymological standpoint because originally its meaning in French was *'to unfold and reveal meaning'*. In this sense, development is the act of bringing to the surface of our being that which is most substantive within us. If we accept that the spirit is the basis of our existence, then by extension, we develop ourselves and others by bringing about an alignment with spirit so that its virtues can be first embodied by us and then perpetuated in the world. As we affect this spiritual unfolding in ourselves and others, we give to life more holistically, and the ode of our calling doesn't just revolve around what we do for work.

Extending to all facets of our lives, we are challenged through this calling to live with integrity and stay receptive to the virtuous promptings of spirit at all times. As exacting as this standard appears to be, it is not one where perfection is the goal, which is unrealistic, but rather an excellence of character that sees us consistently demonstrate these virtues in our daily lives. As I see it, one of the most incredible things about life is that it is impossible for us to out evolve it. What I mean by this is that there is always room for us to learn and grow, even at the time when we are taking our dying breaths. To honour this blessed quality of life is to steadfastly hold the space in which we can bear witness to the transformative power that we have as human beings. Just as the forms of the physical world, such as the concept of time, are never static, so was the substance of our inner lives never intended to remain rigidly set. While we may find comfort in the prospect of being who we are now into the future, living in this way would only stifle our responsiveness to the calling of our spirit within.

Despite the barrenness that this stagnant state of existence produces in the world, in many ways it has come to define the current human condition. While there are a multitude of factors that contribute to this inert way of being, such as fear of the unknown or not wanting to confront the wounds of our past, one of the most prominent causes as I see it is the denial of our spiritual calling. What motivates this eschewal of our innate purpose can be different from person to person. For one person, it might be a rejection of religion from which they perceive their calling as originating. For another, it might be because they are too heavily invested in forging a reputation that values external appearances over internal substance.

A rather frequent justification that I have encountered for this during my time working in the law is the desire that one has for parental approval regarding their career choices. Whether one's parent/s are lawyers or not, if the law is a path that their parents are intent on their children taking, then that can be hugely influential in steering a child away from their genuine passion or felt sense of purpose and towards the profession of law, or other professions such as medicine or finance, that are traditionally perceived to be high status lines of work that offer career security and an increased earning potential over the long term. The pressure that one feels to acquiesce to these parental desires doesn't even have to be overtly exercised by the parent. It can be implicitly applied if there is a familial connection to a particular profession, where the expectation is that the child will follow in their parents, or other relatives, footsteps in order to preserve that connection, and the felt sense of pride or respect that have been garnered through their lengthy involvement in that line of work.

I have also seen this phenomenon at work in the lives of my students who I often counsel on the future direction of their lives. While noble intentions might underpin their decision to follow a career course that was set by their parents, my view is that they are sacrificing way too much of themselves in following this lead, if their intrinsic calling is not aligned with the career in question. What one's calling is, is a part of their spiritual DNA, which is a different thing entirely from their genetic DNA. While we might be genetically tethered to our parents and share aspects of their physical composition and personality, their calling is not ours. Coming physically through them, we are spiritually not of them, as Khalil Gibran reminds us of in *The Prophet*. As Gibran also correctly identifies, each of us are sons and daughters of life that is longing to realise itself through our being. *With the spirit as life, we perpetuate life as we honour the calling of our spirit, and by doing this faithfully, we actualise its potentiality to create a heaven on earth through us*. If you have ever questioned whether your life has any greater value than as an instrument of daily activity, then you need to read the preceding sentence again. You are a saviour of the world in waiting[16], and together, our evolution in consciousness can counteract the negativity and destruction that the presence of ego has wreaked on our world.

At the deepest level of your being, you resonate with the hero's journey and acknowledge that it is not a journey that is foreign to your own heart. Who and where you are now is in the process of living it. This is why your spirit rouses when you are watching an uplifting film that involves a redeemed protagonist, or reading an inspiring tale about someone's 'rags to riches' transformation. In these stories, the protagonist is introduced as living some form of ordinary life in which they are constrained by internal or external factors that suppress who they are or what they really want from coming forth. In some of these narratives, the main character may even be totally

---

[16] Note to the ego: I wrote 'a' saviour, not 'the' saviour. One must be cautious in articulating this role and be cognisant of the meaning which the ego attaches to that concept (the ego likes to play the role of saviour to others as this makes it feel superior to those others and fosters their dependence on the ego-driven agent).

oblivious to who they really are or what their life purpose is, that is they are living unconsciously. In the next phase of the story, their life gets turned upside down in some way. This shakes them to their core and forces them to confront a fork in the road. Shall they retreat into their ego and remain who they were previously, languishing in response to these drastically changed circumstances, or will they self-assess to reveal their veritable face and draw upon their deepest resources to successfully meet and overcome this life defining challenge? This defining moment of truth is normally the most captivating part of the movie or book as it will shape the future life or destiny of the character and the world of which they are a part. As this movement towards integrity extends into the final phase of the story, the hero emerges to deploy the virtues of spirit, that they have unearthed through their dealing with adversity, against the chosen personification of evil or destruction in order to achieve victory or liberation.

I can think of a multitude of well-known movies and books in which the protagonists live out this mythical journey. Luke Skywalker in the *Star Wars* Trilogy. Rocky Balboa in the movies of the same name. Harry Potter and Frodo in *Harry Potter* and *The Lord of the Rings* respectively. The character Santiago in Paulo Coelho's *The Alchemist*. Wonder Woman, Katniss Everdeen from *The Hunger Games*, Disney's Moana and Alice with her adventures in Wonderland, all embody well the heroine's journey from darkness to light. While each of these are fictional examples of the hero's journey in action, I can easily point to the lives of real people who have walked a broadly similar path, albeit in very different circumstances. Václav Havel, Oprah Winfrey, Dwayne 'The Rock' Johnson, J.K. Rowling and boxing champion Tyson Fury come to mind as strong illustrations of how this transformative spiritual journey can be lived out in the flesh.

In the final stage of the hero's journey, the hero/heroine returns transformed to the place from which they came. This homecoming represents the circle of life that starts and ends with the eternal spirit. No matter how much we may seek to ignore our calling in order to preserve an ego centred life of pretence and superficiality, this calling never goes away. Like the spirit, it is ever present and committed to the realisation of the promise that our life holds for the world. While the voice of our calling may become faint as we persist to ignore it, it comes back to life as we turn towards the only form of life that is worthy of us.

To think that we were born to just get by, or live a life that is limited by the sum total of our fears or the bounds of our collective conditioning, reveals a deficit in us, and what we understand our life as representing. The framework of each of our lives was designed to align with a larger plan for humanity, and our contributions towards this end are anything but miniscule or insignificant. Despite appearing that way from our limited vantage point, we can trust that as we choose to live our calling, the picture that we paint within that contextual framework of our lives will beautify and enliven the house in which humanity dwells both now and into the future.

Being ourselves inspired in the pursuit of virtuous excellence and the making of an authentic contribution that will help to move the world forward, we are sure to inspire others to do the same and craft their own unique legacies that serve as a testament to the indomitable power of the human spirit. When I think about the lives of influential individuals like Albert Einstein, Leonardo Da Vinci, Socrates, Vincent van Gogh, Marie Curie, Amelia Earhart and Mother Teresa, I wonder whether in their wildest dreams they ever would have conceived of the legacies that they have enjoyed as a consequence of following their respective callings. Having inspired millions of people across the world who they had never met, or were yet to be born, to reach higher towards their potential, and further to meet the needs of others and the world, their leadership, while perhaps being unintended, was inevitable in the sense that it naturally emerged from their decision to live faithfully to their spirit and calling.

When we genuinely commit to living our calling, we will stand up and stand out, not because we are motivated by the ego driven need to be seen by others, but because we are inspired by the duty that we feel to put our best foot forward and make something happen that serves a positive social purpose. Having validated ourselves by listening to this voice of truth within us, we don't feel the need to wait around and seek permission from others, or society more broadly, before we give our calling a voice. Being authentically empowered through this felt conviction and focused in the direction that we know is right for us, we don't waste our precious energy worrying about what other people might think about our calling, or who we are as we pursue that path.

Whether these people understand us or not, or want to try and define how we live our calling, that shouldn't feature on our radar, as all that these considerations have the effect of doing is distracting us from our core work. If they want to be supportive or get involved in the movement that we are creating, then that is wonderful and their assistance is welcomed, but in us doing what we are doing, we aren't dependent on these people getting on board with us or validating us through their approval.

Maybe they aren't the right people to bring on our journey, or the timing of their involvement is not optimal at the present time. Whatever it is, we have to learn to trust in the timing of the universe, and believe that the right people will come into our orbit at precisely the right time. While there is undoubtedly an element of making things happen with our calling, we also must allow things to happen, and not try to control all aspects of the process, or be too attached to things working strictly in accordance with a pre-prepared plan. It is for this reason that when we are living our calling, we need to hold loosely to 'our' goals, and hold the space for insight or opportunities to potentially take us in a different direction.

Many a lived calling journey has been radically altered by the intervention of serendipity or synchronicity that unexpectedly deviates the course of one's life for the better. I know this from personal experience, as my calling as a husband and a father, in the form that it now takes, almost never eventuated. You see, on the day that I first met Elizabeth, the woman who would become my wife, I had previously left the function that we both attended, and I had no conscious intention of returning. It was only as I was driving away from the venue that I felt a strong intuitive pull to go back. Despite not knowing at the time the reason behind this bizarre happening, I made one of the best decisions of my life to trust this internal call and return to the event. Shortly after re-joining the festivities, I met this incredible woman who would become the mother of my two beautiful children. It was only in hindsight that I could see how this event and other synchronous happenings had shaped my life in profound ways and drawn me into greater alignment with my spirit and its guiding wisdom. Speaking to this co-creative relationship that each of us has with spirit as we engage in the process of living our calling was Patañjali, the author of the Yoga Sutras, when he observed that *"When you are inspired by some great purpose, some extraordinary project, all your thoughts break their bonds: Your mind transcends limitations, your consciousness expands in every direction, and you find yourself in a new, great and wonderful world. Dormant forces, faculties and talents become alive, and you discover yourself to be a greater person by far than you ever dreamed yourself to be."*

When we are too set with what we want to do from an ego standpoint, we block the flow of spirit that is seeking expression in our lives. This is why I prefer to adopt a more organic approach to life, where I allow the promptings of my spirit to inform the thoughts and behaviours that I enact in response to what takes place around me. Assisting me to hold this space from which I can co-create with my spirit is the affirmation, *'Do what you ought and trust what may be'.* When we listen to the call of our spirit and do what we ought to in response to its promptings, there is little that we have to fear or sweat over with the outcomes that we produce. This is not to say that the fruits of this conscious collaboration will work out perfectly, or that 'success' is guaranteed. It simply means that we can live serenely with these results, and not have to experience the dreaded feeling of regret that can hang like a cloud over the lives of those who have chosen to relate to the world in an unconscious manner.

As I write this and reflect upon the findings of my research, I am struck by the recurrence of this theme amongst respondents who didn't believe in having regrets and letting this negative view of the past taint their present moment experience of life. How these people perceived the events of their past were as enablers of growth from which they could more fully mature and become who they were created to be. Being like stepping stones that had got them to this point, they were grateful for these events happening, and as difficult as some of them may have been, they were seen to be necessary to foster both resilience and dedication to that which they have been called to do.

Just as the cold of winter makes us appreciate the warmth of summer, so does our time in life's wilderness steel our resolve to make the most of a good thing while we have it. If you are living your calling in this moment, you understand that it is a blessed opportunity that may at a future time not be available to you, so rather than half-heartedly dabbling in that which you are called to do, you respond to the call eagerly with the intent to immerse yourself in it. From this experience, what you put in is what you will draw out, and while you might be tempted to think that joy, fulfilment, tranquility and lovingness are by coincidence characteristic of these spiritually alive persons who are fulfilling their destiny, their embodiment of these exalted virtuous qualities is actually a predictable effect of living life intentionally from our centre, where we know what it means to be wholeheartedly engaged with life.

The spirit is truly our gateway to life and all the good things that it comprises, and as we make ourselves receptive to its presence by responding to our calling, life becomes receptive to us in a way that it never has before. This is why it can feel like the universe opens up to us when we find our spiritual centre, and express the life purpose that becomes conscious through this connection. Being our point of alignment with this source of creation, it also becomes our locus of attraction for its providential gifts that can assist us in more fully actualising our calling.

Since undertaking this study, I have encountered numerous persons who have relayed stories of how when they connected with their vocation, events in their lives aligned to bring into their orbit people, experiences and/or resources that were needed (sometimes without their awareness) to take the next steps on their calling journey. I have experienced this phenomenon at work in my own life, particularly with books that I have been put onto by seemingly random people which have proved to be quite formative in my understanding of the concepts that I write about here, and when I was younger, with the rather large number of pens that I ungratefully received as birthday gifts or for other special occasions.[17] Given that writing is such a focal part of my own calling, I don't see these specific happenings as having occurred by accident. Taking the form that they did for my learning and evolving capacity to serve humankind in the way that I was designed to, this evidences an undeniable love and elegant beauty in the way that the universe speaks directly to each of us in a language that our soul understands.

This, I have only come to appreciate in my later years since connecting with my calling as a writer. You may find this difficult to believe but when I was younger, I was completely indifferent to writing and it was never on my radar as something that I wanted to do. Even the books that I voraciously consume now, you could not have paid me to read during my teenage years. Being largely disconnected from my spirit and having little understanding of who I was or what I wanted to do with my life, I was only capable of speaking the victimised language of the lost at that time, and of being receptive to the surrogate influence of the ego in my life. By this I mean that in the void created by my disconnection from spirit, the promptings of ego become so pervading that they drowned out any communiqués from my floundering spirit. But my spirit never died, just as yours never dies, and ultimately, the despair and emptiness that this dysfunctional and abusive relationship with ego brought to me, served as a powerful impetus to lead a more purposeful and fulfilling life.

Quite simply, I had had enough of living a meagre form of existence in which suffering and meaninglessness had become the norm, and I therefore had a choice to make. Like the proverbial frog that finds itself swimming in a pot of warming water, I wasn't going to allow myself to slowly boil to death, so I had to jump out of that noxious vessel and into a new holding space where I could begin to rebuild my relationship with spirit and become receptive to its voice again. From this turning point, it would be approximately a decade before I connected to my true calling as a writer, with everything that I became involved with in the intervening years being reflective of new and

---

[17] As you can imagine, my teenage self was not thrilled by this choice of gift and would have somewhat understandably much rathered video games, CDs or sporting equipment instead.

emerging dimensions of myself that were finally being given an outlet to flourish.

How I experienced this path to my calling was as a zig-zagging road, rather than a straight-line journey, and mine was definitely not a case of knowing what I wanted to do early in childhood and then moving with clarity in that direction as I got older. Over the years, I have met individuals who fit into this category, but these people, I have found, are rarer to come across than those who have come into their element through a more winding path. However it is that we come to our calling is from my perspective just as important as us connecting to it. This is because the path that we take to our calling is so formative in how we actually live it out. The worn out saying that it is the journey that matters and not the destination, reflects this truth well.

In addition to working as a crayfisherman after leaving school early, I also worked as a security guard, lawyer, salesman and university academic before I came into contact with the thing that I felt called to do. As varied as these previous zigs and zags were, I don't recall having ever considered them to be a waste of time, or experiences that didn't contribute to shaping me as a person, whether in a character sense or in the development of my aptitudes. It is strange, but for as long as I can remember, I have favoured taking a long term perspective towards my life. This became particularly noticeable when I returned to study as a mature age student in my early twenties when my friends were out earning money in their jobs and using their earnings to buy nice cars and expensive clothes to impress members of the opposite sex. While I was tempted to take a similar path and enjoy the hedonistic gratification that such a path would have afforded me, I knew within myself that I had a different route to take if I was to become the person that I wanted to be, or should I say, the person that I thought I wanted to be.

Despite not having yet grasped who I was at my heart or what purpose I was born to fulfil, I felt strongly that if I sought the answer to these questions with honesty and devotion to the path that was uniquely mine, then these pearls of truth would eventually be revealed in time. This thankfully proved to be the case, and putting my faith in this intuition has been one of the best decisions that I have made in my life. Reaping the reward of these profound responses to my call to the source of life, I have never looked back since receiving these revelations. It was once said by Auschwitz concentration camp survivor Viktor Frankl that *"those who have a 'why' to live, can bear with almost any 'how'"*. As true as this statement is, I also think that it could be amended to "those who search for the 'who' and 'why' of their existence, can bear almost any challenge that stands between them and the revealing of these truths".

While I couldn't always see what was going to unfold in front of me at different points of time, I had found the capacity within myself to trust that my path was going to lead somewhere that my soul could call home. By being open and responsive to my spirit, I can see how I liberated it to lead the way amidst the uncertainties of this world, and as I walked in its company, I experienced the reassurance to look upon my path as a marathoner would. Being vested in the journey for the long haul, my concern was not to sprint towards receiving the novel offer of the day. In taking this road that is less travelled by modern standards, I can completely understand how the journey is its own reward and not bereft of any legitimate value, just because it might not deliver the immediate benefits that we are looking to receive as fruits for our labour.

That which is worth building requires its own time to construct, and we shouldn't fear missing out on what may or may not come in the interim. As we come to trust in the direction of our true path, we also come to trust in the prosperity that this path will deliver. No matter who we are, where we are, we have within ourselves the resources that are required to successfully navigate our calling journey. Whatever it is that we appear to lack, we will draw to ourselves as we step out in faith and put one foot in front of the other. One thing does lead to another when we are on the right path. This observation was made by a number of respondents when they reflected upon the interconnected stages of their calling journey, which at the time of them experiencing those different periods, appeared to be more like independent segments that were not woven together with a common thread.

While these stepping stones are often hidden from view as we contemplate the future of our lives, the potential for their unfolding is already present, lying dormant in the seed of our calling. Awaiting our participatory engagement before they are provoked to appear, we co-create their coming forth through our commitment to manifesting the intention of our spirit in the present moment through which it speaks to us. In every waking moment, our spirit is speaking to us of our calling in ways that are both general to life, and specific to the context that is aligned with our animating purpose.[18] In this sense, our calling is composed of multiple parts. At its foundation, our calling is to return to the spiritual source of consciousness within ourselves

---

[18] This could also be extended to the time that we spend asleep when we may receive visions for our life or counsel about our personal unfolding in the form of dreams. On numerous occasions, I have recalled the details of dreams which symbolically have been very meaningful in allowing me to identify areas of my life in which I was unconsciously stuck, and needed to pay greater attention to if I was to evolve and overcome those challenges.

so that we can enact virtue in our dealings with one another and the world. This is the calling to heal and be whole. Working alongside this is the service component of our calling from which we give to the world of the unique set of qualities and talents that we have been born with. As we channel these natural gifts towards the fulfilment of an innate and spiritually defined pro-social purpose that brings meaning to our life and benefit to the world, we also serve others by providing them with a powerful example of leadership in action. To successfully heal the divide between unconsciousness and consciousness, those of us who live from the light within ourselves must act as a bridge for others who are yet to see light, in themselves or the world. In a moment of inspiration, famed French military commander Napoleon Bonaparte comprehended this responsibility when he remarked that *"a leader is a dealer in hope"*. Being one of the many qualities that define a conscious leader, the next chapter will provide a framework of my leadership model and introduce the five themes of conscious leadership behaviour, which will be discussed in greater length in Section two of the book.

Before I conclude this chapter, I want to address and clarify an important dimension of a calling, or should I say 'callings', which is that whatever our calling is at a given moment in time, it may evolve into something else in the future. Professional athletes know this well when father time comes knocking at their door, and the sporting careers which were the focal point of their lives up until that point, have to give way so that a new purposeful pursuit can emerge to guide the next phase of their journey. Mothers also, who transition from meaningful roles in the workplace, to the most meaningful role in the home (and perhaps the world), can have the experience of feeling that the basis of their calling has shifted. While this phenomenon may appear confounding if we have previously subscribed to the belief in a one and only calling, it shouldn't surprise us if we accept that our spirit is not static and it is continually revealing more of itself as we move consciously through our journey of life.

Who we are becoming will impact our relationship with our spirit, and this can alter our course as we move into different phases of growth. When I first went to university in my early 20's to study sports management, I was so incredibly passionate about the area and I couldn't have imagined being involved in anything else, but what happened, rather naturally, was that as I evolved to deepen my relationship with spirit and connect with the emerging dimensions of my being, I gravitated towards other things. First it was the law, then it was teaching and writing, which is the focus of my calling today. Whether this will change, I don't know, but I strive to remain open to taking an alternate course if that is what my spirit prompts me to do in a future present moment. As for now, this present moment is all that I am consumed with, which allows me to do justice to this work and speak to you through the same medium in which the spirit speaks to me. With this, understand that the means of conscious connection and understanding is not defined by the worldly rules of time that influence so many of our daily movements. What has happened in the past, or will happen in the future, can only hinder our receptiveness to the calling of our spirit in the only time there is, now. Honour thus the present moment as an enabler of your calling, and the flourishing that your spirit centred life will contribute to the world.

If after reading these defining features of a calling, you are daunted or feeling pangs of doubt in your ability to live them out, I want to reassure you that this is well within your power. Nobody I know, or have read about in the course of human history, has lived out their calling in every moment of every day of their life.[19] Being a practical impossibility that isn't worth aspiring to as a life goal, what I am asking you to strive towards is being present and consciously aligned with your spirit in the now which facilitates this most essential relationship, and if we can do this together then that will go a long way towards strengthening the influence of spirit in the affairs of the world and creating the conditions in which more people feel at peace in following the path of their own heart. As you work towards your embodiment of this integral way of being, there will inevitably be challenges and failures that see you fall short in your efforts, and I can assure you that I also experience these trials every day in some shape or form, whether it is at work when I am having a hectic day, or in my relating to my children with patience and understanding. When I am tempted to feel that not meeting this mark makes me a hypocrite for writing a book such as this, I am at the same time reminded to show myself some love and compassion, and to draw wisdom from the lessons that these shortcomings afford me. Without these relapses there can be no recovery of our spirit, and we should draw hope from this, as we should from the calling journey itself which teaches that just because something is extremely difficult to do in its totality, doesn't mean that it isn't worth doing to the best of our abilities.

---

[19] Even Jesus, a paragon of virtue to so many, and an excellent example of someone who was living his calling, acted in ways which indicated that he didn't always live in alignment with his spirit, for example, when he lost his temper at the temple, and doubted the presence of God on the cross when he questioned why his father had forsaken him.

CHAPTER 3: Leadership through a Lived Calling - An Introduction to the Five Themes of Conscious Leadership Behaviour

Let me commence this chapter by offering my own perspective on the leadership question that scholars have ruminated on for decades, which is whether leaders are born, or are they made through the impacts that their life's events have had on them? Before I jump in with my answer, I must first qualify it by stating my belief that the binary framing of this question doesn't really assist us in answering it with the depth that respects leadership as a multi-dimensional construct. In reducing it down to an either/or proposition, we are apt to close our minds off to broader considerations that inform a holistic understanding of how leaders come to be. Now that I no longer have to fall on one side of this discussion, I can offer that each of us is born with the potentiality to be a leader, and that the circumstances of our lives can, and often do, play a pivotal role in bringing these leadership qualities forth in the world.

As neat as it might seem to classify some people as natural born leaders and others as mere followers who are incapable of developing these leadership qualities, I think that this presents an incomplete picture that is injurious in its dishonouring of the innate ability that human beings have to evolve and embody leadership behaviour. Serving to disempower those whose present mode of being aligns more closely with the latter category, this lazy and fixed way of thinking assumes that there are in built limits to how some people can develop if they were not blessed with 'leadership DNA' at birth. These limits however, are largely contrived in the minds of those who subscribe to this erroneous way of thinking, and in those who have allowed themselves to be conditioned to believe that they are inherently deficient in their leadership capability. The future is what we make it, and just as we can intentionally cultivate our relationship to spirit and the qualities of character which emerge from that integral movement, we can evolve to embody conscious leadership behaviour that will become as natural in its demonstration as the very act of breathing. I know this at an experiential level, as the path that I took to become the leader that I am today was one that unfolded over time as I took steps to mine my own soul for its wisdom and insight.

At no stage in my youth was I looked upon as a leader by the adults in my life, and I do not recall having ever been nominated as a captain of any of the sporting teams that I played for. I most certainly was never a prefect at school, and socially, I was not someone who organised events, or was the central hub in a group of friends over which I exerted influence. All too often, I preferred to keep my own company rather than socialise with others, which was likely an outcome of being raised as an only child. While this was suited to my reserved and introverted disposition, it was most definitely not a quality that would inspire others to be led by me. One could say that I started my journey in a shell and I was very comfortable in playing the role of follower. As natural as that seemed at the time, I now know that in many ways I was stifled within myself, and it took me growing as a person and a leader to gain the perspective to be able to see that clearly today.

In stark contrast to the way that I was in my youth, were some of my contemporaries at school and in sports who seemed to innately possess some of the traits that are commonly associated with leadership, such as the confidence to speak up and the courage to put oneself forward in the face of challenging circumstances. Having kept in touch with some of these 'natural born' leaders as we moved into adulthood, it has been interesting to observe that their leadership capacities haven't seemed to evolve much, if at all, since our adolescence, and in many ways their current mode of being actually evinces more of the characteristics of a follower that goes along to get along and thus reinforces the status quo of their daily existence.

I believe that the prime reason for this has been their unwillingness to honour the natural inclination to growth that we human beings have been born with. While these contemporaries no doubt grew physically into their adult bodies, in the spiritual, intellectual and emotional dimensions of their lives, they appear to have fallen into the trap that has become all too common in our society which is to eschew giving conscious attention to evolving ourselves in these areas. Lacking the intentionality to develop these core dimensions of their being, these individuals effectively moved out of step with the part of themselves from which their leadership once sprung, and as a consequence these aptitudes have atrophied, much like the muscles of a weightlifter who hasn't renewed their gym membership in years.

As one of my respondents beautifully summated about this contention, *"Leadership is the peak of the personal development journey"*. Being the place that we arrive at when we have done the work of character formation that enables us to exhibit the most evolved version of ourselves, it is as much dependent on being present in the company of the spirit in the moments of our lives, as it is on doing the actual work of strengthening our capacities. In so many ways, we look upon leaders as doers, and honour those who effectively bring about outcomes through their actions, but this is only one side of the equation. What is often missing is the attention given to the beingness of the leader, which underpins what they do and the spirit in which they do it. If a leader, especially one with power and resources at their disposal, acts without

54

the consciousness of being, then there is a good chance that they will bring about self-serving outcomes that perpetuate unconsciousness in the world. An example of this would be to base organisational decisions solely on the profit to be earned, rather than the furtherance of the social purpose which justifies that organisation's place in the broader economy.

Now more than ever, the world needs integrated leaders, whose yin of being balances their yang of action, to heal the divide that exists between what we know makes for great leadership, and the unconscious way that it is commonly practiced. I can't think of a time in recent memory when the lack of belief in and mistrust of leaders has been this high, and across a range of domains there have been numerous examples of the significant harm that can be caused by leaders who habitually engage in unprincipled and egocentric behaviour.[20] And these are just the high profile cases. What of the leadership practices within the less conspicuous organisations that we come into contact with on a daily basis? If the escalating rates of employee disengagement, burnout and staff turnover are any indication to go by, then the practice of leadership within those institutions is deficient in significant respects as well.

Tempering the damage that these poor models of leadership have brought about is the emergence of conscious leaders who have observed or personally experienced the shortcomings of ego based leadership styles, and resolved not to replicate the harm that they inflict on their people, or the working culture of the organisations that they exercise stewardship over. Having wisely learnt their lessons about how leadership should not be done, they have taken it upon themselves to become purpose-driven agents of transformation who will move the practice of leadership forward and infuse it with the virtues of spirit that I will outline in the next section of the book. When I think of who currently models this conscious leadership in the world, individuals such as Patagonia founder Yvon Chouinard, Naturalist David Attenborough, international sporting captains Siya Kolisi and Patty Mills, virtuoso cellist Yo-Yo Ma, animal behaviourist Temple Grandin, Whole Foods Market founder John Mackey and former national political leaders Jacinda Ardern and Jose Mujica stand out as prominent examples.

---

[20] In religion, with paedophiles in the priesthood and the sanctioning of extremist acts of violence; in politics, with the vain posturing and manipulations of Donald Trump, Kim Jong-un and Vladimir Putin; in entertainment, with the sexual impropriety of Harvey Weinstein, R. Kelly and former Disney/Pixar head John Lasseter; in business, the CEOs of Australia's big four banks at the time of the Royal Commission into the Banking industry come immediately to mind, as do those executive members of global consulting firms PricewaterhouseCoopers and McKinsey & Co. who embroiled their corporations in well publicised scandals.

Quite a number of these conscious leaders who have formally exercised leadership authority didn't start out their journeys as empowered, or even free, individuals, but through the strength of their character forged through the fire of oppression and introspective self-evaluation, they gravitated, like metal filings to a magnet, towards the prescribed leadership roles in which they made the contributions to humanity that they are now remembered for. Nelson Mandela, Vaclav Havel and Mujica spent years of their lives in prison before they emerged to become the heads of state for their respective nations, and icons on a global stage. Serving as potent examples that debunk the leader is born and not made myth, what their journeys have to teach us is that inner leadership through being responsive to our spirit and its calling will often precede the external recognition and formalisation of leadership in the world. Greta Thunberg didn't rise to prominence as a leader in the fight to prevent climate change because of a unique status that made people want to listen to her. Rather, she gave her leadership a voice through the sacrificial decision to take time away from attending school to protest against global warming in front of the Swedish parliament. Calling for urgent action as an anguished member of the next generation whose lives will be affected by the unwillingness of governments to address the problem, her passion and earnestness resonated with many others who wanted to see meaningful change on the issue and this sparked a global movement. By demonstrating the virtuous courage, commitment and conviction that this change needed to happen, Thunberg found herself front and centre as a leading and influential voice on climate change, despite being only sixteen years old and having a series of conditions that could be labelled as disabilities.

As Thunberg shows, leadership that is facilitated by the living of one's calling can be embodied by anyone who has the courage and commitment to live in alignment with their true self. This form of leadership is not reserved for anyone 'special', or available exclusively to those of a particular gender, age, educational qualification or other identity category. Neither is it centralised in individuals who hold formal positions of power. It can thus be practiced outside of an institutional context and across the full spectrum of organisational life. While most people would ordinarily identify certain roles or sectors (i.e. not for profit) as being conducive to the living of one's calling and this form of leadership, there is a much broader scope for its application. Just as one may encounter priests, artists or school teachers who are living their calling, there are also corporate executives, builders, accountants and health workers who embody this highest form of leadership as they enact their novel contribution to the flourishing of our collective human potential.

Having its origins in the human spirit, this leadership through a lived calling is also not dependent on external factors for its realisation, although the bringing forth of the virtues that characterise its practice may be impacted by the enablers and barriers to the living of one's calling that are brought to light in Chapter nine. While these aspects of our worldly experience might affect our ability to lead through our calling, by themselves they don't direct our minds and hearts on the question of who we will become. Being a more fundamental question that we can't help but answer in each of the present moments of our lives, the decision that we are faced with as I see it is, do we intentionally align with our spirit to live our calling, and in the process become as one with the animating force of life itself, or do we allow ourselves to be reflexively led by the ego, as an unconscious follower, into the abyss of delusion and falsehood. It is only when we choose the former that we can unlock our capacity to practice the conscious form of leadership that is outlined in my leadership theory and this subsequent work.

At the most essential level, leadership is centred in the source of our being, not in our behaviour alone, or the dimensions of our personality.[21] Neither is it rooted in a title, rank or position that one may occupy, and it would be a mistake to seek to exercise authority on the basis of these labels, which are artificial, transient and dependent on an institutional context for their legitimacy. Pulling rank in organisational life is rarely a good idea for this very reason, as only a leader who is weak in character would need to rely on asserting the power that is inherent in their position to get others to comply with their instructions. One of the defining characteristics of leadership is the ability to influence others to action which fulfils the broader objectives of a collective entity. The source from which this influence emerges is critical to the effectiveness of this process, and if a leader is to have any real credibility and lasting impact, this influence must be centred in their way of being, and the authority that they derive from living in alignment with their true spiritual self.

If you were to ask any employee what qualities they admire in a leader, and what makes them want to follow a particular person, their answers would be pretty consistent and strongly reflect the presence of the spiritual virtues of character. Respondents in my study to whom I posed these questions specified that they admire someone with honesty and integrity, who they can trust and feel safe with, who is fair and even keeled with their temperament. They wanted to be treated with respect and supported by their leader, to do great work and develop themselves and the core competencies that their work

---

[21] Or as one of my respondents phrased his musings about leadership, *'It's of how you do things and who you are in those things…It is about being and I think that's as much a Christian concept as a Buddhist concept in the sense that it's about transcendence, it's about going beyond self…Leadership is trying to discover how to be a human being.'*

entails. They aspired to be led by someone who was attuned to their calling, on purpose and in alignment with the important work that their organisation is involved in. But perhaps above all else, they yearned for somebody who is humble and grounded, who hasn't forgotten how to be a human being, whom they can relate to, and depend on to listen to their concerns and practice the solidarity that allows for the demonstration of empathy.

Leaders who are truly conscious don't allow themselves to lose sight of the fact that leadership revolves around people, and the quality of the relationships that they have with the members of their team is a crucial determinant of successfully answering the call to leadership. By allowing their spirit to guide the process of leading, conscious leaders resonate with and honour the spirit of their people, which makes treating them well a natural outcome of their leadership. Unlike egocentric leaders, whose leadership is in part characterised by the mistreatment and exploitation of those who are under their control, conscious leaders don't view people as a means to an end to serve their personal or professional interests. Recognising the inherent dignity that every human being has, they understand themselves to be a steward for the upholding of that worth, which they reflect through their treatment of others, even in trying times. While they no doubt experience a wide range of emotions concerning their people, they strive not to allow any negative feelings associated with their performance to obscure the recognition that first and foremost their people are worthy human beings who must be cared for and respected.

Possessing this sharpened awareness of how they want to treat others in their space, their sense of connection to those others also extends to the environment that they inhabit through their conscious presence. Being the life giving space in which culture takes form, they are careful to nurture that environment in a way that serves both the deepening of those relationships and the embodiment of virtues that are sought to guide how their work together will be carried out. In contrast to conscious leaders who have their finger on the pulse of the culture of their organisations to infuse them with the *esprit de corps* that makes for synergistic magic, egocentric leaders are out of touch with these elemental dynamics that make for a thriving and engaging organisation that people want to be associated with. Being a natural consequence of them being out of touch with themselves spiritually, this unconsciousness extends into the spaces that they inhabit and contaminates them with the self-serving and divisive intentions that when manifested through behaviour make for an unbreathable culture that stunts the life of the spirit. When one comes to understand that a fish rots from the head down, it is predictable that a deteriorating culture will emerge through the neglect of the spiritual fibres that tie together the patchwork of virtues which underpin the workings of any transcendent organisation.

Take for example the Australian men's cricket team and the 2018 ball tampering scandal that shone light on the significant cultural failures by the sport's governing body in Australia, which had enabled those events to unfold through years of dubious and unprincipled decision making. In the scathing review that followed the impropriety, it was highlighted that the win at all costs mentality that Cricket Australia had fostered was responsible for creating a brewing storm of ego that not only shaped the toxic on-field behaviour of its players, but also the off-field conduct of their officials. Described by stakeholders in the report as 'arrogant', 'dictatorial' and 'non-collaborative', it was clear that Cricket Australia had eschewed its once strong organisational spirit, and that of the sport which was its duty to oversee. During media reporting of the scandal, it was not uncommon to hear that Cricket Australia and its players had violated 'the spirit of the game', which I saw as no coincidence given the priority placed by leaders on the achievement of ego centred objectives that promoted a disconnect between how the game should be played on the field, and how the team went about winning at all costs to maximise the financial returns that would accrue from their on-field success.

It is worth noting that two of the three players who were found to be directly at fault for the ball tampering incident were the captain, Steve Smith, and the vice-captain, David Warner. By functioning from their ego in planning for and allowing this cheating to occur, these two individuals, who should have been the ones setting the example for the younger players on the team, in effect, created a leadership vacuum that would threaten the career of the third player implicated, Cameron Bancroft, who as a new member of the team had naively agreed to carry out the tampering in order to 'fit in' with the playing group and ingratiate himself with its senior members.

In this void created by unconscious leadership, it is all too easy for a once strong entity or industry to come crashing down like a house of cards. We saw this starkly through the corporate collapses of Enron, WorldCom and Lehman Brothers, and the near failure of the world financial system in 2008, which at the micro-level was predominantly caused by greed, hubris and irresponsibility. While it was hoped that the harsh lessons associated with these events could have been learned by leaders in the financial sector, this proved not to be the case, and a decade on the 2018 Royal Commission into the banking sector in Australia uncovered an array of dishonest and exploitative practices being engaged in, that enriched those responsible for the four major banks at the centre of the controversy, at the expense of their most important stakeholder, being their customers. As was the case with the Australian cricket team scandal, this underhanded conduct from those at the top would come to pervade the workings of these banks, as the front line workers put into action their bosses unethical directives that were sought to be justified by the fierce competition taking place within the sector.

Eroding the trust and goodwill that these institutions had built up with their clientele, it was the manifestation of ego in these employees, and the clear failure of leadership to allow this malformed consciousness to pervade their organisational workings, that affected the divide between what these banks said that they stood for, and what the behaviour of their officers indicated was the priority of those who were responsible for leading them. With their focus being on the maximisation of returns for shareholders and the lining of their own pockets through the performance bonuses which incentivised this crooked conduct, it was the pro-social purpose that justifies the role of these institutions in society that was relegated to an afterthought, if it was even given any consideration at all.

This brings us to something that is extremely important for an aspiring conscious leader to understand. In order for a conscious culture to be cultivated in an organisation, it must be supported by a higher purpose, or reason for being, that virtuously serves a social need that the world has for its betterment. This virtuous purpose, or collective calling if you will, must resonate deeply with those who are to be involved in the day to day activity of realising it, and give their individual calling an outlet in contributing to an advancement that is beyond their capacity to bring about by themselves. It is through achieving this alignment that we see a mutual thriving where the individual puts forth a superior effort in delivering excellent work that is inherently meaningful, and the organisation prospers by leveraging the fruits of this engagement to serve the market in a way that makes a positive difference to how its members live their lives.

In this conscious economy of legitimate exchange, remunerations are well earned and appreciated as being vital to the life and sustainability of the organisations that enable these impacts. Being like the food and water that a healthy body needs in order to function effectively, these profits are not confused by the conscious leader with the overriding purpose which animates that body with life. Having the wisdom to realise that the purpose of that body is not to eat and drink to excess, which would inevitably produce a diseased organism, they are continually mindful not to confuse the need to make a profit as the principal reason for which their organisation exists.

While conscious leaders rightly see profits as a means to an end of fulfilling an organisation's higher purpose, leaders who are blinded by unconsciousness can easily fall into the trap of mistaking the making of profits as the organisation's reason for being. Having descended into their own internal abyss of ego that disconnects them from a recognition of their innate spiritual purpose, this disconnect extends to their inability to properly perceive purpose in the instruments of the world. With the organisation in which they work being one of these instruments, what their inability to connect with its virtuous purpose does is open the door for the flawed rationalisation that organisations exist to make a profit to guide their decision making. How this serves them individually is that it allows their ego to feed itself on the 'benefits' derived from that focus on profits, to the neglect of interdependent stakeholders, such as workers and customers, and the natural environment itself.

Being the creator of the mantra that says, 'more is better', it is the ego that motivates the unconscious leader to prioritise increased profits as the ultimate aim of the business, for fear that if they are not given the utmost importance, they will be lost to competitors and the organisation will thus be diminished in its ability, not to serve the market, but to make more of the profits to which the ego attaches a primary value. In the haze created by this impoverished and misguided zero sum outlook, it becomes understandable why some of these leaders conduct business in a way that is marked by desperation and dissonance in choosing courses of action in the short term that cannot support a prosperous long term agenda. Looking at these decisions from the outside, one might say, *"how did that leader think that they were going to get away with treating their people (or clients) like that?"* or *"didn't that leader consider the clear environmental impacts that their decision was going to have?"*

Unfortunately, what these external onlookers have the ability to foresee is beyond the scope of these unconscious leaders' perceptibility. This is what makes the future prospects of a world led by unconscious leaders so daunting. At no other time in history have these individuals had such powerful tools of technology and social influence at their disposal to amplify the destructive impacts that their ignorance to spiritual imperatives can bring about. Despite this harm being inadvertently brought about in most instances, I am often shocked by some of the statements that are made by these leaders on Twitter, and other social media platforms, which indicate quite clearly the narrowness with which they perceive their scope of responsibility, and the purposes which serve what they personally desire to bring about. These purposes, which serve an individual agenda rather than a broader virtuous end can be seen in the political domain where a leader may prioritise funds being allocated towards erecting a monument that they will be remembered for commissioning, rather than the non-profit or social services sectors, where those additional funds would make more of a difference in improving the quality of people's lives.

In the corporate context, I have seen instances where acting to satisfy a distorted sense of purpose has torn apart a strong company culture and devolved the behaviour of those working within its teams towards the satisfaction of their own personal interests. When people within an organisation see their leader serving a personal agenda at the expense of the organisation's purpose, if they don't determine to leave that role, they will be inclined to start protecting their position by engaging in turf wars, political game playing, information hoarding, or other similarly destructive behaviours. Whether this is done out of fear or resentment towards the leader, this effect of organisational abuse has its roots in the disavowal by the leader of their commitment to do what is in the best interests of the organisation as a whole, which is to act in the fulfilment of its virtuous purpose. Try as they might, unconscious leaders cannot fake the making of decisions that further the common good, and if one looks closely enough at the rationale behind the details, often that will reveal the impure motives which have skewed the moral direction of what is sought to be done.

If one has their eye firmly on the virtuous purpose that the company exists to meet, and the needs of those who benefit from the creation of their products or services, it becomes impossible to justify an exorbitant pay increase, a preference for shareholder interests, or mass layoffs to cut costs while those in the C-suite remain unaffected. To keep intact their own integrity and that of the organisation that is personified in its *esprit de corps*, conscious leaders proactively cultivate the space to stay mindful of this purpose and the attendant responsibilities that they owe to others who depend on them for guidance and support. Being the means by which they mitigate against the risks presented by the privileges that their role affords them, they find themselves, through this practice, better equipped to avoid the temptations that so often get their less reflective counterparts into trouble.

Why the ego is so attracted to leadership in the world is because of the associated freedoms that it values above the exercise of duty and restraint, but to indulge this in such a role precludes us from leading with a solid base of power. We know this because inherently we do not respect a leader who is more inclined to exercise their rights than uphold their responsibilities. In describing such a leader, we would say that they lack integrity in the sense that they are unwilling or unable to hold both facets together in their being and behaviour. While the unfettered exercise of our rights can often lead us down the perilous path of vice, on which we become slavish followers of its instruments, it is our willingness to take responsibility for our lives that redeems our leadability, both from a credibility standpoint and in our practice of dealing with life's inevitable setbacks and conflicts.

To exercise responsibility, and the other behaviours of conscious leadership that are outlined in Section two, is to embody virtue, which needs to be distinguished as a concept from the values that a number of leadership scholars incorrectly perceive is the source from which authentic leadership originates. As its name suggests, 'values' are merely reflective of qualities or objects that a person values, whether that is family, success or independence, for example. Being subjective expressions of our personhood, or who we understand ourselves to be in the company of our ego, they fall short of touching the spiritual heart of who we are as human beings. Goodness, humility, reverence, courage and evenhandedness, to name but a few of these virtues, are innate qualities of our being that are not possessed by some and foreign to others. Being transpersonal in their substance, they emerge naturally from the human spirit when we choose to live in alignment with it.

To the extent that a person's behaviour is not reflective of these virtues, they are living out of alignment with their spirit, and identifying with the false ego self, which leads them to conduct themselves in a way that is best described as incongruent. An example of this would be someone who is arrogant because they believe that they are special in ways that others are not. Representing a value that they hold, but would never likely admit to (being better than others and being seen in that light), this value deviates from the spiritual virtues of humility, reverence and evenhandedness which acknowledges that no person is above or better than any other in the eyes of God. The tension that results from the holding of this misaligned value will naturally lead this arrogant individual to occupy a negative state that tangibly affects how they experience the world and relate to others in it. While they might seek to project blame onto others for those others' unfavourable responses to the unconscious embodiment of that arrogance, this is wholly unjustified for the mirroring of the negative feelings that stem from their internal disconnect is but a symptom and not the cause of their unnatural value being out of step with their fundamental calling to manifest virtue.

Had they the awareness to perceive the artificiality of this ego-based value and others like it, then they could start to take an active role in disavowing them. In taking this responsibility, which is a virtue of spirit that I will expand on in the next chapter, this individual would reclaim, at least temporarily, a direct connection to their source of being, which is not dependent on the contrived values of mind for an identity. From this we can learn that as we align with our spirit to embody its virtues, we diminish the need to define ourselves by reference to an independent value set. With this construction being like a layer of the onion that encases our true being rather than defines it, what we find is that as we search for the source of truth and wisdom within ourselves, we will eventually peel away that values-based layer which lies close to our spiritual centre, but is nevertheless distinct from it. While many people are inclined to perceive values positively because in their highest form they reflect the virtues of spirit, when they are confused as the base of our most noble human qualities that will displace the spirit in our recognition of their source. As a consequence of this false attribution, we encounter a barrier to knowing, not only who we are, but also the attributes that we share with each other at this fundamental level of being.

Goodness, reverence, love and evenhandedness are not just values that you or I can claim for ourselves. Being infinitely more engrained than this, they are our collective virtue, which any person can come to embody when they align their being with its spiritual source. While you might doubt the veracity of this claim and point to examples of 'evil' people in the world, it must be remembered that what we often label as evil emerges from the shadow of ego-centred behaviour. Eckhart Tolle, whose profound spiritual teachings have touched the hearts of millions around the world, acknowledged as much when he wrote that *"there is only one perpetrator of evil on the planet: human unconsciousness."*

I have always found it an interesting quirk that the word evil is 'live' spelt backwards, but I think that there is more to it than just coincidence. As we deny this spiritual source of life (and virtue) within ourselves, we make ourselves vulnerable to the ego's 'evil' proclivities, which can be alternately labelled as vices. Among these vices that prove so obstructive to the recognition of virtue at our core are laziness (not caring to fully live and grow) and ignorance (turning away from truth when we encounter it). Why these traits are particularly divisive to our integrity and flourishing is because at some level they involve a wilful decision to disregard the human spirit that brings consciousness and leadership to life in the world. To adapt a famous quote from John Stuart Mill on the subject, *"The only thing necessary for the triumph of evil is for good people to do nothing."*

Regardless of the era in human history where evil has sought to triumph, it has never ultimately prevailed because the call to virtue by the human spirit is too fundamental to life itself. Whether this was seen in Winston Churchill's unwavering commitment to resist the Nazi advance into Britain, or Martin Luther King's unwillingness to hate those who sought to oppress his people, what our slow but definite march to progress has shown us is that our spirit cannot be defeated or estopped from eventually rousing to action to preserve the embodiment of virtue in the world. While the unconsciousness of ego can often push us to these extremes of division and war, we need not allow the ego to lead this offensive if we refuse to defend its role in shaping who we think we are and what we value as entities that are distinct from our spirit. Whatever it is that you or I proclaim to value is not at all important, and while your ego will be offended at me expressing this sentiment, I can guarantee you that your spirit won't be at all perturbed.

Having established the primacy of virtues to conscious behaviour, let me now extend this to the leadership context by describing the form that this behaviour took in the lives of my research participants. From the thousand pages of data that conveyed the different facets of how leadership was manifested by the majority of sixty five respondents who were living their calling, and my additional research into the phenomenon, the qualities of being that were identified could be grouped into the following five themes: Integrity, Authority, Goodness, Service, and Presence. In the next section of the book, a chapter will be devoted to each of these themes and the specific qualities that are associated with them. I have headed that section 'The Fruits of Faithfulness' to convey that as we devote ourselves to the spiritual life of our calling, these virtuous qualities and associated behaviours will emerge forth as fruit that feeds our practice of conscious leadership, and nourishes the lives of those who we lead from that inspired realm of being.

Just as we don't live completely in alignment with our spirit in every moment of every day, so will we sometimes sacrifice the bringing forth of these qualities of conscious leadership at the decadent alter of vice. As transcendent as King and Churchill were as leaders for the majority of their lives, at different times they each succumbed to frailties or temptations that weakened their character and temporarily detracted from their leadership ability. To the extent that we use the present moments of our lives to indulge similar vices, we stifle our ability to embody conscious leadership in those moments. As harmful as those lapses in judgment may be, they will only briefly preclude us from consciously leading, if in the other present moments of our lives we are aligned with our spirit, and receptive to expressing its virtues in the world. What qualities of virtue that we evoke in any given aligned moment will be shaped externally by the context of our environment (along with those present within it) and the circumstances that each of these present us with. Prompting our internal response to this stimuli will be the spirit and the mind made conscious by our willingness to surrender our ego and its agenda. Consequently, the virtues that we may manifest in the unique circumstances of one particular moment can be quite dissimilar from those that are exhibited in a different moment and context. Take for example the following two scenarios. In the first scenario, our conscious agent is trying to mediate a dispute between two team members at work, and in the second, they are engaging in a reflective self-care practice to find a deeper sense of balance amidst the incessant demands of their daily life.

In working to bring a resolution to the dispute in the first scenario, our protagonist may demonstrate respect for each party by actively listening to their positions, as well as solidarity in empathising with how the conflict has impacted them. However, with the alternate scenario that requires a different response which is more suited to that unique context, the virtues that are more likely to be demonstrated are commitment (becoming vested in that process to realise that balance and better understand the habitual patterns that work against their aim), along with openness and patience (this type of spiritual growth work is particularly challenging because it requires us to be vulnerable, and the changes that we seek to realise from it don't happen overnight).

As much as we might like to condense this form of conscious leadership into a routine formula that can be predictably applied in all situations, the nature of how each of these virtues find life in a given context precludes the reduction of their manifestation into a set blueprint. With the conditions of our responsiveness being more nuanced and considerate of the unique form that each moment takes, this way of leading reflects elements of situational leadership theory[22], in the sense that it requires an attuned receptiveness to how life is unfolding around us.

Before we can open up this organic space of spiritual responsiveness, we must subdue the strong urge of the ego to impose itself on the conditions that confront us. Being convinced that it has all the answers and can make the right call to resolve any predicament, we are urged, in its company, to rush in and close down this space so that it can take centre stage and impose its will on the world. The problem with these attempts at forcing an acceptable outcome is that as we quash that spaciousness of the present moment, we inevitably become reactive to what is taking place within it. Having deprived ourselves of the spirit's insight and guidance that is birthed in this spaciousness, the best that we can hope to bring forth with our decision making is the logic of the mind and the stilted expression of emotion that may be conducive to transactional leadership, but is inadequate in being able to support a transformational leadership dynamic.

---

[22] The theory of situational leadership posited by Paul Hersey and Ken Blanchard centres on the idea that no one style of leadership is better than any other, and the most effective leaders are those who are adaptable in meeting the needs and challenges of a particular context.

In order to bring one to a higher place in their life, a safe space must be established, which allows them to vulnerably come forth, speak their truth and draw connections between the state of their internal and external worlds. Enabling also the building of trust that forms the foundation of any conscious relationship, this generous act of creating space for the evolution of another liberates them by releasing their need for defensiveness that can so often arise when one feels exposed in the judgmental company of another's ego. Being its own form of reactivity, this is what we want to be careful of not eliciting in others by relating to them from the wounds of our false self. No matter who we are, we carry with us scars from events in our lives that have hurt us, sometimes very deeply, and if these wounds are not healed then they can serve as a great impediment to consciously relating to others and being able to lead them towards wholeness. Without having reconciled these wounds in the spiritual depths of our own being, we will be unable to transcend the reactiveness that has us blame, lash out and project our negative feelings onto others whose words and behaviour form the stimuli that we encounter in our everyday interactions. As actress Ashley Judd expressed so powerfully in her TED talk about the online abuse of women, *trauma that is not transformed is transferred to others*. What this teaches is that our abuse of others is an extension of the abuse that we have inflicted upon ourselves by not responding to the voice of our own pain that speaks of its torment and desire to heal so that we can be made whole.

An aspect of this pain is the denial of our vocation and our want to escape from the responsibility of unfolding a life that is oriented towards virtue and purpose. To run in reaction to what can shatter the illusion of the false self is a convenient course, but it is a lot more challenging to test our self-concept, which if done honestly will cause us to face and address the spiritual deficits that keep us and our world locked in perpetual patterns of bondage and discord. Being the duty that the conscious leader bears willingly, they are not afraid to engage with the tough questions concerning their own existence and how this intersects with the broader life of the world. This existential wrestling is what makes them capable of reconciling the divides that stand between where we now are, and where our spiritual source of being has called us to be. Rather than building the walls of separation that is the ego's way of dealing with challenges to its identity and will[23], the way of spirit is to bring down those walls so that the consciousness of love, peace, reverence,

---

[23] Think of the Berlin Wall, and the proclivity of ego-oriented authoritarian rulers such as Viktor Orbán, Benjamin Netanyahu, Recep Tayyip Erdogan and Donald Trump to erect these barriers. The latter famously sought to erect a wall across the length of America's southern border to protect the country from Mexican immigrants.

hope and solidarity can move and touch the hearts of those who sleep but yearn to wake to the journey that their calling would have them take.

As we deal with the daily challenges of staying connected to what leadership really is, it helps to remember that the ancient root word for leadership was *laitho*, which meant 'the way' or 'journey'. While the aim of leadership can often seem to revolve around a future end point, it is not a finite exercise, as Simon Sinek points out. Being a perpetual unfolding that takes form in us, and others who will be born to make a positive impact on the world for future generations, it is our awakening that will pave the way for the free expression of their conscious contributions and their flourishing in the light that we will have kept ablaze by our courage and commitment to live our callings. Let us not abdicate this highest of responsibilities and allow the infirmities of ego to write the story of what humanity will become. A quote that is pertinent to this comes from Nike founder Phil Knight when he wrote that, *"The cowards never started and the weak died along the way. That leaves us, ladies and gentlemen. Us."* It is the ego that makes us timid and fragile in our self-concept, but in truth that is not who we are. We were created to manifest our destiny by living our calling. We were born to be virtuous leaders. Let us now explore these noble qualities that are ours to express as we traverse the way to conscious life.

SECTION TWO: THE FRUITS OF FAITHFULNESS

CHAPTER 4: Integrity – Putting the Pieces Back Together

Integrity is what we embody when we are aligned with our spirit, and functioning from this state of wholeness within ourselves, what we bring into form in the world are aligned and whole movements that positively impact others and enrich the institutions in which we work. This became evident after talking to my respondents about the concept and having them explain how their demonstration of the quality impacted the environment around them. In different forms, their ways of being brought people and things together and synchronised how they thought and functioned. Whether it was building complimentary teams to take on challenging projects or mentoring others to connect them with their life purpose, the effects of their actions reflected the inner alignment and connectedness that they had cultivated with their spiritual source. Having largely disassociated themselves from the corroding identity of ego, this force was less of an influence in leading them towards destructive and fragmenting behaviour.

Unlike the behaviour that ego-centric leaders are predisposed to engage in, these integrated individuals did not create factions, dissention or cultures of blame that isolated members of their unit from the collective entity. They also were not content to allow their organisational departments to work in silos and compete with each other in ways that undermined cooperation, the sharing of information and the broader fulfilment of the business' core purpose. Being themselves in alignment with their animating purpose which resonated with this organisational purpose and drew them in to contribute to its fulfilment in the first place, the guiding vision that they present to their people is oriented around this purpose, which inspires others as they themselves have been inspired to put forward their best efforts in shared service. By rallying their teams in this way, they orchestrate superior performance which organisations that are culturally deficient and rife with political game playing are incapable of delivering.

Emerging from the dominant thought in the leadership literature is a definition of integrity that revolves around values. Pursuant to this way of thinking about the concept, if one lives in accordance with their value set then they can be seen to be demonstrating integrity. But how useful is this definition when one considers the subjective nature of values which may not necessarily be oriented towards the good? As I highlighted in the previous chapter, the best that values can hope to reflect are the universal virtues of spirit, but by themselves they are not the source from which the purest form of integrity emanates. If you think about the qualities that one would use to describe a person of high character or integrity, they would go straight to the heart of what it means to be a genuine human being. To be honest, trustworthy, committed to others and a worthy cause, empathetic, in harmony and willing to enter into solidarity with the world so that they may authentically contribute to its functioning. This is the incontrovertible embodiment of spiritual virtue.

As we proceed throughout this chapter, I will expand on the above qualities that give life to integrity in different forms, but for now I would like to present an alternate definition of integrity that is grounded in my research findings, which is *a person's ability to create and maintain a state of internal and external wholeness.* To be whole in any given moment requires one to have entered into union with their spirit, where there is no divide between who they essentially are and what they are presenting to the world with their being. As this connection is preserved, and the divisive influence of ego is held at bay along the journey, the thread of integrity is weaved into the tapestry of their life, with their modes of being and doing not being reflective of an actor or actress playing their part on a social stage.

With these people, what you see is what you get, and what they say they are going to do, they follow through with, not because that is what is expected of them, but because the keeping of their word is the standard that they have set for themselves. Appreciating at a fundamental level that saying one thing and doing another tears at the fabric of their character, they are intent to avoid this happening, particularly in the face of pressure to go along in order to get along.

One of the great challenges of life can be dealing with these expectations that the world places on us to bend to its will and do what is popular or comfortable in preserving the narrative of the status quo. This is especially the case when our adherence would come at the cost of living our calling and expressing truths that run against what these external forces want us to conform to. Faced with this dilemma, we must ask ourselves, shall we step up and step out, and lead by revealing our true face, or should we acquiesce and remain as followers of convention that has us marching out of step with the beat of our inner drummer.

If we make the decision to lead by not compromising ourselves, then that necessitates allowing ourselves to be guided by the call of our spirit in all manner of circumstances, even those in which great temptations are present.

By trusting in our spirit as the source of our strength and discipline[24] we can vulnerably move forth, expressing our essence as we relate to the world, while resisting these temptations and the other ego-based influences that would have us relinquish control over the course of our lives.

It is no coincidence that those who are not whole within, and struggling for direction as a consequence, are the easiest to be manipulated by external agents whose offerings promise to solve their problems and reconcile their broken lives to an ideal state (an artificial claim to wholeness). Marketers of products are experts in crafting such messages that lead us to acquire things that we don't ultimately need if we are centred in integrity, knowing who we are and what purpose we have been given to fulfil. Whatever the items that are being spruiked, whether they are cars, clothes, make up or jewellery, they cannot remedy an internal deficit, or lack of integrity, regardless of how much of them we bring to ourselves. Those who possess inner integrity know this, and they are not fooled by the exaggerated nature of this puffery because they are not dependent on anything external to themselves to heal an inner divide, or instruct them on who they are and what direction their life should take.

Having this clarity which emerges from their alignment with spirit, they are free of the inner conflicts that so often undermine the honouring of our calling and the ability to lead ourselves and others effectively. This allows these integral agents to act as peacemakers, or healers of the conflict that is initiated by the ego, with its zero sum mindset and concocted belief in 'otherness' from which it can stand apart and gain strength by opposing and overcoming those who espouse different ideologies or ways of living. With the spirit having its focus on drawing others close to it so that the common basis of our existence can be acknowledged, respected and built upon for mutual benefit, it doesn't buy into this notion of being separate from others who we must overcome in order to make life better for ourselves. To fracture the whole is to diminish the sum of its parts, and expose them to a form of suffering that, in their integrated form, they were never intended to endure.[25] What this teaches us is that we can't thrive in an interdependent system when our focus is limited to asserting our independent mindedness.

---

[24] Discipline as a leadership quality is one that we paradoxically come to embody as we become followers, or disciples, of spirit in our lives.

[25] To join is to separate. As we allow the ego mind to bind us to worldly identifications or ideologies that teach us who we are in limiting terms (for example, being a member of a certain political party, religious denomination or activist cause), we disconnect ourselves from the broader knowing of who we are in spirit and the recognition of interconnectedness that characterises life at the most essential level. It is only when we renounce these superficial identifications as defining features of

While we possess autonomy, in our thinking and being, that blessing must be exercised wisely with a broader recognition of what we affect through our choices and behaviours.

I believe that this is one of the key learnings to come out of the current climate predicament that is crying out for the emergence of leaders who can drive integral change at the systems level. But before we can change a system, we must evolve our understanding of how that system is composed and functions symbiotically, which is not a process that can be circumvented or 'hacked' by those who are looking for a shortcut to solving the complex challenges that confront us. In order to make sustainable change last, we must actually learn our lessons by reconciling our capacities for both worldly knowledge and spiritual wisdom. As fond as we are of the mind and its workings, we must humbly submit that it alone does not have all of the answers to life's pertinent questions. Perhaps it was this realisation which prompted Czech statesman Vaclav Havel to muse that *"the salvation of the world lies in the human heart"*. To achieve that balance is to locate our inner compass of consciousness that gives integrity a voice through action. This is but one of many truths that need to be understood from a holistic standpoint.

Truth

To lead consciously, one must humbly submit to spiritual Truth and allow themselves to be guided by the immutable reality of what humanity was conceived to be. This legitimate form of Truth doesn't emanate from the mind that is disassociated from the heart, which is prone to misunderstanding the nature of life and the role that our existence plays in its unfolding. One of the great weaknesses of the ego is that it is compelled to impose a story over that which we perceive in its company, and throughout our lives, we craft these narratives which become the subjective truths[26] that we live by, and seek to impose upon the world in order to establish our legitimacy and righteousness as independent entities.[27] With this myopic view, what we are easily prone to confuse is our own personal truth with the underlying Truth of the

---

who we are at the deepest level that we atone for our unconsciousness and restore integrity to our present state of being. Atonement in this sense (or at-one-ment) represents this reunification with the spiritual dimension of who we truly are.

[26] Where I have written Truth with an upper case 'T', I am referring to the immutable universal Truth of the spirit that is distinct from the subjective truth of our ego, which I am describing when I write truth with a lower case 't'.

[27] We don't just do this at an individual level but also at a collective level through our cultural or religious norms, for example, that reinforce our constructed identity by distinguishing us from other groups who subscribe to different thought systems or value sets.

universe that can only be glimpsed as we remain integrated and faithful to our spiritual nature.

What those who are living their calling do well is the work of discerning the truths of their ego and the deeper Truths of their spirit that they have come to encounter through reflective practice and other forms of spiritual exploration. Having become conscious of the presence of their ego and how it works, they are able to create some distance from its false narratives to achieve a level of clarity and authentic purpose in their lives. With this clarity and purposeful direction comes an alleviation of suffering because they are able to navigate around these false narratives and avoid having their identity caught up in the dysfunctionality that they inevitably produce.

Take for example an accepted cultural imperative to save face in order to preserve one's reputation or social standing, and the negative consequences that can produce in the form of passive aggressive behaviour or blaming others to avoid responsibility for having erred in making a decision. Rather than choosing to play this false game of keeping up appearances and a harmonious facade, those who are living their calling opt for the respectful expression of Truth which is offered to serve the good, and further the guiding purpose of those individuals or institutional agents who they are communicating with. Having disassociated from the ego in delivering the substance of those messages, what they have to convey is measured, wise and extremely useful in resolving any tensions that are being encountered.

I think that most people have had the experience of being in a room with others whose egos have locked them into a standpoint from which only their self-interested position can be seen. Whether this was at a negotiation or work meeting of some type, what you find in these people is that they have separated themselves from the Truth that would implicate them in some way if they had the courage to look at their situation from a broader and clearer perspective. As these parties stubbornly adhere to the subjective truths that underpin their differing perspectives, conflict inevitably ensues and the means to generate a positive outcome becomes harder to envision. That is until someone who is committed to a Truth that is bigger than their own personal truth, and those of the parties, is invited to intervene. As this arbiter demonstrates the honesty and integrity to act impartially in the best interests of all the concerned parties, both trust and influence can be established to pave the way for a reconciliation to occur.

When we enter into the company of someone who embodies Truth and selflessly conveys it for our benefit and personal growth, our defences are melted away to allow us to become receptive to their offerings, because with the recognition of our spirit, we appreciate that their ego is not animating their input or presence. Laying the groundwork for the practice of a deep form of trust, our givenness to the Truth of another holds tremendous potential to align us more closely with the path of our calling. In many of the interviews that I conducted for my research, respondents spoke about experiencing a turning point in their lived calling journeys upon encountering a Truth-teller who was courageous enough to tell them what they needed to know at that point in time, and not just what their ego wanted to hear to validate their existing course. You yourself may have experienced one of these pivotal moments, where a wise man or woman lifted the lid on your naive or closed view of the world by imparting something that incisively resonated with you at a foundational level. Perhaps it was someone who saw something in you before you did and challenged the false conceptions that you had concerning what you were capable of. By helping you to actualise the Truth of what you are, as testified by you actually manifesting that reality, they played a facilitative part in the Truth of spirit guiding you more consciously in your life.

I can write to this thankfully, as I have had many mentors who served this purpose for me, and helped me to emerge out of the shadows of my ego to live a more Truth centred life. Having led by their spirited presence that I intuitively came to trust, my following of them gradually evolved into me leading others as I came to more fully trust my spiritual nature as the guide of my calling journey. Without cultivating this trust in one's authentic identity, our efforts to establish a deep level of trust with others will be frustrated, particularly in a leadership context where our ability to influence others is dependent on them buying into us as persons of integrity and character. With this, it is important to appreciate that Truth is transparent, which is evidenced by people not being easily fooled, and being able to sense a dissonance in someone who is being untruthful with themselves. Though they may not be able to properly articulate why they feel this way, they will nevertheless feel an internal reservation which will lead them to recoil from that other person's attempts at persuasion.

We therefore must lead ourselves away from the denial of Truth that prompts others to want to deny us. On so many levels this denial imposes a cost on our wellbeing that if we were truly conscious of the toll, we would be unwilling to pay it. Whatever it is that we base our subjective truths on, when that house comes down, it crashes to the ground, and we are left emptied, hollowed of the false narratives that we had righteously clung to in order to experience a sense of power, control and faux leadership over our lives. With this breakdown having revealed the starkness of the illusion, we are liberated to breakthrough and find our source of power anew. As we take steps to become who we were created to be, and give voice to the Truth within, we might be surprised to experience the world treating us differently, with more reverence and authority. Tempted as we might be to think the world has changed, in actuality we have, through our diminished interest in placating the ego by making ourselves heard, and instead favouring the expression of Truth that others naturally resonate with and are receptive to listening to.

Before we can consciously lead we must free ourselves of the need to justify our truths and find approval of these in the minds of others. Acting to perpetuate such a need signals our insecurity in not having a strong enough base to give voice to who we essentially are. This helps to explain why people often get defensive as they express their opinions which are presented to others as truths. Requiring others to validate these opinions in order to reinforce their fragile sense of identity, what emerges from these interactions is an affirmation of unconsciousness, which is the antithesis of what conscious leadership seeks to affect. *"It is better to be hated for who you are, than loved for who you are not"* said French writer Andre Gide, and it is only when we know who we are that we can summon the courage and conviction to express Truth in the world.

To mitigate against any unconscious resistance being raised in another, it must also be appreciated that how Truth is expressed is just as important as what that Truth has to convey. Conscious leaders understand this and they are cautious to engage in respectful dialogue that walks with another rather than speaks at them. To garner respect for the Truth we convey, we first must be respectful to others and nurturing of their receptivity to Truth's way. This becomes much easier when we can humbly accept that we are receptacles through which Truth passes through, and are not the primary source from which it comes. By surrendering to this realisation, we keep our integrity intact and affirm our commitment to answering the call of our spirit by giving voice to virtue in the unique context that our leadership finds life.

Commitment

Underpinning the call to serve a virtuous purpose in the world is a commitment that was made by our creator to each of us, which precipitated the bestowal of gifts that we would require to fruitfully answer that call. While it is clear that we must be committed to this calling if we are to live out our obligation to fulfil it, what is less appreciated is God's commitment to invest so heavily in us by endowing us not just with life, but with a form of life that is unlike any other. Nowhere in this world is there another person who has the animating purpose that you do *along with* the unique blend of personal qualities, aptitudes and contextual presence that would enable them to usurp the function for which you were created. Your being then was not intended to be superfluous, or something that this life force did not take seriously in enacting. When looked at through this lens, our mandate to fulfil our calling takes on a renewed importance that honours the commitment that our creator has demonstrated in giving a particularised form to each of our lives.

To reciprocate this commitment, we must dedicate ourselves fully to the process of unfolding our highest potential in the realm that we have been given to occupy. Requiring a sustained effort that is diligently applied over the course of our lives, we will find ourselves being confronted with the temptations of short-termism that prioritises the immediate gratification of the ego above the more challenging work of building an enduring legacy that is congruent with our spiritual calling. In the face of these enticements, the choices that we make will have a great impact on whether we will keep our integrity intact, or forego it in favour of doing what feels good to our ego in the moment.

While it may temporarily please one to take on a job that earns them more money, or couple with a lover who doesn't require the emotional investment that their partner does, the cost that this imposes on our spirit diminishes our overall ability to experience wellbeing, and leaves us devoid of the true substance of life that makes for meaning and intrinsic fulfilment. This is why the money chaser and the promiscuous player are compelled to keep searching for someone or something that they can attach themselves to in order to feel complete. Being bereft of wholeness within, this is what they have become addicted to pursuing in the world. But neither the high paying job, nor the revolving door of lovers will grant them the solidity or solace that they crave through their vain efforts.

This is because what they do, they do only for themselves and not to uphold or strengthen a deeper union that transcends their ego. Both an authentically loving relationship and the participation in vocational service require our selfless generosity and concern for the other partner, client, colleague or stakeholder, who we are in relationship with. Wanting for them the same blessings and prosperity that we want to receive, we have held the space of integral functioning within ourselves, from which comes the recognition that beyond identifying with the 'I' and 'them', is the 'we' and 'us' that can support the making of lasting commitments in the world.

To lead consciously by being committed is to embody this quality in a variety of ways. What was evident by hearing my respondents speak of their animating purposes, was that they were heavily invested in the process of enacting them, both in the short term and long term contexts of their lives. Unlike the money chaser who is prone to vagrantly hop from one job to another to placate their ego in the moment, those who are living their calling are not inclined to stake their futures on any imminent gains that the present may deliver, especially if these gains would come at the cost of nudging them off their destined path. With their current course of action supporting a longer term agenda that is consistent with what they want their calling to contribute to the world, the energy behind their efforts is not dispersed in directions that pull them away from where they know they need to be, doing the core work and supporting those who have supported them over the journey.

Related to the quality of commitment is loyalty which was a theme that was quite pronounced in what my respondents felt that they owed to others in their lives. Contrary to the churn and burn mentality that is attributable to egocentric actors, particularly in the workplace, those who lead from virtue stand by their people with a solidarity and respect that honours them for who they are as people, not merely for what they have brought to the organisation or the leader personally. Recognising the efforts that their people had expended through their involvement in the shared enterprise, both gratitude and a reciprocal desire to give back were embodied by these respondents to enrich the lives of their people in ways that extended beyond the earning of an income.

Not discriminating in their devotion and willingness to take care of others, these conscious leaders are unlike their unconscious counterparts, who, if they are committed to anybody, will only bring along the 'yes' men and women who sooth their ego and prop up their base of power within an institution. Inherent in this transactional dynamic is the proviso that no favour will be bestowed by the person in control unless the allegiance of others is first pledged to serve them. Being like a conditional form of care that falls far short of what genuine loyalty displays, it will prove incapable of fostering a committed union because neither the safety nor autonomy of the dependent followers is present to allow trust in their leader to form.

When we are not wholeheartedly present and open to giving of ourselves for a common purpose, the people in our environment will sense that and be reluctant to go all in with their contributions, even if all the right things are being said by the person who is guiding the group. While words can signal an intention to commit, ultimately it is our actions that will speak loudest to those who we want to follow our example. For many of the respondents in my sample, the way that they chose to lead others was through setting the right example for how they wanted things to be done. Appreciating the importance of not only role-modelling behaviour to set a certain standard, but being seen to be hands on and engaged in the front line work that is being undertaken, what this clearly demonstrates to others in the organisation is that the leader is committed to something more abiding than what they have to gain through their involvement.

Ultimately, when we honour our commitment to live our spiritual calling, we prosper as the world which we enrich through our service does, in an integral way that sustains rather than drains our reserves of energy. While they work extremely hard to fulfil the commitments that they have made, those in my sample who were vocationally aligned found themselves to be invigorated by the challenge of meeting their responsibilities and becoming more fully functioning people in the process. Being something that supported their disciplined approach to continuous learning and improvement, what they desired for themselves was not for life to be easier to deal with, but to become more capable in handling what life had to throw their way. With such a perspective that reflects the possession of an autonomous inner locus of control, the barriers that may have presented for others to stifle their commitment were not as present and impactful in causing these empowered agents to waver in their dedication to their higher purpose.

A lack of faith in others being there to support their calling, for example, can cause one to lose hope in their vocational path and retreat in giving a lukewarm and uncommitted effort in applying their gifts, but if one has actively nurtured their connection with God as the source of the calling that they have been given life to enact, then growing from that will be both a conviction in their ability to bring that calling to fruition, and a profound trust in God's ability to provide those means of support. Fortifying their commitment to answering that call, they have circumvented the obstacle that presented to those of little faith, whose belief in the workings of the world to overpower them has superseded the intrinsic faith in themselves to be able to meet its challenges successfully.

When we are committed to bringing our calling to life, part of the integral movement affected by this commitment will be the coming together with others in a spirit of solidarity and community that holds and honours them in the same sacred space in which we have come to connect with and know ourselves. As comfortable as it might be to treat the enactment of our calling as a solitary exercise, if it is to have real impact by supporting a broader flourishing, then we must be willing to move beyond the boundaries of our own ego and humbly join with others to take the journey of becoming fully human together.

Solidarity

Solidarity is the tie that enables this unitive functioning and the formation of communities that we can all find a home in, regardless of our gender, race, socio-economic status or the other means of defining ourselves and others in worldly terms. Beneath all of these things, at the fundamental level of our humanity, we are intimately connected to each other in our experience of life, which our capacity to feel and express empathy testifies to. Even when we hear of difficult things happening to people who we have never physically encountered, we can internally recognise how that might feel, with this recognition being all the more pronounced if we have experienced those same difficulties on our path. Bound together by this understanding, we will enter into solidarity with those people if we can disassociate from our ego that wants to judge them for how they have handled the events of their lives, and take a superior position from which it can feel a false form of empowerment.

Think here, for example, of how one might negatively perceive somebody who is homeless and living on the street. When functioning from their ego, their internal voice might say something like that person brought their plight on themselves by making bad choices and not taking the proper responsibility over their past circumstances. By looking at the homeless person and their predicament in that way, in isolating and diminishing terms, our capacity to feel solidarity and empathy for them is stunted because the judgmental dictates of our mind have silenced our spiritual willingness to recognise and embrace that other as an equal and worthy member of the human family. To somebody else who is living their calling in alignment with their spirit, they are not taken by the judgments that the ego evokes in an attempt to direct their mind. Being grounded in the fundamental realisation that who they are is not separate or different/better or worse than this person before them who is struggling, they are able to relate to them as another human being who has also experienced adversity at different stages of the journey. Even if they have not known what it is like to be homeless, this doesn't act so much as a barrier to the expression of solidarity and compassion because in their openness to receive who that other person is at the core of their being, they are capable of non-judgmentally listening to their story and understanding what that form of struggle feels like to live through.

While you may doubt that it is possible for one person to walk in the shoes of another, I put forth that at the deepest level of our humanity, one size does fit all. So often, we blind ourselves and overlook this spiritual reality because we are too entrenched in our ego identity and the points of difference that it emphasises to legitimise its want to separate from others in the world. While your spirit yearns to feel solidarity and the connection that comes from being conscious of our commonalities, the ego opts for special-ness and the visibility from the top of the mountain where they are removed from others who occupy lower vantage points. After all, what better testifies to your personal success than pointing to the failure of that homeless person, or the inferior station of the subordinate who works for you, and not with you?

Try as one might to distinguish themselves in this way in order to ground their leadership, they will no doubt fail in its most fundamental task, which is to bring others with them. Nobody wants to follow a person who can't connect with them at a human level, or who needs to derive legitimacy from the belief that they are special. Even people who are highly competent in their fields will struggle to connect with others, if at the human level they have unresolved tensions around who they are, or past wounds involving others that have not been healed. Such evidence of a fracturing in integrity, or misunderstanding of who one is, will inevitably cast doubt on their ability to be trusted as a source of safety and belonging, being two of the most fundamental needs that followers require their leaders to satisfy. With this, these people may be asking, how can this person tend to my garden when in their own domain they can't even tend to themselves?

Lacking in this self-nurturing and fertile connectedness with their spirit, a unit or community that extends beyond their ego's conceptions will not able to be formed into anything concrete. This is why there is such a deficit in the culture of many organisations today that strive to build thriving commu-nities, but must settle in their place for a looser coming together of persons who consequently are not bound by a shared awareness of what their collec-tive purpose is. As the etymology of the word suggests, solidarity finds its basis in solidity, and to affect the former in their environment, those leading a cultural reformation must be grounded in the latter. In a similar way, being open to enter into community with others is a natural extension of occupying a state of communion with one's true self.

In the end, we can't pave a way for others down a path that we have not traversed ourselves, and if we do try to artificially lead others on that journey, then we shouldn't be surprised to experience that path crumbling under our feet. Just as with any relationship that is built upon the humble willingness of each participant to live into the Truth of who they are so that a trusted bond can form with their significant other, communities emerge to exhibit this cohesive quality when they have been laid to rest on these same pillars of virtue which animate the lives of their members.

What respondents who were living their calling often emphasised in their interviews was the importance of community and connectedness in their personal and professional lives. Yearning for their contributions to extend as far as they could into the world, these aligned agents were not content to just tend to and enrich those who were closest to them in relational proximity. Being conscious of the spiritual imperative to give generously of their giftings and the blessings that flow from occupying a state of internal abundance, what they had to impart was not limited by any ego centred considerations of what they had to personally gain from such acts of benevolence. By comprehending in clear terms the connection that they shared with those broader groupings of people, what was able to be recognised was that as they served these communities and helped them to enhance their capacity for prosperity, so were they themselves nourished and their vocations fortified.

Whether it was charitably serving the underprivileged or marginalised groups in society, or working to assimilate people into the culture and workings of their organisation, what these behaviours evinced was the coming together movement of the divine spirit that in its unceasing love for all that are human, wills that no person be left behind. Resonating with this sentiment, are two things that can be observed from leaders who are animated by the virtue of solidarity. Not only are such leaders inclusive and welcoming of others who they feel called to serve and collaborate with, but what they are conscious to keep before their eyes is the principle of the common good that informs their integral 'big picture' perspective on how decisions should be made and resources allocated amongst groups of people who work alongside them to achieve the organisation's fundamental objectives.

As they do this, they avoid the situation of solidarity being eroded amongst members of their team who have been adversely impacted by ego driven decisions that don't serve the best interests of the whole enterprise. In many organisations, this is the match that ignites political firestorms where people try to align with the leader or other dominant factions if those entities stand to be enriched by decisions that are made to advance the lesser good. With this lesser good, what it frequently entails is the powerful elite benefiting at the expense of others, who are diminished in their significance and thus denied the dignity of belonging and being able to buy into the core purpose that brought them to the organisation in the first instance.

Rather than denying and invalidating these members and their contributions, what a leader who is an advocate of the common good does is create the space for meaningful participation and the offering of input that can enhance the ability of the collective to serve its core function. By these leaders being willing to listen to and enable these contributions, a greater cohesion and harmony is realised in both the culture and daily functioning of the organisation. While this doesn't always translate into a state of organisational equilibrium, it does present a firm footing on which the collective body can navigate the changes of the world without losing touch of its conscious heart.

Harmony

When we are aligned with our spirit as we live our calling, our functioning becomes more centred and harmonious, with the effect that we can navigate the everyday challenges of the world with less stress and tension on our being. By knowing ourselves to be at one with life, what it throws our way is nothing that we can't handle when we are grounded in the source of our peace and strength. Being two among many virtuous qualities that characterise our natural state as spiritual beings, we are never without the power to return to our centre, despite what the ego has conditioned us to believe about our personal limitations or the futility in taking that inner journey.

What wisdom, another one of our spiritual gifts, teaches is that the objects of peace are not to be found in the external world, and as we insist on finding tranquility through this outer searching, we will never stop to realise that all along we have had the capacity within to gift to ourselves and others this most valuable of treasures. Sitting alongside love and joy as the highest gifts of human flourishing, this quality of peace is cultivated as we remain present to who we are in this moment and the movements that the spirit's energy makes in the world. But how many of us consciously have our fingers on the pulse of this transcendent dimension of our life? Not as many that are needed to shift the prevailing energy of the planet from chaos to harmonious order.

Perhaps the most predominant reason for this at the level of the individual is that we haven't tended the internal space from which we can discern the reality or Truth of our existence from the stories that we tell ourselves about who we are in relation to the physical world. As a result, the default belief that we have come to hold is that we are these stories that the ego has crafted on the back of our personal histories. So even though those events and circumstances have come and gone, the influence that they have on how we see ourselves in the here and now is so strong because we have not stopped to look deeper into ourselves or challenge whether those figments of our memory are still useful in defining who we are at present. By being stuck in the past in this way, particularly in the wounds that have left a deep impression on how we define ourselves, we stunt our own ability to evolve and move freely into the present from which we can make peace with who we are anew.

With this, think how differently life would feel if you allowed yourself to drop all the baggage from your past that incites your current feelings of guilt, shame and regret. By being liberated from the tyranny of these destructive emotions, your relationship with this moment and who you are in it would not be charged by anything other than the energy of spirit that invokes this peacefulness. For anyone who has engaged in serious spiritual practice, such as prayer or meditation, they know that the recognition and feeling of peace that arises from this empty state of connecting with our divine source is intimately connected with the mind releasing its grasp on the past. Through creating the conditions for silence and stillness to wash over us, we present the mind with an opportunity to stop its incessant chatter so that a deeper awareness can emerge to direct our thoughts towards consciousness.

Impacting our present orientation and the state of our future present moments which they lead into, this practicing also better equips us to release the fears and other negative emotions that we hold about what lies before us. Just as our thoughts about the past rob us of harmony in the present moment, so do our foreboding feelings about the future cast us adrift from our inner oasis of peace. Incessant worrying about whether we will have enough monetary security to sustain ourselves and the fear of the unknown are but two examples of these emotional blocks that scatter our mental and spiritual bearings, and keep us locked in a state of self-preoccupation that sabotages our best attempts at leadership.

When we are disconnected from the source of peace within, what tends to happen is that unconsciously we become consumed with filling that void, and in this process we are prone to become indifferent to and neglectful of the needs of others who rely on us for a sense of stability and direction. The affect that this has in a leadership context will be the diminishing of belief and trust that the person in charge can properly manage their responsibilities and the working relationships with their people that are vital to sustained success in any venture. How a conscious leader handles the operational and relationship challenges that they encounter is with an even-tempered composure that naturally engenders the trust and respect of the people who follow them. By being self-possessed in this way, they are wise to avoid the mood swings and lashing out that unconscious leaders are prone to engage in when their ego confronts stressful circumstances. While these stressors are still felt by the conscious leader, their negative effects are largely offset by the calm inner centeredness which acts as a buffer to those otherwise destabilising stimuli.

The question that a leader should not want their people to be asking themselves is, 'which boss am I going to encounter when I come into the office today?' If people within an organisation are asking such a question, it would indicate that their leader is lacking in the equanimity and consistency of character that go to the heart of how integrity is demonstrated and role modelled for others. What a leader wants to avoid with this is being so unreliable with their temperament that their people give up in dealing with them and tune out what they have to say. On this point, it has been said that, *"if people don't know what to expect from their leader/s, then they will stop expecting anything at all"*. Whether a leader likes or is comfortable having these expectations placed upon their shoulders is really immaterial, and they need to make peace with the fact that expectations will naturally arise in the minds of followers, who by virtue of their dependency on their leaders, remain vulnerable to arbitrary exercises of authority that could cause them to suffer harm. A part of the reciprocal obligation and inherent responsibility of the leader in this dynamic is to accept the expectation reasonably placed upon them to temper their own ego and enact a way of relating to others that is palatable to their good nature.

As a leader does this, they tangibly demonstrate an honouring of the privilege that their position affords them, and can more effectively temper their ego's expectations about what it feels entitled to gain from occupying the role. By obtaining some distance from these vain hopes, what these leaders are better able to grasp is the reality that exists before them. Rather than only seeing what they want to see to bolster their false and fragile sense of self, what emerges from within is the wherewithal to, as Eckhart Tolle puts it, accept what is happening in this moment as if they had chosen it. As they retreat into this space of surrender and experience the attendant solace that accompanies it, what they are able to release and transcend are the traditional earthbound attachments to wins or losses, success or failure and acclaim or scorn by which the ego measures itself in a leadership context.

When legendary NFL quarterback Aaron Rodgers expressed in an interview that he's *"been to the bottom and been to the top, and peace will come from somewhere else"*, I believe that he was touching upon this same sentiment. Despite winning a Super Bowl title and numerous Most Valuable Player awards during his illustrious football career, the realisation that Rodgers has inevitably come to is that 'success' or 'failure' in the physical world are decoupled from the peace or disturbance that we respectively associate with them. While so many athletes at the highest level seem to struggle with the ups and down of the fickle environment in which they forge an identity, Rodgers is exceptional among them, primarily due to his unflappable demeanour and poise under pressure. Having freed himself to play his own inner game within the larger game of football, he role models a rare form of sovereignty that imparts repose in exchange for the offering of one's best self to what they have been called to do.

Such is the integral connection that exists between the fulfilled heart and the fulfilling hand, and if we were to look at our own lived calling journeys we would see that when we are the most tranquil is when we are immersed in serving a meaningful purpose in our respective domain. As Mike Yaconelli wrote of this interdependent relationship, *"when you follow your calling, you feel at home, at peace - you feel as though you're where you're meant to be"*. To claim our spiritual leadership authority, or inner seat of power, is to allow our soul and worldly role the liberty to this rightful union in our lives. From integrity comes authority, or the power to author the story of our own lives. Are you willing to write this story, for your spirit and the prospering of the world? Let us now turn our minds to the qualities that will inform your answering of this question.

CHAPTER 5: Authority – The Inner Seat of Power

Why would you fly with the wings of a sparrow when the wings of an eagle have been given you already? This question from *A Course in Miracles* is a powerful one because it prompts us to challenge the source of power from which we function in our daily lives. Metaphorically, the wings of the sparrow represent the transient powers of the physical world which the ego aspires to gain in order to substantiate its identity. To the ego, the principal power to be valued comes from status, acclaim, being desired and possessing resources such as money. These are the things that we chase after with sparrow's wings in the hope that they will inoculate us from the frailties of perceiving ourselves as such feeble creatures. Conceiving of ourselves through this ego lens as being innately weak, we feel the need to be made strong through acquiring the external means which we have been conditioned to believe will compensate for these deficiencies.

While this is an intoxicating and drama filled search, the problem with this approach to being made whole is that what is acquired must eventually be divested and let go. The money we earn is eventually spent or lost. The high ranking position that we have now will need to go to someone else at a future point in time. Praise for what you have done today can quickly turn into disapproval and resentment for what you will fail to do tomorrow. So what are we really left with to ground our own self-worth, and the capacity to make a meaningful contribution to the world?

When one strips away all of these material preoccupations along with the erroneous belief that one is dependent on the world for their empowerment, what is able to be discovered and connected with is our innate power to fly with eagle's wings. This transcendent and immutable form of power is of our spirit, and it is the locus from which its agents are oriented towards the demonstration of virtue and leadership. All of the great statesmen and stateswomen that we revere from history and in the modern day, are conduits for this type of authority. Like the eagle, who resides at the apex of the species of birds, these individuals stand apart as exceptional embodiments of the human capacity for good, solidarity, justice, and all of the other qualities that enable our highest contributions to be made in society.

Having connected with and functioning from this true source of power within themselves, they are liberated from the illusion that worldly forms of power are goals to aspire to. To people who don't know them, these spiritually vibrant beings may seem unambitious or lacking focus in a status quo sense. While everybody around them is preoccupied with achieving success and being celebrated for their efforts, these sovereign individuals couldn't care less about those strivings. Marching to the beat of their own inner call, they are inspired in their movements along that path to derive meaning while being engaged in the process of serving their higher purpose. For them, there is no end beyond this purpose that 'motivates' them to do what they do. Where others may be driven by the recognition that comes from receiving awards, for example, these intrinsically aligned individuals don't require that external validation for their contributions, which they experience as being rewarding enough to their soul.

Often it is the case that what we are motivated to bring to ourselves has its origins in our inner feelings of deprivation or lack. Not believing ourselves to be enough, we won't ever feel that we have enough to be complete, so the impetus in our lives then becomes to fill that empty cup with externals that the ego values as being important. But this clamouring to gain from without is a tiring and ceaseless endeavour that disempowers us through the diminution of our autonomy to intentionally choose a meaningful path to life.

As we allow ourselves to become beholden to the objects we pursue, we give them a power of control over our lives. Leading us to become like automatons who can only act in the way that they are programmed to, what we lose from this material subjugation is our spiritual agency and the resourcefulness to draw from our full inner cup of virtuous blessings. Being what some might term as the quality of self-reliance, when we are absent of this independent recognition of our own power, we will be prone to mistaking in our mind, encumbrances for beneficial additions to our life. An example of an erroneous belief that testifies to the truth of this is the one which holds that having money or material goods will make us happy. Anyone who has ever subscribed to such a belief for long enough would be able to verify that not only does its promise fall far short of reality, but that our holding of it actually presents a latent barrier to the experiencing of peace, gratitude and joyfulness which lie at our core.

When we clear up misconceptions such as these, we reclaim the authority to write our own story and deploy the abundant trove of inner resources in service to our calling. In its highest sense, authority describes the ability of one to self-determine and direct their life with intentionality. The clue with this is in the word itself, where the term 'author' is prominent. Regardless of what we are confronted with in life, we always have the agency to reside within the gap that exists between these stimuli and our response/reaction to them. In this space is where our true power is expressed. Being the central tenet of Viktor Frankl's philosophy in *Man's Search for Meaning*, this ability to consciously choose how we will respond to life's happenings also lies at the heart of what it means to lead oneself in the fulfilment of a calling.

Even with our calling itself, it is not mandated by our creator that we follow that path, otherwise we wouldn't have a choice whether to live it or not. With this ability to determine our course, comes the opportunity to lead ourselves and others into a life of consciousness and spiritual power that radically exceeds whatever solitary power we understand ourselves as an ego based agent having. A metaphor that is useful in understanding this contrast in power involves the ocean. When you remove a drop of water from its ocean home, it loses the potentiality of the larger body of water through that act of separation, but left as one with its source of existence and it holds the immense power of the whole ocean. What the ocean represents here is the expanse of spirit that amplifies the force of each of those droplets of water that remain connected to it.

A leader who is conscious reciprocates in their relationship with this life force by preserving their connection to the ocean of spirit within themselves. Becoming integrally empowered through this union, the natural outpouring of that is endeavouring to empower others through the same means. Inspiring leaders do this by taking others under their wing as mentors, sharing of their stories of transformation, and by imparting the wisdom that they learned along their journey. Believing in the power of a single human being to shape the world profoundly, they honour the intrinsic worth of others and the potentiality that they hold to serve this purpose for the good. Being the reason why they are willing to invest their time and effort in others, what also enlivens their benevolence and commitment with this is the recognition that for as long as there are people who are ego bound and disempowered as a consequence, our collective ability to embody this spiritual source of strength will be stunted.

To really look at and acknowledge our innate power takes real courage because that light can be blinding. Putting an onus of responsibility on us to live into our purpose and actualise our potential, we must exercise autonomy and resilience in these tasks, and not yield to the pull of our base ego self that is inclined to misuse power rather than harnessing it to evolve ourselves and achieve progress in the world. Be like the conscious leader who is powerful enough within themselves that they don't have to absorb the external forms of power that others or a formal position offers them. Being unnecessary for your validation and virtuous leadability, hold that power loosely and give it back wherever possible so that those whose capacities you are looking to build can say with conviction that they produced good work by their own hands. This is the gift that spiritual authority brings to those who encounter it. Enlarging them, while magnifying its own affects, what it reflects is the abundant love and generosity of our creator who held nothing back in endowing us with the eagle's wings that are necessary for free and full flight.

Actualisation

When we are living our calling, what we come to learn and accept pretty early on in that journey is that life does not intend to enable our comfort or staticity. With our spirit being pregnant with the potentiality of our purpose and virtuous flourishing, it wills that we be in order to become. To be is to live a life of presence that is aligned with this spirit, and receptive to its call. Our becoming, that flows from this being, is affected by our responsiveness to this call, and the conscious steps that we take to grow into our fullness as human beings.

To know peace and fulfilment in our hearts as we travel down this authentic path, we must surrender the ego's desire for sameness and the rigid keeping of structures that preserve its means of control over our lives. When we fear change for example, this is a defensive block of this false self that keeps us locked in a perpetual state of resistance against the naturally shifting movements of life. This is why when we live this way, we feel uninspired, bereft of direction and agitated, like we are missing out on a richer form of life that could be available to us. Intuitively, as we languish in this dormant space, we are aware of the disconnect that we are experiencing, but because we feel so disempowered within ourselves, we lose faith in our ability to progress forward and create a more prosperous future that we can find freedom in.

Contrast this state with one that honours the spiritual impulse to grow and evolve into our fullness. When we are continuously learning about ourselves and relating to the world through what we discover, we become more confident in navigating life, and our ability to forge a meaningful path that challenges us to actualise the best version of who we could be. Leading us to experience ourselves as having a greater capacity for autonomy and living into our purpose, we find strength in the progress that we have made, and remain inspired to keep improving our means of contributing to the world through our calling.

As we create momentum on this path for our deepest gifts to come forth, what we come to realise is that it is the spiritual intention to become our best which enables this unfolding. Being a very different aim than the egocentric notion of being the best, when we are focused on becoming the best version of who we can be, the battle that we face is internal, to become the master of our destiny and spiritual warrior who can cast out the life-stifling ghosts of ego from our character.

Unlike the goal of being the best, our striving to become our best is not a zero sum game of external competition that must see others lose in order for us to 'win' at life.[28] Having connected with our own wellspring of spiritual strength that we can draw from at any time, we don't feel compelled to seek to take power from others by opposing and defeating them. While the world values these games highly as its players vie for trophies, commendations and other forms of victorious signalling, to those who are committed to living their calling, their intention is to engage others in a spirit of co-operation so that the value offered in service can be added or multiplied.[29] Being the path to prosperity that makes things better for everyone, this drive to enrich the human condition and make a difference is testament to this actualising quality being alive in us.

When I conduct my leadership workshops for executives who are often steeped in this 'winning over others' mentality, I ask them the following question to challenge their conditioning on the point: *'In anything that is truly meaningful in life, is it possible to be the best, without you first being at your best in doing that thing?'* After this provokes a thoughtful silence, I advise them that invariably it is not. It is therefore clear that we should give primacy to the inner journey of evolving ourselves to reach our potential, which we exercise full autonomy over, over the exterior goal to be the best, which is largely beyond our ability to control and accomplish. By affecting this shift in focus, we can take the energy out of our ego's crazed and desperate play for this misguided form of symbolic recognition, and paradoxically give ourselves the best chance of fulfilling our particular legacy.

As we live our calling in this way, we save ourselves much of the negative stress[30] and anxiety that accompanies trying to control the uncontrollable in

---

[28] A more enlightened characterisation of 'being the best' can be stated to mean the striving of the human being towards the ideal of what our actualised potential and virtuous embodiment enable us to reach. Such an interpretation can be contrasted with how we understand the concept from the level of ego consciousness, where it is seen as a final winning outcome to a competitive endeavour that subjugates the losers to a lesser station than the victor.

[29] The ego, engaging in competition, is the exponent of the two other well-known elements in the order of operations in math - it divides and subtracts/detracts from the life of other entities.

[30] Contrast this harmful form of stress with the feeling of eustress that accompanies our growth on the actualising path. Eustress is the enlivening tension that we feel when we are pushing back the boundaries of what we believe we are capable of, by,

our environment. When I talk to these executives after our sessions together, it is not uncommon for them to admit to me how under pressure they continuously feel to meet their KPI's and other performance goals, which measure success by the narrow metric of being number one in their chosen industry. With so many of the factors impacting this 'success' being beyond their scope of influence (for example, the state of the economy or changes in the legislation/regulatory policy that govern their industry), it is little wonder that this tension exists to dissipate the energy that they are capable of extending towards making their organisations the best that they can possibly be (the applying of this actualising impulse in an institutional context).

Before we can play a pivotal role in making something external to ourselves the best that it can be, we must be open and allowing of this actualising impulse within ourselves. Whole Foods Market and Conscious Capitalism founder John Mackey found this out as he was going about the process of building his company. In describing the connection between his vocational unfolding and the development of his business, he conveyed that, *"more than once in the history of Whole Foods Market, the company was unable to collectively evolve until I myself was able to evolve - in other words, I was holding the company back. My personal growth enabled the company to evolve."* Often, when we experience a failure, or a block to progress on our worldly path, it is our unwillingness to evolve as necessary that is the cause of the frustration. By resisting the pull of our lesser self, we can realign with our spiritual source of power to lead the transformation of these impediments into opportunities for new growth to be realised.

Conscious leaders are proactive in this process, challenging themselves and others to unfurl the boundedness of their nature. What they realise is that no matter where we are in life, there is still room to grow and improve, not only the quality of our own individual lives, but also the collective standard of life on this planet. To these individuals, the notion of remaining stagnant is anathema to their soul, and they can't imagine being the same person today that they were yesterday. Provoking them on their path of evolution, they allow inspiration to guide the way forward so that an alignment is maintained between who they are and what they have been called to do. They don't therefore seek to grow just for the sake of it. With their growth being intentional, it serves to support and strengthen the depth of purpose that they carry in their hearts.

---

for example, running a marathon or learning something new that challenges us to think in a more nuanced way.

Being what makes their participation in this growth process so meaningful and fulfilling, what they invest of themselves in this journey is commensurate with the rewards they derive from their efforts. With their enhanced capacity for service and contribution that flow from this application of personal leadership, the returns that they realise are often multifaceted and aren't just limited to the experience of intrinsic enrichment. Having cultivated deeper levels of self-awareness, social understanding and expertise in their discipline, they have much more value to offer to the market than individuals who are going through the motions without this growth orientation. Making them hard to ignore, these curious and eager students of their domain, and life in general, are often brought up through the ranks by mentors and other leaders who have identified their rich potential, and want to play a part in cultivating it.

With this elevation by influential others can come the opportunity to advance materially at a more rapid rate than individuals with a fixed, or stagnant, mindset. While this may be tempting for their ego to exploit, what keeps these actualising agents grounded and in alignment is the awareness of their calling is the primacy that following it takes above any accompanying benefits that present themselves along that path. For them, what preserves their authentic power is faithfulness to their purpose, or *'keeping the main thing, the main thing'* as Stephen Covey was fond of saying. Without purpose we have no authority, or base of influence for leading either ourselves or others to any destination that is worth venturing to.

Purpose

Why are you here on this earth? To be and affect what in this unique moment in time? These are sobering questions if we have not previously cultivated the space to answer them, or consulted with the spiritual dimension of our being that knows what this purpose is. Emerging from a thorough investigation of who we truly are, our animating reason/s for being will struggle to reveal themselves if our point of relating to life is located in the shallow pool of the ego self, from which we can only ever scratch the surface of understanding who we are in relationship to the world.

As desperate as we might be for answers to the question of our life, we will not gain the insight or wisdom to see how the thread of our existence ties into the greater tapestry of life if we are so insular and consumed with indulging the ego's vein whims that we can't stand above its smallness to discern our larger calling to serve the world beyond ourselves. Beneath all of the ego's bloviating and chaotic attempts to distract us from living a life of significance is a still point of clarity from which we can reconnect to the spiritual foundation of our human identity, and the vocational path of meaningful contribution that emerges from it. Being the interior space that we are required to enter into with humility and stillness, it also takes a great amount of courage to walk through that inward facing door to awareness, where much of what we have been taught and believed about ourselves and the world will be tested.

Part of the reason why Truth is so powerful is because once we have encountered it, we can't turn our back on its presence without experiencing some significant repercussions for our inner life and wellbeing. Whatever superficially motivated path that we might have pursued to this point in our life will reveal itself as a dead end that we need to move on from. Similarly, the roles that we have taken on to unconsciously strengthen our ego's standing in the world will be seen in a new light, and become subject to abandonment if they cannot be redeemed to serve the purposes of the higher self that we have awakened to. As we come to realisations like these within ourselves, we enliven our power of intention and authority to enact that which the spirit rouses in us. No longer are we mindlessly bound by what the world tells us we should be and do, and with these constraints removed we can begin the journey of becoming a clearer vessel for our calling to come forth. As this purpose emerges to guide our decision making and we become more confident in the new direction we are taking, the passion that we feel towards this subject of our calling will rise to the surface of our being and lead us to engage with it more deeply. Being the emotional component of living on purpose, what we see with passion is that it is inextricably linked to a calling being lived out. In countless interviews that I reviewed from my study and a broader range of sources, these mutually reinforcing qualities of purpose and passion were consistently observed in individuals who had chosen to travel down the authentic path of their vocation.

It should not be surprising that a great number of these people could also be described as high performers in their respective fields, who have gravitated to leadership through their embodiment of these qualities. For leaders to be successful in building a following and initiating effective action, they must be animated by both a compelling cause and a fervent zeal to bring people together in service of that cause. Being the potent combination that enables them and their teams to make a real difference in the world, these impacts would not be able to be affected without the spirit's infusion of love for that which their individual and collective missions involve.

With this love being like fuel for the journey to live our calling, purpose reciprocates to anchor that passion, and harness it toward the accomplishment of a worthy end. When it is decoupled from a purpose, passion becomes a scattered energy that if we are not aware enough to consciously channel it, can easily lead us to become hedonistic in our pursuits. This is why some caution against the advice to 'follow your passion'. When we whimsically give in to what makes us feel good in the moment, we lose our vision for the bigger picture which puts our calling in its proper perspective. In order to transcend, one must rise above, and being able to keep their focus on this bigger picture is one of the conscious leader's greatest strengths. Endowing them with a systems level understanding of how things come together, they are better positioned than their more myopic counterparts to effectively align and work with stakeholders in their environment who share the same animating purpose. Another positive effect of embodying this perspective is that they don't get bogged down in the weeds of what they are dealing with. By working as a part of a larger team who they trust to take care of the details, these leaders preserve the attention to be guided by their conscious instincts, or intuition, in the fulfilment of that purpose.

Where this purpose can get lost or distorted however is where a leader falls into the ego made trap of micromanaging every detail because they don't trust the members of their team to effectively do their work. Leading to information and task overload for that individual, the other problem that this excessive need for control causes is a diminished bandwidth to prioritise and execute the core objectives that align with the organisation's mission. The flow on effect of this is deleterious to the life of the entity. Not only does it cause a disconnect with others that undermines their loyalty and engagement, but it also plants seeds of confusion regarding the fulfilment of roles and how they work to serve a vision that is no longer clear.

As we are told from the book of Proverbs, *"where there is no vision, the people will perish"*. This vision is the articulation of what the fulfilment of a purpose would look like. It shepherds, inspires and brings others into service who resonate with it. When an organisation strays from its collective 'why', this will draw into question the personal whys of its members, and how much of it they are willing to compromise by working out of alignment with the vision that stimulated their involvement in the first place.

If through our offerings to the world we are not answering this *why* question of our life, then we will be diminished in the meaning, joy and fulfilment that we derive from our work and relationships with others. Our inner state of feeling can therefore be a valuable indicator of how on purpose we are with our being. When we are unfocused with our direction and drifting aimlessly from one moment to the next, it is inevitable that we will come to doubt ourselves and become distressed and indecisive about what the right way

forward is. Having allowed our purposelessness to suppress our spiritual instincts, this accounts for much of the errant decision making that leads life
to present us with some of its harsher lessons. While the suffering involved
in these lessons will tempt us to resist them, our surrender to their teaching
comes with the recognition that even they serve a valuable purpose in our
evolutionary journey. Bringing us humbly back to a point of Truth in our
lives, what these missteps and travails uncover is the path back to purpose
and meaning.

As the world emerges out of the isolation bubble brought about by the coro-
navirus pandemic we can reflect on how our perspective towards life and
our priorities may have shifted. Being a period of great disruption to our
'normal' routines of living, what our forced time out has bought to our
awareness are the significant questions that we were previously too busy to
ponder. This has especially been the case for those among us who have lost
work or loved ones during this period of upheaval. As challenging as this
time has been, I believe that it has served as a valuable opportunity to stop
and reassess our individual and collective courses to ensure that the future
we are all playing a part in creating will be conducive to not only the material
enhancement of our condition, but to the flourishing of the human spirit.

An inspired purpose is an enduring purpose, and it will see us through existential crossroads such as these if we are committed to giving it a voice in
our lives. Whatever the void that exists in our heart, our purpose can heal it,
and lead us back to the seat of power and wholeness from which we can lead
others in the world consciously. Now let us explore the role of responsibility
in the conscious exercise of authority.

Responsibility

One of the many blessings of our lives, that is easy to take for granted, is
that we are born free. As children who were eager to explore our environment and understand who we were in relation to it, the world was our oyster.
Presenting an infinite range of possibilities as to what our life could hold, we
learned as we grew up that a key determinant of where we would end up was
how we exercised our freedom of choice. All of us, no matter what external
circumstances we find ourselves in, possess the fundamental ability to
choose the direction that our life will take in the present moment. Even
someone who is physically imprisoned has the choice of who they will become through that experience, and while many will emerge out of their con-
finement with hardened hearts, and minds that are resistant to the lessons of
their hardship, others such as Nelson Mandela, Viktor Frankl and Vaclav
Havel come to connect more deeply with their spiritual source of strength,

and the power to decide how they will respond to external circumstances that are beyond their control.

This ability to respond is otherwise known as the quality of responsibility. Meaning more than just one's willingness to own their behaviour, it also encompasses the fundamental authority that each of us has to steer the direction of our life with intention. In any moment where there is a decision to be made, we can deny ourselves this power by choosing to remain unconscious, or we can assert conscious control over our thinking and choose a life giving course of action. This is what Viktor Frankl did amidst the horrors of life in a concentration camp to realise meaning and purpose to his human existence. Whilst to all appearances he enjoyed no physical freedom, within himself he had complete dominion over his mind and spirit, which nobody external to him could deprive him of. Despite being in reality a victim of these unjust circumstances, this was not how he saw himself because he had not abdicated the responsibility to determine the state of his inner life.

What made his journey of survival and personal growth so extraordinary is that he had every reason to slink into the role of a victim. Nobody who was looking at his predicament would have blamed him for giving up, and yet the choice he made was to plumb his depths to connect with that transcendent dimension of his being that would allow him to endure this suffering with grace and equanimity. I believe that the power of his example lies in it reminding us that in the much less dire circumstances which we find ourselves, we can self-determine our course and overcome challenges that we might once have believed were insurmountable.

While it imposes a burden on us to accept this response-ability, the cost of sitting in the passenger's seat of our life is heavier in the toll that it takes on our being. As we fail to exercise this autonomy for our own purposes, we in effect announce to the world that we are victims in waiting, to be used and abused for others self-serving agendas. Putting this in theatric terms, Canadian psychologist Jordan Peterson explains that *"If you're not the leading man (or woman) in your own drama, you're a bit player in someone else's – and you might as well be assigned to play a dismal, lonely and tragic part."*

As Peterson alludes to in his quote, the quality of responsibility is a prerequisite for leadership. Before one can lead others effectively, and with credibility, they must first prove capable of leading themselves, and it is through the medium of response-ability that we demonstrate the possession of ourselves to chart an intentional course for our life. To look at this another way, if you were told that you were going to be led by an individual who was impulsively triggered by other people's comments, or reactive to their environment in the decisions that they made, you would struggle to find respect for this individual, and resist being led by them, because their behaviour demonstrates that they are not in control of themselves.

A large part of what makes great leaders so valuable is that they are able to bring stability and safety to environments that are inherently unpredictable and chaotic. By being in control of their inner state, conscious leaders are able to bring calm and centeredness to their sphere of influence, and buffer their people from the uncertainty that surrounds them. From the cohesion that forms through this infusion of consciousness, the collective mode of being can begin to mirror the character of their leader and effectively deal with the challenges of responding to the changing dynamics of their environment. As the group evolves along that path, they can even progress to become proactive in setting a direction that other players in that environment will want to follow.

We see this in operation all the time in business where a conscious leader with a transcendent vision changes the landscape of an industry by responding to the deeper needs of their customers, or opportunities that spark an inflection point for that industry. Instead of merely reacting to what their competitors are doing, or where the broader winds of their industry are blowing, these conscious businesses blaze a trail to a future where corporate social responsibility becomes more than a perfunctory act of goodwill that is engaged in to strengthen the bottom line or create a positive perception of the company in the minds of its stakeholders.

To be conscious in perceiving the wider needs of our world naturally imposes a responsibility on us to play our part in meeting those needs to the greatest possible extent. Our avenue for achieving this and making our most impactful contribution to the flourishing of the world is to live our vocation. By awakening to our innate gifts, we can put them to the best use in service of a cause that aligns with the call of our heart. To allow these gifts to go unoffered would be an irresponsible waste of life that flies in the face of the need that the world has for our being. With so much work that is still required to be done to restore equity, peace, love and wholeness, we can't allow the ego to deter us from that integral path by allowing it to demand of the world the satisfaction of our entitlements and rights. While the upholding of these rights at the level of our humanity is no doubt important, the other side of the equation is equally vital if we are to achieve a more balanced state of equilibrium.

On this point, one will begin on the path to significant growth and transformation when they cease asking the world 'what it can do for them' and instead ask 'how they may serve its highest purposes'. Not only is this the fundamental question of our calling, but it is also the answer to solving much of the current dysfunction which plagues the human condition. If we take the scourge of racism for example, great progress could be made in a very short time if those who held prejudicial views took responsibility for correcting them so that those who belong to the affected minority groups are seen and treated in a more equitable light. Part of what perpetuates the cycle of ignorance around the issue, stems from a stubborn refusal by those who hold bigoted views, to look at and change behaviour, which serves to reinforce their perceived superiority over those who are marginalised by its enactment.

If one were to call out these individuals for this or other dysfunctional behaviour, chances are that it would lead to blame deflection from them who don't want to change behaviour that they believe serves them at some level. Even if the call being made to their fundamental humanity centres on responsibility, which if exercised would empower them to evolve and embody their best self, because they are already disempowered within themselves, their deciphering of this plea would be predisposed to take on a victim narrative that seeks to justify their prejudicial perspectives. Prompting them to say something to the effect of 'that group of people are really bad for what they did to my in-group in the past', this will evidence a defensive lack of introspection to discern the true basis of their accusatory thinking (the ego self), and understand how they or their forebears may have contributed to the conflict that was experienced. From this righteousness of the ego being professed on both sides of a divide, we have a perpetuation of grievances that exist across generations.

Much like children, who in their outlook on life are all about themselves and what they want to do, when we are preoccupied about our rights and what we feel entitled to from life, we create a very infantile state of existence that limits our individual and collective ability to evolve beyond ego consciousness. Imagine how radically different the world would be if each of us was driven by a deep sense of duty to uplift others and be stewards of the planet that supports our life so generously. By serving to actualise this vision in the context of our calling, we would demonstrate leadership in the most human way possible. While leadership can take a multitude of forms, at the heart of how it is embodied is the sowing back into the world the seeds of our spiritual growth.

When we look closely at the usual progression through life stages, it becomes clear that we are called to manifest greater levels of responsibility towards the world and those in it as we venture further along that path. As children we exercise minimal responsibility and it is only as we grow into teenagers and young adults that we start to give effect to this virtue. As we then move to have more intimate and mature relationships with others, our circle of concern and responsibility widens. Not only are we looking out for just ourselves anymore, but also for those who we have committed to share our lives with. If children are born from these relationships, then that expands this circle even more, and we have to take on the added burden of parenting these children to the best of our ability. In my own experience, the growth that is stimulated as we take on this role is pivotal in nurturing a sense of global responsibility that can enliven our legacy work in mid-life and into our later years. When we think about the world that we are creating for our children, this also encompasses the intertwining fortunes of other people's children, with whom our progeny will have to work alongside to move the world forward and make it a better place for succeeding generations.

By coming to hold this integral perspective where our concern for the world beyond ourselves runs deep, we find all the purpose we need to stay inspired and committed to living our calling. As Fred Kofman reminds us, *"in full consciousness, we take full responsibility"*, and leading from that space of being causally responsible for the experience of life that we are creating, we come to accept that we are not helplessly affected, or powerless, to overcome the challenges of life that test our ability to respond to them with resilience. To be human is to be hardwired to endure, as we will learn in the next section.

Resilience

The quality of resilience is one of the most prominent ways that the power of the human spirit reveals itself to the world. To be resilient is to demonstrate the capacity to positively adapt to the adverse circumstances that are a part of life. No matter who we are, we will inevitably experience significantly jarring events that lead us to question our perceived ability to endure them and move forward. The pain of having someone we love die, losing a relationship that means the world to us, having a battle a serious illness, or sustaining a life-altering injury. Each of these are common to the human experience, and how we deal with those challenges plays a pivotal part in the direction that our lives will take.

Look at the people in your own life, for example, who have undergone trials like these, and you will see the key role that their responsiveness to these events had in determining how well they adapted to those challenges. While some people fall apart and into a pit of despair from which they don't believe they can bounce back, others amazingly rise out of this trough with courage and the determination to forge a new way forward in their life. Being unwilling to give up or give in to the suffering which such experiences evoke, they instead find a way through that pain by relying on the strength of their spirit, and the quality of resilience that it inspires in them. When we witness these individuals' journeys, we might be tempted to label them as extraordinary or superhuman compared to what we think we would be capable of enduring in similar circumstances, but having this perspective belies the truth that the capacity to embody resilience is our birthright, and as natural to our being as breathing, or having our heart pump blood to every extremity of our body. Right here, right now you have in your treasure chest of inner resources the ability to allow your spirit to see you through the storms of your life, and fundamentally you don't need anything external to yourself to bring this virtue into manifestation. Since humans have been habitating this planet, we have faced serious threats to our existence, yet we have overcome and prospered. Parker Palmer, a man whose writings I greatly respect, likens our human soul to a wild animal that is not only resilient, but tough, savvy and self-sufficient in its makeup. Knowing how to stay alive in even the most unforgiving of habitats, it does so primarily because it doesn't stray from its nature as members of our species are want to do.

As I write this, I think of my grandmother on my mother's side, who had to flee her village in Italy with baby in arms to escape the bombs that were dropped by the Allies and the Germans in World War II. Nobody had to offer her resilience training to make her way through that hardship, and as absurd as that sounds, I am pretty sure that at that time there was no such thing on offer. It is only in recent times that people have tried to pedal this type of training to individuals who feel totally disconnected from their spiritual source of power. When we don't have a spiritual basis to our life, and identify with the ego too strongly as a result, we become increasingly vulnerable to its frailties and falsehoods that diminish us and our feeling of being in control of our own life. This is why we feel so threatened and victimised by unanticipated circumstances, and struggle to cope with them effectively when they arrive. Having given our power over to the ego and become resistant and reactive to life as we experience it, what we have forfeited through that relinquishing of autonomy is the authority to persevere and bounce back from our trials and tribulations.

I think this helps explain why we put leaders such as Ernest Shackleton, Abraham Lincoln and Helen Keller on a pedestal without properly allowing their example to inspire us to emulate the quality of resilience in our own lives. To see them in this artificial light only masks the universal nature of this quality, which does a great disservice to the workings of spirit in the world. Part of the blessing of resilience being embodied is that it can inspire others to draw on their own inner strength in ways that they may not otherwise have done. Giving them the hope and tenacity to dig that bit deeper in meeting the challenges they are confronted with, they are momentarily led to align with the presence of spirit within and glimpse their own true power. While we may not always be conscious of the movements that our spirit makes in response to others embodiment of this quality, we will feel it and be inclined to label that swell of emotion as 'inspirational'. This is not a coincidence, for underpinning this exchange of life giving energy is the presence of spirit at work in us.

Even the hardships that we face carry within them life giving energy that is waiting to be harnessed by those who answer the call to embody resilience. In his classic work *Think and Grow Rich*, Napoleon Hill made a similar point, being that, *"every adversity, every failure, every heartache carries with it the seed of an equal or greater benefit"*. Like a magnet that simultaneously holds both a negative and positive charge, so do the trials of our life that our ego, denying this potential benefit, readily labels as terrible and unfair to us for having to experience them. By subscribing to its perspective here, we then slide into the role of victim from which we fail to learn anything constructive about what we have had to endure that can help us grow into the person we were born to become.

For our spirit, these difficult events are not processed in the same limiting way, and are therefore not shied away from. Realising that they present an opportunity to bring consciousness more fully into form, these happenings are accepted and responded to, as if the person experiencing them had chosen for them to occur. While this individual would never consciously invite or choose severe forms of hardship to come to their door, upon them arriving in any event, they are determined to be positively dealt with and used as a catalyst to create a better form of life for themselves and others. With this, I will forever be astounded by people who experience unimaginable suffering and come out of that deep valley to serve the world with the profound growth and clarity of purpose that they have found. Presenting a powerful form of leadership in its own right, one would be hard pressed to dwell in the despair of their own disappointments when exposed to these harrowing stories of surviving tragedy and finding a way back to life. When we see or hear of others go through difficult things that make our hardships pale in comparison, not only does it inspire us, but it strengthens our belief in being able to find a way through. *'If they can overcome, then surely I can too'*, we may say to ourselves.

As I was interviewing for my research, one of the things that drew forth my deep admiration for my respondents was their sharing of the lowest moments of their lives and how they allowed those happenings to make them better people. By just listening to their stories being told with vulnerability, self-love and forgiveness towards those who had caused their hurt, I felt myself become more emboldened to address the unresolved tensions that I was experiencing at that time of my life. Being a wonderful gift in retrospect, it was the consciousness born of their spiritual growth that led me to venture down a path that I had previously tried to avoid. While this may seem like a trivial example, there are numerous other ways in which one can be led by the resilience that others embody. As an aspiring writer who has previously experienced rejection of my work by publishers, I know to put this in its proper perspective and not to give up because of the rejection littered path that great authors such as J.K. Rowling and Stephen King have travelled.

When we encounter someone who has gone through the same challenges that we face and come out the other side, what they have to convey of their experience carries great weight to influence us, and conscious leaders, aware of the good that they can bring about through sharing of their lessons learned in hardship, are comfortable with being vulnerable and creating a space for others to grow into. Being also mindful that human beings are bound together more closely by their frailties and failures than by their successes, they use these shared experiences of struggle as points of connection and empathic understanding of what others have gone through along their journeys.

It takes a truly powerful individual to not have to hide behind their successes, and unconscious leaders fall short in that area of openness and vulnerability. Fearing that what other people think about their challenges and inadequacies will dismantle the veil of artificial strength that they have allowed their ego to construct as a protective armour for their weakness, they unknowingly weaken themselves further and compromise their ability to overcome future challenges because they are not being honest in confronting the reality of their disassociation from the natural form that life takes. With the sunshine comes the clouds that sometimes obscure it, and never have we been guaranteed a smooth run in life where we jump from one success to another. To believe such a fiction will make bouncing back from life's inevitable hardships that much more arduous, for if our script is written to only accommodate the ease of our perceived entitlement to order, it will come as a more severe blow when unanticipated events happen to jar against these expectations.

In order to grow into our fullness by aligning with our calling, we can't forego the work of journeying through the suffering that these hardships evoke. On the other side of that darkness is a light that illuminates the virtues of goodness that lie at our heart. Representing our Godliness that spirit has made manifest, these staples of character form the basis of the good life that conscious leaders have evolved to create in themselves, and the spaces that they grace with their presence.

CHAPTER 6: Goodness – Your Godliness made Manifest

Whatever good you have is all from God, whatever evil, that is from yourself. This verse from the Quran succinctly encapsulates the essence of what this chapter is about. When we live in alignment with our spirit, we will naturally bring forth in the world the virtues of goodness that are characteristic of our creator. To be acquainted with the presence of God within is to know the benevolent, loving, gracious and peaceful nature of this life force. Being among the highest qualities that humankind is capable of giving expression to, as we live our calling to enact these virtues, we allow the light of the divine to shine through us and illuminate the dark corners of the world where unconsciousness has become prevalent.

The greatest men and women to ever live and lead, each allowed themselves to become instruments of this purpose. By choosing to be consciously led by the spirit in their own lives, they each played a prominent role in furthering the common good, and evolving humanity towards a more integral state of functioning. Having subverted the influence of their ego in what they applied themselves towards, they were able to meaningfully contribute to the world by offering their deepest gifts in service. When we give generously to others from our spiritual heart, the reward that we receive are the positive feelings which affirm to us that what is moving from us into the world is characteristic of our true nature. Joy, enthusiasm, fulfilment, gratitude. By allowing ourselves to become a conduit of these energetic movements, we embody the wisdom of the maxim: *To do good is to feel good.* Providing his own perspective on this was Frederick Streng who put forward that *"a spirituality provides considerable benefit to the person, and typically views the person as being in a positive and fruitful relation to other people and the larger world."*

Contrast this with the kind of emotional debris that is left behind when we do wrong by others or intentionally cause them harm, and this helps to demonstrate this causal relationship between our actions and how they lead us to feel internally. When we lie to, steal from or cheat another person, we will likely feel shame, guilt and regret as a result, and those negative emotions will taint our present moment experience of living. Despite getting what we thought we wanted by engaging in this unconscious behaviour, the unintended but inevitable consequence was that our feeling state would become depressed. Given the metaphysical interrelationship that we have with other people[31], this shouldn't be surprising, and the energy with which we act towards others will leave a residue on us that cannot be shed easily.

Whatever is the state of consciousness that we are living from, we have in hand a boomerang which we cast out into the world through our words, deeds and emotional energy. By being mindful of that imagery, and allowing it to anchor us in faithfulness to our true self, we can exercise conscious responsibility for what we cast out, and avoid indulging the unconsciousness of the ego as a habit. All too often, the harm that we cause to ourselves and the external world comes about because we are acting reflexively, without presence, and a honouring of the space it provides for the spirit's energy to move to and from us. Because we are out of balance in this way, what we find is that it doesn't take much for our ego to become triggered and lash out at the world. Being a projection of the negative feelings that we harbour in its company, we won't prove capable of stifling their embodiment and externalisation until we stand to correct the misperceptions around our true identity, and the goodness that lies at the centre of it.[32] To eschew this responsibility and seek to blame these external 'triggering' events for what is wrong with our life, is to continue giving the ego our implicit permission to cast out boomerangs of negativity at its own discretion. For those who take on this victim role, nothing good comes from the anger, resentment, helplessness and fear that they allow themselves to be controlled by, and if this way of relating to the world describes us then it shouldn't be any wonder why we too are failing to create the prosperous life that we desire.

While prosperity, being a state in which our life is infused with goodness[33], is our birthright, in the rapidly moving and complex world that we have created, it is easy to find ourselves struggling to reflect this reality. Rarely do we have the time to revel in the good things in our lives, even when these blessings are right in front of us. Taking them for granted, we choose to attend to more pressing matters that demand our attention in the moment. While of course this busyness has its place in the scope of our life, if we are not aware of and attuned to the spiritual need that we have to connect with its

---

[31] The Golden Rule, do unto others as you would have them do unto you, reflects this interrelated quality of our human existence, and provides a forewarning of how we can expect to be treated if we allow the ego to guide how we relate to others.

[32] Misperceptions such as humankind being born into sin, and evil being a natural force in the world.

[33] Prosperity, as I define it here, means more than just being financially wealthy, which is but a component of what can flow into one's life when goodness is exemplified in their character and contribution to society. For leaders serving in an organisational context, the goodness that they enact has been statistically shown by Batz and Hillen to correlate with better financial results for their business.

intrinsic goodness and physical manifestations, then this busyness can easily become a conditioned response to what is going on around us. To break this cycle, or interfere with it before it begins to take hold, we must become more intentional about perceiving what is good in our life. What this looks like in your life may be different from what it looks like in mine, but trust me it is there, and once we humble ourselves to acknowledge it, then we can begin to feel gratitude for its presence.

Humility in this context teaches that just because we can't see something, doesn't mean that it isn't there. Therefore, if we can't perceive this goodness in the world then we need to face up to the encumbrances within ourselves that have the effect of distorting what we look upon. Forms of pain and suffering can bring this about, and lead us to believe that the world is a hostile place that is not conducive to our flourishing. But just because we experience this grief doesn't mean that it is God's doing or willed by this life force. As the spirit is all-encompassing, transcending the dichotomies of the physical world, it holds both the capacity for goodness and that which is not good, without being the cause of the latter. Only the wounded and victimised ego proclaims that God is not good because this life force allows terrible things to happen. Clearly, it cries this for the less than pure motivation of turning us against our creator so that it can exercise greater control over our lives.

Seen in a conscious light, even this pain and suffering is ripe for transmutation, pregnant with a transformative potential that can be harnessed for good. Giving effect to this transformation by allowing our spirit to process the events and powerful emotions of hardship, we become like the alchemist who has turned base metal into precious gold for our life. The way in which a number of respondents to my study overcame tragedy and other forms of adversity in their lives testifies to this. Leading them into greater alignment with their calling and a more integral recognition of its nature, many of their characterisations of this animating purpose encapsulated the theme of goodness:
doing good things for others/in the world; doing something for the greater good; doing something in life that you are naturally good at; being a good person/spouse/parent/leader; fighting the good fight; seeing and appealing to the goodness in other people; helping other people to live good lives; providing good service to others.

These findings testify strongly to our inherent goodness, and the spiritual mandate that each of us has to breathe that goodness into the world as we live our calling. In the following sections of the chapter, I will highlight the prominent associated virtues of goodness that were demonstrated by these respondents and other conscious leaders: Love, humility, evenhandedness and optimism.

Love

When we evolve to reflect our spiritual essence to the world through our calling, agape love is what we impart. Being a universal love that catches everything in its sweep, it is the same love from which we were created, and which our creator continues to feel for us in this moment. To remain conscious of the presence of this life force in us is to remember that we have never been without love. Like the inhalations and exhalations of our breath, it is always moving to and from us, sustaining our connection to the world and our relationships with those in it. Even when we don't give it any mind, it is still present surrounding us because the life that it has is not conditional on us being aware of it.

But how much this preeminent virtue of love infuses our being will be determined by how receptive we are to all that it is. In this, we can't be selective, choosing to love only those people and things which our ego identifies with and derives strength from. Such a malformed version of love is not only conditional but superficial, which explains why when we embody it, our spirit is not evoked and nourished in any meaningful sense. If you listen to people talk, they will tell you about the things that they 'love': foods, locations and Netflix series for example, but this is a pseudo love from which they gain shallow and fleeting pleasure. Requiring nothing of real substance to be given by them to those objects, their relationship to those things can't deliver the rich rewards that come from being in a genuinely loving union, or engaged in work that makes their heart sing.

What I found in speaking to respondents who were aligned with their spirit as they lived their calling was that the love they awakened to in that alignment was what infused their relationships with those they encountered on their path, and the carrying out of their vocational work. By allowing themselves to be led by love, it powerfully shaped how they led others along a shared journey, and themselves in the challenging process of actualising their calling. Having the ability to radically transform our relationship with others for the good, love can also recast our identity into the virtuous mould of what our creator intended when giving us life. Being universally recognised as the chief virtue for this reason, it is through love's gate that the other virtues of the spirit come to pass into our heart.

Take the qualities of actualisation, commitment and resilience for example. When we are filled with love, it makes us want to be better people for those who have roused it in our lives. Those others may be our children, a romantic partner or someone who we serve through our calling. As we invest this energy in giving more of ourselves to these valued others, we strengthen our commitment to them, and will endure further in protecting what those relationships represent. With a fortified resilience towards that end, we are not so easily derailed by the challenges that confront us on our path.

For the conscious leader who leads from love as they relate to stakeholders in their environment, one of the primary barriers that they can encounter, particularly in the commercial sphere, is the reluctance to accept the word 'love' as a part of the established vernacular. For years, many have viewed business as a combative endeavour where the goal was to win at the expense of others to secure greater financial rewards, but in recent times this perspective has started to shift which has allowed leaders to become more emotionally vulnerable and engaged in expressing care, empathy, charity and compassion in the workplace. Being altruistic behaviours that at the deepest level are inspired by love, it was these characteristics amongst others that conscious leaders were seen to practice in their personal and professional lives.

While we ordinarily think of love as being embodied through its extension towards others, conscious leaders also extend this love towards themselves by engaging in self-care practices such as exercise, meditation, healthier eating, developmental learning and restorative breaks from work. Serving the important purpose of buffering them from stress and burnout, these practices also had the beneficial effect of making them more mindful of their inner emotional state as they went about their lives. With this inner orientation and awareness of how they could become self-critical and punitive when failures hit or they made mistakes, they were able to cut themselves some slack and forgive their shortcomings by directing their kindness and compassion inwards. One of my respondents even described this extension of self-love as being inherent to her calling when she remarked, *"That is I think a sense of vocation to come to a place where I know and I accept and I love this self."*

It cannot be emphasised enough how important self-care is to the fulfilment of our calling. If we are denying ourselves what is needed for wellbeing, and running with a depleted tank as a consequence, then that will compromise our ability to answer our call in service. When I interviewed the priest who presided over my wedding for this research, he expressed this same sentiment in a unique way. Conveying that for him the key to good ministry is self-care, the value of this wisdom lies in the concept of 'ministry' not being limited to the enactment of the religious role that he occupied. Whatever form our calling takes, our ministry is how we bring it to life in the world, and to do this to the best of our ability, we must honour the physical vessel through which our spirit undertakes its work. If we refrain from consciously attending to this in the present, then over time we increase the likelihood of poor health or a premature death coming to our door. Being barriers that respondents' recognised as hindering one's ability to live their calling, they also can effectively stifle the zeal and joy that emanate from the love which one has for their work.

For many people who are living their calling, the area in which this love is most evident is at work. When asked to describe their feelings about their work or vocation, a pervasive response was, *"I love what I do and have a great passion/enthusiasm for the work"*. In drawing a connection between a lived calling and leadership using love as a link, it is important to understand the power inherent in having and, perhaps more significantly, demonstrating, passion and enthusiasm in our work. Both of these qualities are highly infectious and effective in sparking passion and enthusiasm in others who resonate with our area of interest. This phenomenon was evident from the subsequent segments of respondent interviews:

"When you are enthusiastic about it, people are like, 'tell us more, we want more'. It is like a positive infection. It is contagious because then people say, 'if he can do it, why can't I do it?' It is almost like an instant injection of passion. It is something that is a fantastic result. // When I was working in India I always remember that when we worked on the streets of Calcutta that we never had a leader, that for each of us, the person who was most passionate about a particular situation was given, if you like, priority to lead in that moment. // I'm passionate about it, and people can see that which is why they follow me. // I'd heard so much about the organisation, understood her passion for their work, and that was why I committed to take on the Board position."

Even if we don't hold a formal leadership position, having love for what we do will attract others to us and build influence among that group. From love comes immense care, for both the quality of the work we are producing, and the value that those we serve derive from it. Giving rise to an excellent offering that others will want more of, what also enlivens their engagement towards us is the recognition that our work is an extension of who we authentically are. When there is no disconnect between who we are and what we do, the love that we have for it becomes energetically palpable to others. Being unable to be hidden or faked, this explains in large part why we respond so differently to people that we encounter in service situations. If the person we are speaking to is disinterested and unengaged in their work, then we are more inclined to be indifferent towards them, and by extension, whatever they are offering. On the other hand, if the person we are dealing with loves what they are doing, then by them being in their element as they relate to us, our spirit will open to receive their aligned and inspired energy. Being what it resonates with, and therefore trusts to bring goodness into the world, how our spirit reciprocates this extension of love towards them is by acting as an outlet for their gifts to come forth and be seen, appreciated, and nurtured. By this willingness to engage the love we encounter, we play our part in restoring a lost sense of oneness, or spiritual connection to the holistic mode of life for which we were created. As Sam Keen says of this centripetal movement, *"To love is to return to a home we never left, to remember who we are."*

Humility

For any integral leader who would direct their hand to achieving good works, humility can't be bypassed as a quality of being that is necessary to ground that contribution in the world. Emerging from the English word *'humus'*, which means *'from the earth'*, humility is the connection that we must preserve to the natural part of who we are. Being the virtuous spirit that allows for birth and renewal of the life force through us, this growing forth would not be possible without the accompaniment of fertile soil that nurtures the flowering of our potentiality. Having metaphorical but also literal significance[34], we are taught to be wary of moving out into the world without an anchoring point that can sustain our connection to life and the calling that we were given life to enact.

To ungraft ourselves from this base of flourishing is to be like Icarus from the mythological Greek tale that warns of the dangers of hubris and being unbridled in our wilfulness to affect outcomes that are self-serving. Having the opportunity to escape from the island of Crete with his father, Daedalus, Icarus ignored his father's warning not to fly too close to the sun, lest the wax on his wings melted and sent him descending towards earth and an inevitable death. Being unable to temper the thrill of flight which tempted him to find freedom on his own terms, he met his demise because of his ego's unwillingness to follow the wise counsel of his father. With this father character in the story being symbolic of God, we are reminded of whose we are in relation to our calling, and the problematic circumstances that we create for ourselves when we close our inner ear to the promptings of this higher counsel.

I know in my own life that when I have fallen off the path of my calling and acted deleteriously towards myself and others, it was my own stubborn or arrogant insistence on affecting certain outcomes which benefited my ego that was responsible for causing that dysfunction. By needing to have things

---

[34] In the field of Botany (the study of plants), humus is the organic component of soil that stimulates the healthy growth of vegetation.

fall my way in order to feel satisfied with what was taking place, what I didn't consider as much as I should have was the indifferent treatment that I showed to others along the path to getting what I wanted. When we put ourselves at the centre of our attention and ambition, the natural consequence of that is for others to be marginalised to the periphery of our awareness. As we do this, it can be very easy to get taken away by the false belief that we are in some way superior to them and thus entitled to their respect and allegiance. For a leader on this ego trip who exercises formal authority over others in an institutional setting, the harm that they inflict upon 'their' people can be particularly severe.

Having experienced this phenomenon at work in previous job roles, it was observed that these unconscious leaders were liable to mistreat others, use them for their own ends, and even cast them out if their allegiance wasn't unequivocal. When we treat others who would follow us in this way, we effectively disqualify ourselves from leading them. Just as people will be reluctant to follow a selfish leader, they will find themselves being repelled by a leader who is arrogant and close-minded. Causing them to withdraw their engagement and support at a rapid rate, before long the leader will find themselves left in the company of the only person who matters to them: themselves.

Often times this individual is so insular and out of touch with their people and the toxic situation they have created, that they will be caught off guard by the fall that they experience. While this may be surprising for them, it won't be for those who understand how lacking in the quality of humility leads to a disconnect from reality. To the extent that we don't allow the practice of humility to preserve our integrity, what we look upon will be perceived unwholly and have its purpose/s distorted to justify their serving an ego based objective. This explains how unconscionable leaders can make the objectification of others or the misappropriation of resources for their own benefit appear so normal. Bearing no deep and abiding connection to what they use and abuse, they are victims of their own separation from spirit, which they reflect outwards to cause drama and discord in the world.

Underpinning this quality of humility is the recognition that at a spiritual level we are connected as one, with no person being superior or inferior to any other. As we relate to the world from that Truth, the way in which we treat others will be with the same dignity and reverence that we know we are deserving of. By actively embodying the golden rule in this way, and 'doing unto others' from the benevolent heart space of being, we demonstrate the virtuous form of leadership that multiple respondents in my study mirrored in their relational behaviour.

How these individuals, and others more broadly, come to hold the capacity for humility will be shaped by their upbringing and the calling journey they have taken. For some, humility was effectively role modelled for them in their childhood by parents or teachers who practiced the virtue. For others, they had to return to humility the hard way through a fall or humiliation of some kind, which had the effect of breaking down their strongly held identifications with the false ego self. In the course of my interviews with them, many respondents recalled jolting life experiences such as going broke, the loss of a loved one, relationship breakdowns, life-threatening health problems, and vocational or existential crises as being pivotal to their lived calling journey. Being significant turning points that put them on a more authentic and prosperous path, they represented the falling back to earth moments that their spirit used for the purpose of replanting the seed of their calling, and deepening their roots of solidarity and empathy for the plight of fallen others.

As they reclaimed their lives in the aftermath of these trials, there were other ways in which they reported demonstrating humility. Having opened themselves up to continuous learning, and being willing to learn from other people and experiences that had something valuable to teach them, they also evidenced an elevated awareness of their own shortcomings, and their role in bringing about the hardships they encountered. Without possessing this quality of humility, this growth would not have been possible because they would have become too entrenched in their existing understandings of the world to expose themselves to new sources of learning. Similarly, these individuals intimated that they would have been incapable of owning their failings or misgivings if they lived from the deflecting ego, because its need to not appear flawed or wrong doesn't allow for the vulnerability that reflection and the taking of responsibility require.

For a leader, the ability to be vulnerable is a great source of strength that can draw others to them with the humility and humanness that it reveals. Providing a powerful point of connection from which trust and credibility can be established, its proper embodiment requires us to allow our spirit to shine through the cracks of the protective ego shell that ordinarily impels us to defend ourselves from the criticism, judgment and exploitation that it perceives will come our way if we open ourselves up to the world. Being where weakness lies in the constitution of this false identity, it is not, as the ego would have us believe, to be found in the act of making ourselves vulnerable. For those of us who have the courage to challenge this false narrative and unmask, what we are likely to find is that the negative perceptions that the ego projects onto those who we reveal ourselves to are misguided and informed by its fear of losing the artificial power that distinguishes it from others. With superiority by separation being how it wields control in the worldly context, its vested interest is in keeping us ignorant to the even-handed quality of spirit that humbles us in our understanding of who we are in relationship to each other, and the good treatment to which all are entitled to receive as they move about in their daily lives.

Evenhandedness

When we humble ourselves to see the world clearly, and perceive the inherent value that each human being possesses by virtue of their existence, it becomes very difficult to justify treating some people less favourably than others. This is especially the case when we base that treatment on superficial or egocentric considerations. No matter what race, religion, sexuality, gender or socio-economic class that one belongs to, at the more fundamental level of spiritual identification there is an inseparability from the God source that can't be denied or stripped away from them. Being the foundation of their essential belonging in the world, there are no conditions that the ego can impose over this to make them earn the acceptance and good standing that is already theirs. What has freely been given us has already been earned, and the spirit asks no questions about the dignity we hold, and the respect to which we are entitled. Even our laws on human rights, and the justice system more broadly, acknowledge this latent worthiness, reinforcing what in our hearts we know to be true. Former Chief Justice of the US Supreme Court, Earl Warren, recognised this when he made the incisive comment that, *"It is the spirit and not the form of law that keeps justice alive."*

In spite of the self-evident spiritual imperative called the golden rule being a guiding light for how we should treat each other, there still exists a great divide between our abstract understanding of the concept of evenhanded-ness, and our ability to construct a social reality that genuinely honours the virtue. At no other time in human history has the gap between rich and poor within nations been so wide, and the stratification of our social structure been so intensely demarcated along political, racial and ideological lines. Leading us to virulently oppose each other in our private and public dis-course, civility often emerges as the first casualty of this uncompromising mode of dialogue. Contributing to this economic disparity are the powerful elite who routinely wield their influence to advance their own interests without considering how they could better serve the needs of their communities, or protect the environment that we collectively rely on for our survival. Rather than promoting equitable and meritocratic organisational systems where people can advance by their own diligent efforts and character, what we often see being built in their place are mirror-tocracies that stifle diversity by preserving the status quo, and only provide a pathway for those who remind the powerbrokers of themselves.

While this ego-reinforcing system benefits those who reside at the top of these structures, those benefits often don't flow down to those at its base and middle rungs. Being kept in their place and exploited by the dynamics of the dysfunctional hierarchy, and the strivings of others to carve out a larger share of the economic pie for themselves, they are objectified as ladders to be climbed upon for others' egos to gain leverage in the play for dominance. Through the taking of these steps, we see at work the ego's proclivity to stand apart and above those who it perceives as being inferior and a threat to its own sense of specialness and entitlement. Separating itself from those others, it has those who align with it lose feeling and understanding for their plight, even if the one looking down has experienced similar hardships or barriers in the past.

This is why in the state of ego identification, we are bereft of the empathy and compassionate urge to uplift, that ordinarily moves us to reach down to those beneath us, and elevate their standing. Being our spiritual inclination when we are faced with an inequitable disparity, we will only be inspired to attempt to rectify that deficit through our vocational efforts when we remain connected to the unifying and infinite consciousness that has abundance enough to support everybody's flourishing. Unlike the ego with its conceptions of scarcity surrounding the availability of status symbols and the other material cravings that it defines itself by, others gains are not experienced by the spirit as a loss to its identity, but rather as an affirmation of the mutual thriving that is possible when we resolve to play our part in the actualisation of the collective good.

For the conscious leader who is centred in the integrity that can hold others successes along with their own, they are not thrown off balance by the prospect of others advancement. Knowing it to be a precondition to the improvement of society that the enactment of their calling serves to affect, they are not threatened by this outcome, or protective of what their ego fears that it will forego through this developmental recalibration. Being a willing ally in the cause, they are active in the cultural transformation of our institutions and the reformation of systems that in the future will be connected as much by the tendrils of consciousness as they have traditionally been by the workings of commerce.

With the fair treatment of others being a prerequisite of leadership, the person at the top of an organisation can't allow themselves to play favourites and denigrate those who don't serve to bolster their ego in the way that their sycophants do. To indulge this vain need would create a toxic culture of underhanded behaviour and political game playing, in which those who are being used as a means to an end are not having their deepest spiritual needs met in the workplace with the effect that they will not flourish or put forth their best work, particularly when having to deal with a leader whom they cannot respect because of their flawed character which is absent of this virtue. Such a situation perpetuates suffering not just in the person working in this noxious environment but also for the organisation, whose performance is bound to decline with the morale of its people. Contrast this leader with one who truly values their people, treats them as equals and is transparent with the standards that they expect everyone to adhere to. Being behaviours that build trust and loyalty when they come to infuse the cultural workings of any organisation, they also provide a level of psychological security as those working within the team come to realise that they are being treated the same as everyone else. Strengthening their sense of belonging, these members will be intent on putting their best foot forward for the organisation because they respect the character of their leader and feel valued for what they have to contribute. Being not made to feel like an outcast because of the leader's inclusive style of relating to them, they will be much less inclined to partake in passive aggressive behaviour, become actively disengaged in their work, or exploit their position for personal gain.

One of the strongest threads to run through my research data was this spiritual quality of evenhandedness, with multiple respondents who are living their calling and demonstrating leadership in the process expressing that the virtue of fairness is one that they hold dear and practice in their life. These respondents also associated the poor treatment of others and underhanded behaviour with individuals who have denied their calling. When asked to provide examples of individuals who have denied their calling, names like Robert Mugabe, Adolf Hitler and Richard Nixon were mentioned, primarily for the demonstrated absence of this virtue in their lives (in Mugabe and Hitler's example this involved the oppressive treatment and murdering of innocent people as both sought to engage in ethnic cleansing, while in Nixon's case the Watergate scandal evidenced a flagrant breach of the law - he was a lawyer by training before he ran for political office - that he willingly authorised in a desperate attempt to maintain political power).

As we indulge these egocentric desires to suppress and conceal so that we can preserve and enhance our own base of power, we are unwittingly cutting off our nose to spite our human face. With every unconscionable imposition that we make on others dignities comes a counter force that we must reckon with, often at a scale that is commensurate with the cumulative negative effect that these acts have produced. This could be seen in the intense civil unrest brought about by events such as the unlawful killings of George Floyd and Mahsa Amini, and the Arab Spring which were fuelled by long held grievances that those in privileged positions of power were loath to appreciate. Try as we might to use our co-opted power as a shield to protect us from these shockwaves, it can't inoculate us from the reality of our interdependence and the disturbances to that system that injustice wreaks. A cancer in any part of the body threatens the life of the entire organism, and if that being has any hope for survival, it rests in understanding the causes of the disease, and reconciling them with what is required for life to be first sustained and then enhanced. By turning towards a life lived in consciousness, we initiate this healing process, and being a remedy that is within our individual ability to provide to the world as we live our calling, I believe that we have strong cause for optimism concerning the building of a future which adds to the tremendous progress that humankind has achieved thus far.

Optimism

With the human spirit being the source of goodness in the world, when we live from that realm of consciousness, the primary lens through which we see and process our physical experience of life will be tilted towards the positive. Making us glass half full people, this was a quality that those in my sample who were living their calling commonly saw themselves as possessing. In my own experience of taking that path, optimism is intimately associated with our relationship to this life force, and without possessing a connection to spirit, life appears dull, devoid of substance and meaning for our being. By becoming a tributary for this life vein, we enliven our perceptual ability to take in and appreciate the inherent beauty and wondrous nature of being that animates all forms of life at the most essential level.

Being a gift that transforms our experience of reality, when we open to the world in this way, it doesn't however mean that we turn our back on what is not good in it. Clearly there is evidence of the negativity brought about by ego driven behaviour that we encounter daily, and the inescapable slings and arrows of life will present themselves at our door regardless of how we choose to look at them when they arrive. Not even the donning of Pollyanna's rose coloured glasses can obscure this actuality, and the more that we might try to sweep their presence under the rug of our attention, the more that we will deny life its extraordinary impacts on our being.

Despite the propensity of these things to get us down, we need not allow them to have us sink so low that we begin to lose faith in humanity, and virulently oppose the natural movements of life. What provides us with great perspective here is the awareness that what takes the form of unconsciousness in the world is but a distortion of our original nature as spiritual beings. While we may commit violence against others or bring harm to the environment, for example, we were not created to do these things. Going against our virtuous inclinations, this explains why engaging in these unconscious acts has the effect of tangibly suppressing our spirit and the inspired feeling of being attuned to life.

By allowing this to teach us about ourselves, we can peel back the veil of unconsciousness and relate to life from a base of Truth that gives proper context to reality. As bad as the news and digital media can make the world look with what they choose to report on, when we observe their stories through the broader lens of consciousness, we won't find ourselves getting carried away with the visceral negative emotions that these agencies strive to evoke in order to keep our attention. What the bigger picture that can be seen with conscious awareness tells us is that all across the globe, every day, the vast majority of human beings are diligently engaged in service that makes the world beyond themselves a better place in which to live.

Making these contributions which affect the secret silent miracle of human progress that Hans Rosling spoke about, there are numerous other socioeconomic trends that testify to the human condition being better now than it has been in past times. In the second half of the 20th century, we have seen a decline in warfare and violence across the globe[35], and the rates of extreme poverty have been dramatically reduced since the year 2000.[36] Together with this overall rise in prosperity, we have witnessed a steady increase in literary rates[37] and the quality of our health that has ensured we will live, on average,

[35] Fagan, Brennen T., Knight, Marina I., MacKay, Niall J., & Jamie Wood, A. (2020). *Change point analysis of historical battle deaths*. Journal of the Royal Statistical Society: Series A, Statistics in society, 183(3), 909-933.

[36] Moatsos, M. (2021) *Global extreme poverty: Present and past since 1820*. OECD (2021), How Was Life? Volume II: New Perspectives on Well-being and Global Inequality since 1820. OECD Publishing, Paris. The World Bank in its 2022 Poverty and Shared Prosperity Report notes however that this trend has slowed due to factors such as the Covid pandemic, the war in Ukraine and rising inflation.

[37] Roser, M. & Ortiz-Ospina, E. (2016). *Literacy*. OurWorldInData.org. https://ourworldindata.org/literacy (Online Resource).

far longer than our forebears did.[38] While the wealth inequality within populations has become the focus of much media attention in recent times[39], that metric by itself doesn't present an accurate picture of just how far we have come in significantly improving the collective state of our existence.

If facts such as these aren't cause for tremendous optimism, I don't know what is! By trusting in the spirit as the principal source of creation on the physical plane, we are empowered to enact in form circumstances which justify our hopes for a more prosperous and harmonious future for humanity. Demonstrating leadership as we do this, we become a charismatic beacon of light for those who hold the intention to contribute to a better world, but have not yet come to trust in their spirit as the mechanism through which they can live their calling to affect this change. Having the positive expectation that things will get better in the future rather than worse, a conscious leader buffers the resolve of their people, and stimulates action which leads to that end. But before leaders can provide hope to others, they must be filled with it themselves, which necessitates them being embodiments of the spirit led life. Being connected to our true self which holds the intention for us to grow and flourish into our fullness, we see that same potential inherent in the world, even with its current condition not reflecting that potentiality, and the uncertainty of the future presenting as a looming cloud over the horizon. Taking this position does not fly in the face of pragmatism, but rather it reflects the ultimate reality that the arc of history bends towards our individual and collective evolution.

Respondents who were living their calling and demonstrating leadership in the process characterised themselves as hopeful, and saw it as their function to bring hope to others during challenging times. Feeling a stewardship responsibility towards their people not to leave them mired in a state of desolation, they took it upon themselves to lift their spirits and provide reassurance that they could weather those turbulent periods. For some people on the receiving end of that encouragement, the act of somebody else being that rock for them can be life-changing when they have found themselves teetering on the edge of hopelessness. No matter what we appear to possess as a potential buffer to the adversity that we encounter, when the hardships of

---

[38] Roser, M., Ortiz-Ospina, E., & Ritchie, H. (2013). *Life Expectancy*. OurWorldInData.org. https://ourworldindata.org/life-expectancy (Online Resource).

[39] Coy, P. 'Wealth Inequality Is the Highest Since World War II', February 2 2022, https://www.nytimes.com/2022/02/02/opinion/inequality-wealth-pandemic.html (accessed November 3, 2022); Taylor, D. 'Rich getting richer and poor slipping further back, with youth inequality growing fastest, ACOSS says', September 1 2020, https://www.abc.net.au/news/2020-09-02/wealth-inequality-rising-sharply-especially-among-young-acoss/12618120 (accessed November 3, 2022).

life knock us off kilter, we will need more than our material crutches to re-balance ourselves. Finding a solid foothold in the presence of these others who have offered their support, we can begin to re-ground ourselves through the recognition that our life has a purpose which we have been tasked to fulfil.

As we do this, we reinvigorate our hope for what our life can be, and how it can contribute to the unfolding of a more conscious world. Giving us something profoundly meaningful to aspire towards, and experience in the present moment, we will find all the impetus that we need to actively engage with our calling and follow where it leads us. Even with the future that we face being unclear, we will be able to tolerate that uncertainty and stay faithful to our given path because of the impact that we will see ourselves making in the lives of those whom we serve. Where I think that we fall into trouble and become vulnerable to feelings of hopelessness is when our efforts don't contribute to something meaningful in society. Even if they do make a difference, but we cease to perceive that to be the case, then we will suffer under the belief that we are laying waste to our life. With this, I can't think of a feeling that is more hollowing than waking up with the belief that the world has no need for what I have to offer today.

Perceiving hopelessness to present a barrier to one's ability to live their calling, respondents also ascribed this disempowered feeling to individuals who they have experienced as denying their calling. When we live our lives devoid of spiritual connection, what will come to drive our motivations are the ego's cravings for power, money and hedonistic indulgence. As we move in that direction and satiate some of those cravings, we will inevitably want more of the thrill that they provide us with, which will lead us to invest more of ourselves in the process of acquiring them. While we might appear to be achieving success in this endeavour, what we are actually doing is laying the foundation for a disappointing fall when we realise that what we had pinned our hopes for happiness and significance on can never deliver those feelings in any meaningful or lasting form. Leaving us shattered of those aspirations, part of the suffering that we will experience from that realisation is a hopelessness concerning our direction. Having travelled down the wrong road for so long, we will inevitably come to harbour strong doubts about our ability to navigate our way to a prosperous path, and we might even start to question whether a right road for us actually exists.

While this hopelessness can be highly destructive if as a result of this fall, we indulge the woundedness of our ego, it can also present a fertile opportunity to correct our course if the void that it produces is entered into with honesty and a willingness to take responsibility for how we have lost our way. Rarely

122

are we more open and receptive to connecting with the fundamental nature of who we are than when the bottom has dropped out of our artificial identity, and the ego's pretences and false narratives are exposed as a lie. With its narrative of hopelessness being one of these fabrications, we will distance ourselves from this depressive thought form the further that we travel into the void, towards the light of our soul. Once there, we will be bathed in the elixir of our calling, and cleansed of the confusion surrounding our mandate to serve the purpose of good in the unique context of our life.

CHAPTER 7: Service – Offering the Essence of Who You Are

Central to the living of our calling is being of service to others, offering to the world the essence of who we are, and what we have to consciously contribute to its enrichment. Through the meeting of this need that the world has for our being, our God-given gifts find an outlet and point of impact which brings meaning to our existence and fulfilment to our heart. Regardless of the context in which this generosity takes form, it is what we allow to move from us that nourishes our relationships with the people we encounter, the substance of our work and even with ourselves. As we act to reflect back the givenness of our creator to the world, we enliven our spirit and open up the channels of abundance that life intends to bless us with.

As we look into the natural world, there is untold evidence of the generosity that has been laid at our feet. Every day, the sun shines its rays to bring light to what would otherwise be a very dark existence. Every day, trees oxygenate the earth and provide us with the opportunity to breathe in its wonders. Every day, food and water sources are in the process of replenishing themselves, and this is in spite of our interference with these regenerative systems. And the receiving of all this has not been made dependent on us demonstrating an appreciation for them. Even if we are unconscious of these blessings, they are still present and made available to us, as and when we need them to sustain life.

If only we could reciprocate this willingness to open ourselves up and give of what comes most naturally from us. Being the fruits of our calling, we will be challenged to share these gifts if the consciousness from which we function is rooted in ego and its insatiable desire to bring to its host the things which enhance its artificial sense of identity. Serving this purpose while also acting as a stimulating distraction from the ego's dysfunctionality, we see this impulsive urge to acquire at work in our consumerist society where the primary motivation for 'earning a living' is to source the means that can fund this addictive habit. As we find ourselves joining this never ending pursuit for more, what sadly becomes lost to us is the sacred potential of work to enact in form our deepest spiritual inclinations and virtuous purpose. Settling because of this for jobs or careers that leave who we are disconnected from what we do, we deprive ourselves of the meaning and fulfilment that above and beyond monetary compensation and recognition from our peers, are the real rewards of partaking in work that is in service to our calling.

Also underpinning this reluctance of the ego to freely give is the paradigm of scarcity which has it believe that there is not enough of the material things that it defines itself by to go around. Fearing the losing out of those objects and the subsequent humiliation of not having them to prove our worth to the world, it is this apprehension that accounts for our preference to serve our wants before looking to see how we can work with others to meet the broader needs of society. Despite having so much, and a surplus of what we could conceivably need to enjoy a good life, we are led to hoard and withhold these blessings, which paradoxically serves to diminish the quality of our lived experience. From an integral perspective, a deficit within the whole detracts from the ability of members of that collective to experience fullness. How this manifests itself in the lives of individuals and the community is as an absence of peace and security, that has become dependent on those externals to provide us with. Having given away our power in that way, whatever we possess is seen as ours to lose, and tormented by this protectionist urge to guard our resources, we resist mightily their moving away from our control.

Draining us of vital life energy that inhibits our ability to give to the people and places in our life which mean the most to us, we would be much better served by evolving to adopt the paradigm which views the want to give away as the source of our richness. While we no doubt derive pleasure from what we bring from the outside to take in with our physical senses, what provides that deeper sense of fulfilment is what moves from us to enrich the quality of others' lives. By being a facilitator of others living into their spiritual potential, we are pulled like gravity towards that flourishing in our own life. This act of serving as a bridge between where one is and where their spirit wills them to be goes to the heart of conscious leadership. Despite the best intentions that we may have for others, and wanting to assist them along the path of their calling, we will not be able to bear that responsibility if our bandwidth is consumed by the selfish need to indulge our ego's pleasure seeking whims. Being like a straightjacket for the enactment of our leadership capacity, these hedonistic impulses must be tamed by the filling of our own spiritual cup through practices which ensure that we have what we need to be able see beyond ourselves and meet the needs that others have for our vocational offerings.

Without possessing this spiritual maturity, we can't embody the selflessness in service that is so endearing and respected as a leadership quality. For respondents in my sample who were manifesting conscious leadership through the living of their calling, they identified this willingness to put others first, and to surrender or suspend the gratification of personal desires to meet the needs of a larger unit as vital for gaining the support and loyalty of followers.

As one of these respondents, a founder of a construction company, put forward on the point, *"I am always thinking about everyone else first. Keeping the team good, or happy...But everyone else first, us [him and the other co-owner] last."* Warning of the dangers that ego-oriented would be leaders face in eschewing this quality to act out of self-interest was another respondent who offered, *"A lot of so-called leaders are very selfish. Selfishness is a characteristic that is easily picked up by people as being a weakness in the leader, and often those in leadership who are selfish, they get found out very quickly....Selfishness or I suppose chasing glory, is something that a leader - a good leader - just doesn't have anything to do with it, he [or she] shares the glory."*

Throughout my research data, there were countless examples of how those leading through the enactment of their calling rendered service to others. These behaviours included, but were not limited to:

helping, supporting and guiding their people; mentoring emerging leaders within their organisations; engaging in voluntary work that benefited the less fortunate; creating/adding value in others' lives that exceeded what they received from those relationships; enabling others with opportunities and equipping them with what they required to make the most out of them; advocating on others behalves; offering to share their expertise beyond the scope of their work role; and demonstrating care for their people on both the personal and professional levels.

When asked to provide examples of individuals who are living or have lived their calling, respondents mentioned individuals on both the global level (Jesus, Mother Teresa, the Dalai Lama, Barack Obama, Queen Elizabeth and Bill Gates, for example) and the local level (not for profit/community leaders) whose contributions have been characterised by generous acts of service. Contrast this to the examples of individuals who respondents cited as having denied or betrayed their calling (church leaders who covered up allegations of child sexual abuse, media tycoon Rupert Murdoch, golf star Tiger Woods, and despoiled politicians like Bill Clinton, or former Western Australian Premier Brian Burke).[40] These individuals, who were overly focused on meeting and protecting their ego needs, habitually demonstrated a selfish inclination to serve their personal interests above the interests of the broader collective of which they were a part. Being a quality that inherently we don't respect from a leadership, or basic human, perspective, it is our spirit that bristles at these individuals eschewal of this most essential human virtue.

---

[40] I would also characterise individuals such as corrupted healers Joao Teixeira de Faria (John of God) and François Duvalier (former President of Haiti), Theranos founder Elizabeth Holmes, comedian turned conspiracy theorist Russell Brand and Lance Armstrong as belonging in this category.

Providing a narration of Gandhi's service oriented leadership style was Keshavan Nair who wrote that *"if the single standard is the foundation of a higher standard of leadership, the spirit of service is the material with which the structure must be constructed."* Nothing that is beautiful or effectual can be created without inspired hands that make manifest the spirit's impulse to move into the physical world. With leadership being the mechanism by which we affect this outward movement, it is incumbent upon us to turn our calling loose so that we can harness its energy and direction. Imbued with this focus and enthusiasm, diligence is no chore, and paired with others whose callings align with ours, we can be potent forces for the betterment of humanity, and have a more far-reaching impact than the smallness of our ego could ever conceive as being possible for our life.

Enrichment

Those who are rich in spirit will by their givenness enrich the lives of those whom they serve. To enrich another is to tangibly add quality to their life or nourish their being, and contribute to making them a more holistic conduit of spiritual expression in the world. Meaning so much more than just providing them with a financial benefit that can be easily spent, this gift of imparting our inner richness for their exaltation amounts to an investment in their future self and vocational unfolding that money simply can't buy.

Unlike those who function from the ego, and subtract and divide by their self-consumed behaviour, those who are guided by spirit have an enhancing effect on the wider community that they inhabit. Of the many qualities that I have observed individuals who are living their calling as embodying, one of the most prominent is that they add value to others lives, and by so doing amplify the positive impact that they are capable of having in the world. They may do this by coaching others in their work teams, for example, where they are transferring learnings and skills that will improve the competence and performance of those team members. On the individual level, the capacity of these team members is being built by this input, but the impact that these contributions make to their development does not end there. Through this act of servant leadership, the seeds have been planted for these team members to pass on these learnings to those who they will go on to lead in the future.

By possessing the vision for how they want to make a difference through their calling, these progressive actors are not so short sighted to believe that their actions only carry weight in the here and now. Having orchestrated their own transformation and seen the ripple effects of that on the people with whom they interact, they don't underestimate the potential of others to light a fire from the spark that has been ignited in them. Being their inspiration in doing what they do, they know that the scope for having this impact is possible because of the interconnected nature of life and the rapid expansion of our social networks. Like compound interest, what we invest in people today bears significantly greater rewards over the long term arc of our and their lives.

For the individual who is living their calling and manifesting conscious leadership as a consequence, all of this factors into considerations surrounding legacy, and the streak of light that one will leave behind once their time on earth comes to an end. I believe that everybody in their heart of hearts yearns for their life to stand for something meaningful, where in their final analysis they can honestly say that the world has been made a better place by them having lived in it. The following sample of answers that respondents provided to my question about their drive for living their calling bore this out also:

What's kind of kept me going and there have been times in running this organisation, that have been extraordinarily personally challenging, is the impact that you can have on the community. // So those sort of things drive my leadership to say where can I impact, what can I do, small as it might be, to try and have an equitable experience for everybody. // Well, at the end of the day I reckon it's the collective impacts that are going to come together to make the differences. So I try to lead in a way that we might have different strands of strategy underway, but we're all going the same path to make that impact, so that's why I do it. // I think what I'm doing here is really valuable and important, and I actually can see that what I'm doing is making a difference. // So it was making a difference in the community at that stage, was the turning point for me, the fact that I could make a difference.

Doing what they do to make a positive difference and progress things forward so that a more prosperous and harmonious experience of life can be created for all, their efforts towards this end push back the ever widening circles of human consciousness that awaken in others the latent desire to give themselves in service to something that is larger than themselves. So often, people want to join in fellowship to make this positive difference, but they either don't know how, or they have an inner blockage that prevents them from taking the important first steps to orient their calling. The conscious leader, in dealing with these obstacles to action, clears the path and offers direction for how it can be navigated in unison.

Possessing the clarity of purpose and intense conviction to serve that virtuous end, they are worthy guides for this journey. Others who yearn to walk the path that they beat believe in them because what they see the leadership as facilitating is an integral movement towards the wholeness that makes mutual thriving possible. Take for example, the work of a company like TOMS that has utilised a one-for-one business model to put shoes on the feet of impoverished children and fund restorative eye surgery to the visually impaired. People will get behind those who drive these initiatives, by providing capital or purchasing their goods, for example, because they know that by offering their support the consequential benefits for society will be tremendous.

Even if those benefits flow to the world long after we are gone, when we function from an infinite mindset there is nothing more compelling in the shorter term which we wouldn't willingly forgo to work towards the future achievement of the higher end to which we are staunchly committed. While many cancer researchers would no doubt be motivated by the possibility of eradicating that disease in their lifetime, they still diligently go about the work of experimenting to find a cure, even when the likelihood is that their efforts will not bear fruit, or at best will only contribute to resolving a small part of the epidemiological puzzle. By just putting one foot in front of the other, we still leave an imprint on the sands of time that is not easily forgotten by the people who we have served and shared the journey with. While it might be nice for the world to trumpet our name and memorialise our contribution, this public recognition doesn't validate our work anymore than the excellence with which we do it, and the knowing that it was done in furtherance of a worthy goal.

Here, I think that we need to be mindful of the contaminating influence of the ego which can seek to convince us that unless we are contributing on a large scale (and being recognised for our efforts) then these contributions don't hold much value. Clearly that is not the case, and we shouldn't allow grandiose edicts such as this to deter us from participating in the inconspicuous core work that must be undertaken at the coalface of our communities. If there was a silver lining to come from the COVID pandemic, it was the stark realisation of the importance of essential workers such as nurses, teachers and mental health professionals to the healthy functioning of our society. Despite not ordinarily getting the recognition that they deserve, and being underpaid for their committed efforts, the immense value in what they were asked to do on the front line of the crisis reinforced what a critical impact that we can each have when we start serving from where we are.

Something else that has really struck me as I observed these heroes lead the way out of this valley is that it is in these professions where we often find individuals who are living their calling and doing what they do for the central purpose of making things better for others. Being not principally motivated by money or status, but the intention to enrich, they provide an inspiring example to others who yearn to have a meaningful impact on the world around them.

American country music star Dolly Parton once made a very insightful comment about leadership that is enacted through the enriching effect of engaging in legacy work. According to her, *"If your actions create a legacy that inspires others to dream more, learn more, do more and become more, then you are an excellent leader."* At the heart of what she is attributing this leadership as emerging from is our calling, for it is our spirit which inspires us and others to actualise in the ways that she sets forth in her quote. Though I included the quality of actualisation under the theme of Authority in Chapter five, I could have just as easily integrated it into this chapter because the journey of actualising our spiritual nature is what unlocks our capacity for genuine service in the world. Unless we know who we truly are, we will have very little to give, or what we will have to give will be ineffectual in serving the higher purpose we are ignorant to. If we are on the path however to becoming more fully ourselves and expressive of our spiritual gifts and virtues, then not only will we have a greater capacity to give, but the potency of that offering will be enlarged because we are serving from our inner source of fulfilment. To be fulfilled is to be enriched by our relationship with spirit, and connection to the purpose for which we were created. By serving in alignment with that calling, we externalise that fulfilment which has an enriching effect on those who are on the receiving end of our offerings. I know in my own life that when I have added the most to my family, friends, colleagues and students, strides were being made in my personal and spiritual development which supported and enabled that impact being made. Through this movement towards congruence, channels will open, and in terms of allowing our inner fulfilment to transfer into the world, the medium of calling oriented service makes all the difference.

Diligence

If we are to actualise our calling in the form of service then we will be required to exercise discipline and work hard, not only in the application of our talents and skills, but in developing ourselves to become a force for good in the world. While God gifts us with enormous potential and the latent abilities to affect our given purpose, these blessings are instilled in us in a raw form that requires much nurturing and conscious development if they are to flourish towards their full expression. Being like a fertile plot of land that carries the unbroken seeds of what could one day be a resplendent garden, we will have to exert a lot of effort over time in tending to that plot. Only by doing this will we facilitate its blossoming, and reap the rewards of having contributed to the creation of something so glorious.

While not all of us would identify as gardeners, we are all tending to something or someone that means a lot to us, and requires the best of what we have to give in its service. Whether that is our work, building a business or the raising of children, we will find ourselves being continually challenged to bring the fullness of who we are to these domains, and embody excellence in our engagement with them. Rather than resisting this as an inconvenient encumbrance to the easy life that we find comfort in, we should accept it as a natural part of the journey to making a meaningful impact in the world. In order to learn and grow in the way that the fulfilment of our calling will require, we need to be tested on our path, and how we deal with these trials will determine how far we are able to travel towards our destiny.

If we aren't willing to confront and deal with much, and sacrifice our comfort for the opportunity to evolve, then we will stop taking strides forward and grow static in our relationship with life. The consequence of this is that whatever character defects that we have which are holding us back will become more ingrained and determinative of our future direction. Our laziness, for example, intensifies as we indulge it, so if we have become habitually inert in the face of challenges, then when an opportunity presents itself to advance in a promising direction, we won't feel the impetus to exert ourselves towards that aim.

When respondents to my study were asked to detail some barriers to a lived calling, this quality of laziness was identified as a significant impediment. Being indicative of an absence of initiative and purpose that the data showed were inversely symptomatic of a calling, this attribute was seen by respondents to characterise individuals who were not living their calling. In exhibiting this laziness, these individuals essentially are failing to lead themselves, and as a consequence will prove incapable of leading others towards any worthwhile goal. In order for members of a group to want to come together and involve themselves in the accomplishment of something meaningful, they must care about the cause. Setting the tone for this is the leader whose investment in the work to be done not only provides an example for others to follow, but the energy for engagement of their best efforts. Of the leadership styles that respondents who were living their calling reported themselves as demonstrating, leading by example was the most prominent, with many of them expressing the sentiment that they would never expect their people to do things that they themselves were not willing to do.

Without the leader embodying this care and commitment, it would be hypocritical for them to expect the other members of the team to demonstrate these qualities, and pull the weight of the collective effort. Knowing this, the conscious leader bears the weight of the responsibility for driving progress, and they can be relentless in that pacesetting. Driven by personal excellence and high performance in their work life, these individuals might not always be the easiest people to work for as the standards that they set for themselves can become the standards that they expect other in the sphere to live up to. This blind spot, if one could call it that, seemed to afflict Mother Teresa and Gandhi, who by many reports could be very obstinate in what they thought needed to be done, and how those who followed them were morally required to conduct themselves.

A more modern example of this propensity was basketball legend Michael Jordan, who during the height of his success as the leader of the Chicago Bulls, was known to ride his teammates mercilessly. So intense was his drive to be the best player he could be, that he often ridiculed them for making mistakes in practice, which in some instances led to physical altercations. While this blunt form of challenging had the desired effect of winning championships, it no doubt contributed to a tumultuous journey for those who didn't possess the same level of skill that he did.[41] Clearly, Michael Jordan was right in the element of his calling on the basketball court, but what could be seen to taint his leadership was the ego interference that prioritised winning above all else. While some may argue that the ends justified the means, particularly given the hypercompetitive nature of professional sports, this argument doesn't account for the fact that there are other proven means of bringing others along the journey and achieving the same outcome.

Whatever are our efforts to prod others to reach another level of performance in their lives, they can be judiciously exercised and marked by restraint, so as not to have a deleterious or counterproductive effect on those people, but one walks a fine line when they are trying to get the best out of others, especially considering that no two people are the same in their disposition or motivation. While those who challenge themselves as a habit, will be inclined to challenge others to grow and develop their areas of weakness, how this is done will make all the difference in how receptive others are to these prompts. Underpinning these relationships should be a mutual trust and basis of understanding that what is said and done to stimulate growth in that other is motivated by a benevolent intention to serve that aim.

The virtue of love can also animate this intention, as is acknowledged by the label that we place on this confrontational style of challenging others to be

---

[41] For Jordan, his philosophy towards training and team practices was that you should work so hard during these activities that performing in games comes easily. This, in combination with his otherworldly talent, should provide some insight into how difficult it was for his teammates to meet him at his elite level.

better, 'tough love'. Being perhaps the most powerful force there is, love has a tremendous ability to move us towards the fulfilment of a higher order purpose, and serve those who we want to see become all that they can be. This became clear when I was interviewing one of my respondents, and asking about why he was expanding the scope of his normal business operations to include the construction of an artificial reef in the ocean where he could grow abalone. Being already a very accomplished and busy man, he explained to me that he saw that endeavour as a 'labour of love' that he felt he needed to partake in. Were this love not present in that pursuit, I doubt that he would have spent the better part of a decade working on the project, which had no guarantee of success at the outset.

Not only did this love conceive of the work, but it also sustained his hard work over that prolonged period of time. Just like love itself endures, so does it have an enduring effect on us when we are possessed of it while working towards a purpose that is meaningful to our spirit. Whatever it is that we are called to do, which as we fulfil it will be our legacy work, will not be able to be completed in a day, week or month. Taking generally much longer than that before our efforts will amount to something truly substantial, we will need to gear ourselves up for the duration of the journey, and be willing to leave some of the things that we have brought, or find along the way, by the side of the road as we move forward.

When asked what advice they would provide to others about living their calling, a number of respondents cautioned that living your calling requires personal sacrifices to be made. Being a feature of leadership which respondents characterised in the same way, it would appear that the sacrificial nature of living one's calling prepares them for bearing the responsibilities of leadership, which of itself indicates a linkage between these two phenomena.

A balance though needs to be struck here to mitigate against the risk of focusing too much energy in the workplace, to the detriment of the other areas of one's life that require their own time and commitment. Those objects cast to the side of the road should not thus include one's spouse/dependents, health and spiritual practices. To do so would be clearly counterproductive to our integrity and wellbeing, and make the journey towards the workplace component of our calling not worth the sacrifice. The respondents to my study, being the wise men and women that they are, also appreciated this, and emphasised the focus that they give to maintaining an equilibrium between the different areas of their lives that mean the most to them. While this of course is not able to be done perfectly, it is no doubt better managed when our conscious attention is given to how well we are doing at keeping our various plates of responsibility spinning in the air.[42]

Collaboration

When we live consciously, one of the fundamental understandings that guide our thoughts and behaviour is that by nature, human beings are in a relationship of interdependence with one another. With all people needing each other in order to create a mutually thriving global community, the best way of achieving this is to work together in a manner that is consistent with our commonly shared interests. What makes this endeavour so challenging, but rich with potential, is the differing nature of our capabilities. While some people are gifted at technical trades, for example, others are more proficient in caring roles or intellectual fields of study. With each of these diverse skillsets having their own contextual utility, when they are applied in novel ways across fields, the new ground that is capable of being broken reminds us of the far-reaching possibilities that are inherent in collaborative undertakings. One of the most amazing developments that I have seen with this in recent years is robot assisted remote surgery that allows medical surgeons to operate on patients in other locations using advanced robotic technology. Having been made possible by the coming together of medicine and the nascent field of robotics, this breakthrough carries tremendous potential for improving the outcomes of surgical interventions in countries that per capita have a shortage of highly skilled surgeons. Being but one example of many that show what innovation can emerge from a cross-pollination of ideas and applications, it is this expansion of our realised potential that promises to move humanity forward with a more holistic understanding of the complex systems that form the circuitry of the modern world.

Despite having evolved in numerous ways since our inception as a species, one thing that hasn't changed is the improved prospects for survival and prosperity that result from working effectively with others in groups or teams. While we no longer spend our time in tribes hunting and gathering the means by which to live, we still have the basic unit of the family to maintain, which requires two or more people to co-ordinate and participate in

---

[42] Paradoxically, what I have found in my own calling journey is that as I nourish the different areas of my life that I derive meaning from, I have a greater zest for engaging myself in each of the individual domains that together constitute the whole. The energy that I give to my writing or lecturing, for example, invigorates the relationships that I have with my family and friends. Conversely, what I have observed is that when I give too much energy to one particular domain, that diminishes my ability to be present and effectual in those other important areas of responsibility.

activity that serves to sustain its functionality. Extending this out to the institutional and communal spheres, we can observe that the greater the cooperation is between members of these broader units, the more sweeping are the benefits which flow to them and others who are on the receiving end of their offerings.

With companies for example, it is generally those who have the most cohesive and supportive cultures that are rated as the best places to work, and not coincidently this also translates into success in the marketplace because what is produced by them is of a superior quality compared to the mediocre makings of their competition. In organisations that do not have this integrity, and whose cultures have been compromised by ego based self-interest, we see a range of fragmenting behaviours that lead its parts to function in opposition against each other. Working in silos and their attendant hoarding of resources and information, political game playing, corruption and nepotism are but some of the ways in which this dysfunction manifests itself in these settings. Being behaviours that directly contribute to declining levels of performance, they will need to be promptly addressed and corrected otherwise it will be a matter of time before these inferior types of organisation will have to forfeit their place in the market, and give way to other players who can embody this spirit centred quality of collaboration in their mode of operating.

Darwin was indeed right when he said that the species who are most likely to survive are the strongest, and those that are most adaptable in dealing with changes that threaten their existence. In using the word 'strongest', or 'fittest', as is more commonly applied to his theory of evolution, I think that the message which he sought to impart has become distorted and misunderstood by many who think of strength or fitness in a purely physically domineering competitive sense. From this perspective, the biggest and the most capable of overpowering weaker members of their species take their place at the top of the hierarchy, and enjoy all of its attendant spoils. While no doubt this physical quality factors into an evaluation of strength, there are broader considerations that characterise the strongest or fittest as those members of a species who are best able to contribute to and preserve a functional social order that can endure threats to its survival.

To understand this in greater depth, it helps to look at our primate relatives, and what behaviours are exemplified by the 'strongest' alpha members of their troupes. While the common misconception is that the alpha males spend their days brutalising their more feeble counterparts and mating with their choice of females in the group, the behaviour that primatologists such as Frans de Waal have observed them to display reflect a more benevolent and unitive inclination. In his 2017 TED talk, de Waal describes how chimpanzee alpha males demonstrate generosity, the empathic ability to console, and social negotiation strategies to keep peace within their group. By serving this range of relational and cohesive functions, these alpha leaders embody a strength that ensures their fitness to lead the troupe. Interestingly, the research into their hierarchical dynamics also shows that alphas who attempt to rule through physical domination increase the risk of them being overthrown by a collaborative effort to promote a rival to that alpha position, which if successful is likely to result in the death of the deposed chimpanzee. This type of outcome, notwithstanding the death of the vanquished, can also be seen to occur in our organisational lives, when a leader relates to their people from their ego, and seeks to impose their will on them in a way that is self-serving. Fraying the connections that are necessary for alliances to be formed over the longer term, their loss of support will likely result in them losing their position, or the resignation of key people around them which makes the keeping of their position untenable. In this respect, the leader's lack of fitness, or weakness, has undermined the stability of the entity which they exercised responsibility over, which consequently posed a threat to its ability to survive and adapt successfully into the future.

While it is of course possible for an individual to successfully adapt to changes in their environment, in the bigger scheme of things this is unlikely to move the needle in affecting significant progress forward for the community of which that individual is a part. For this larger scale evolutionary movement to gain traction, there must be a synchronous working together by the members of the collective, which has been facilitated by the intention to cooperate. Competition, as a stimulus for this movement forward, should be restricted to the challenging of each other's best efforts in working towards the collective purpose of first surviving and then thriving.

I say restricted here because unbridled competition becomes the ego's tool in pursuing domination of others for its own intents and purposes. We may feel envious of what another has, for example, which wounds our ego and makes us feel diminished in relation to them. To alleviate that feeling and tip the balance of perceived power in our favour, we will then be inclined to take steps to acquire something better than what they have. While this may seem like we have bested them, the game has now been set up for them to outdo us on that measure of 'superiority' or another, which is an inevitable outcome given that nobody across the board of their being has more, or is better, than any other (however physically attractive one may be, for example, there would be others who are less attractive, but enjoy other advantages such as greater wealth or status with their work).

By orientating ourselves in the world this way, our collaborative ability becomes stifled internally as well as externally, as people generally don't want to work alongside others who perceive and treat them as nails to be hammered down. Leading them to become protective of their standing within the group, the taking of this defensive posture also has a deleterious effect on what they are able to contribute to the accomplishment of the group's objectives. The solving of problems, which in effect is the end goal that collaborative endeavour seeks to accomplish, requires openness, creativity and a good dose of humility to recognise the limits of our individual thinking. Being qualities that are dependent on our ability to be vulnerable in company, we won't be able to find the freedom to give them wings if an adversarial tone has permeated the group dynamic.

In the face of a threat we naturally close up, and how the presence of ego-based competition is received is as a threat to our identity. Seen also from the standpoint of the one who is compelled to compete, competition can be understood as a protective mechanism for their ego. Opposing others so that they don't have to be vulnerable in their presence, this participatory movement still has a reactionary motivation behind it because it is fear that is driving their behaviour. That fear may be not appearing smart enough to the group, or not getting credit for our input, if we have been burned by others taking credit for our work in the past. Whatever form that fear takes, we shouldn't allow it to stand between us and those who we are called to collaborate and serve with, for without them there is no viable avenue for the practice of conscious fellowship.

Enthusiasm

As the source of life, the spirit enlivens us, and as we align with its energy to live our calling, we will naturally feel enthusiastic about taking that journey. Being as much an animating force as it is a positive feeling, we will find ourselves more engaged with our calling and hungry to experience the depths of its richness when we allow it to consume and guide us towards the fulfilment of our higher purpose. In doing my research for this section, I was surprised to discover how resonant the etymological underpinnings of the word 'enthusiasm' was with this understanding. Meaning *'To be inspired or possessed by a God, to be rapt, to be in ecstasy'*, we see in this an acknowledgement of our spiritual being as the force which imbues our activity with fervour.

Respondents who were living their calling and demonstrating leadership in the process expressed their enthusiasm for their calling as they talked about their passion, deep interest, excitement and having a high level of energy for the work which they used to rally others around their common cause. Having this quality of enthusiasm is vital for a leader as was highlighted by a respondent who opined that a person cannot be a reluctant leader. Needing to work together with other people and bring them on a journey of meaning, those following will not desire to take that journey if they sense that the leader is not as invested in reaching the destination as they are, or is disconnected from their spirit and motivated to occupy the leadership position to meet their ego needs.

Another reason why it is so important for leaders to possess this quality of enthusiasm is because of the energetic nature of the relationship that they have with followers. If leaders are themselves enthused about what they are doing, then this will be passed on to others, and they will be engaged and likewise enthused about the journey ahead. Ego driven leaders, on the other hand, will be incapable of transferring this passionate energy because they have inhibited its flow within themselves as a consequence of aligning with the false self. This however doesn't prevent them from embodying and conveying a shadow form of this energy which they can craftily use to manipulate others into supporting their malevolent objectives. Cult and terrorist leaders, such as Jim Jones and Abu Musab al-Zarqawi, were masters of that dark art, and could whip their followers into a frenzy with their zealous rhetoric that denounced others as threatening influences to their corrupted way of life.

The key difference between how this shadow energy is applied in the world, and how enthusiasm is deployed in the context of a calling, is that the latter serves a purpose that extends beyond the leader. Both Jones and al-Zarqawi used their zeal in a very extreme but focused way, to further their own agenda. Beyond this, there was no genuine care for the welfare of the people who followed them, as evidenced by both of these men being so willing to sacrifice their lives for the religious causes that they espoused. By contrast, the enthusiasm of the spirit is manifested in service to others that not only brings vitality to their lives and the world, but also the actor who has made that contribution through their calling.

In the first interview for the main component of my research, I spoke to a CEO of a drug rehabilitation facility who expressed that despite the taxing nature of the work that his organisation did to serve this marginalised group, he experienced the journey of walking alongside people who were committed to changing their lives as sustaining rather than draining. Being inspired by both their successes and struggles in this regard, it was clear that he found himself invigorated by the opportunity that he had to make a difference in that role.

What I found interesting about this gentleman was that he didn't describe his initial decision to become involved in that field as being reflective of a calling, yet he acknowledged that the work that he and his colleagues were engaged in couldn't be done as just a job. With this admission, he reminded me of a quote from famous Dutch painter, Vincent van Gogh, who mused that *"your profession is not what brings home your weekly paycheck, your profession is what you're put here on earth to do, with such passion and such intensity that it becomes spiritual in calling."* From the language that the respondent used to describe his embodying of many of the virtues that I have outlined in this section, I have the impression that his givenness to the work was in the process of becoming something that he would one day recognise as being synonymous with a vocation.

Compared to a job, or even a career, a calling will stimulate greater levels of enthusiasm that can be utilised to break new ground in the field to which it is diligently applied. With passion comes engagement that generates the momentum to affect significant progress. Even with a career that is experienced as a longer term grind to fulfil our ambition and acquire what we want, our enthusiasm will be diminished by the idealised future state which animates our present moment activity never seeming to materialise in accordance with our expectations. This is not to say however that if we live our calling, we will find ourselves brimming with enthusiasm in every moment of every day because from my experience that is not what will happen. Regardless of the path that we choose, there will be challenges and hardship that can subdue the arising of this emotion, and make our existence feel less vital than it otherwise could be. What living our calling does ensure however is that within our being we will have a much deeper well of enthusiasm to draw from, which can sustain our engagement for longer periods of time.

Being an antidote to the disengagement that plagues work which is experienced as a job, and to a lesser extent a career, the embodiment of enthusiasm is a natural outcome of the spirit being given an unhindered outlet for the joyful expression of what it seeks to manifest through us. The task then for the institutions we work for is to not step on this hose of inspiration that keeps us connected to and in love with work which is experienced as a calling. Through the medium of conscious leaders, institutions can succeed at this task by, firstly, bringing in the right people to occupy roles that resonate with their calling and, secondly, ensuring that those within their current workforce are suitably aligned with work that allows them to give expression to their higher purpose. For those who would find themselves on the outer as a result of this integral re-alignment, my view is that they would be best served by going elsewhere to find a fit that will allow them and the organisation that incorporates them into their operations to thrive.

As much as we may be tempted to try, enthusiasm can't be hacked, so the idea of faking it until one makes it won't get them to a place where the work inherently turns them on. Before that can happen, there must be an internal shift where clarity is gained on how they have been called to serve. Only once this occurs will they slide into the slipstream of enthusiasm that moves them to grow in their work, help out colleagues with challenges they are facing, go over and above what is asked of them by their superiors, and above all, enact leadership irrespective of what position they occupy in the organisational hierarchy. In my own working life, I have seen examples of enthusiastic colleagues garnering tremendous amounts of informal influence through the championing of ideas and initiatives that they were at the forefront of driving. Leading by example in this regard, they were able to infect others with their energy to achieve outcomes that would have been very difficult to accomplish otherwise.

From all of this we can surmise that aligning with the energy of spirit to live our calling is a causative movement that facilitates the emergence of leadership, and while we may choose to constrain the leadership potential that enthusiasm holds as we relate to others, this does not diminish the inherent potential that it carries to serve that purpose.

CHAPTER 8: Presence – Holding the Space that is Receptive to Spirit

To connect with our spirit we must cultivate presence in our life, where our awareness is given to who we are beyond the surface layer of our ego identity. So often amidst the busyness of everyday life, we don't take the time out to question our understanding of who we are, and whether that reflects a deeper reality that is resonant with Truth. When we fail to engage in that introspective investigation, the world that we see and relate to can't help but reflect the shallowness of perception with which we have seen ourselves. Seeing ourselves as a solitary and disassociated entity that is vulnerable in the world, we play the game of life tentatively within the conventions that our society has set to ensure our comfort, and acceptance within that order as a benign contributor.

Becoming however only a bit player through that mode of participation, what has facilitated our diminishment here has been the external conditioning that we have internalised as the rules to live by, and the constructions that our ego has made in physically defining itself pursuant to that conditioning. One such construction that directly subverts the spiritual primacy of being is that the world will define us by what we do, and if we aren't engaged in activity that reflects what the world values then we will lose ground in the social system. How beliefs like this orient us away from presence is that they lock our focus on measuring up to a set of expectations that take us outside of ourselves and toward a fear based striving for validation and getting ahead. Impelling us to action that is not informed by the consciousness of being, it is inevitable that we will diverge from our calling because we have not given our spirit the interior space that allows it to speak to us of our path and guide our way forward.

To hone our receptivity to its promptings and find clarity in what is sought to be communicated, we must create the conditions for stillness and silence to permeate our life. Whatever the form of practice that we introduce to serve that end, what is most important is that we find a mechanism for loosening the ego's influence over our mind so that we can keep open the connection between our being and spirit, and stay centred in that union. Respondents to this study who were living their calling and manifesting conscious leadership in the process, demonstrated behaviours that cultivated this quality of presence in their lives. The practices that they reported engaging in for this purpose included meditation, prayer, solitude (often in nature), mindfulness, gratitude reflection and journaling. Having engaged in many of these practices myself over the years, I can attest to their utility in concentrating our emotional energy in the here and now, and not allowing its positive forms such as gratitude and contentment to be crowded out by the regret and fear that can so often accompany our haphazard ruminating about the past and future respectively. As Jim Afremow insightfully comments on this point, *"when you are not thinking about the future, it is difficult to fear it."*

Without being able to anchor ourselves through these means, we will experience a barrier to leading consciously because our mind won't be free to respond to the stimuli that we have in front of us. With decision-making being one of the key responsibilities that a leader must bear, we are destined to perform that skill poorly if what we allow to drive our decisions are reflexive impulses that project forward what has happened in the past, or what we anticipate will take shape around us in the future. Not only can we not predict the future with our current schema of the world, but the past schemas that we have put together cannot be directly applied to emergent circumstances with any predictive accuracy.[43] Perhaps within a simple system this applicability is less problematic, but in the complex systems that characterise modern life, decision making must be highly adaptable and integrative of new and relevant information if it is to be effective in real time.

What presence also adds to this decision making process is the wisdom that can complement knowledge to deliver holistic solutions to problems that have been ill defined or created by the fragmented consciousness of ego. As Albert Einstein, who for all of his scientific genius was also very spiritually attuned with the natural workings of the world, mused on higher order thinking: *we cannot solve our problems with the same thinking we used when we created them.* By creating the cohesive and coherent interior space to break through that limited mode of thinking, we can avoid the insanity of repeating it and expecting a different result to ensue. Recognising the important role that solitude has in this transcendental practice was another well-known scientist and philosopher, Blaise Pascal, who famously commented that *"all of humanity's problems stem from man's inability to sit quietly in a room alone."*

---

[43] We know that change is a part of life and thus inevitable. In attempting to deal with this change, we can fall into the trap of thinking that we can effectively plan in advance for it, when to a large extent we cannot. All of the algorithms and models that forecasters use, for example, have only a limited use when emergent factors arise that these algorithms and models can't reliably account for (there is no past pattern of behaviour for these novel factors that can be reliably integrated into an analysis using these tools).

So many of the problems that we see in the modern world have been brought about by the application of tremendous intelligence in industrial and technological development that was not balanced by an integral understanding of what the negative longer term ramifications of those advancements could be. Take the contemporary issue of climate change for example. While the introduction of fossil fuel technologies opened up a range of possibilities in the world as to what could be powered by those sources of energy, there was a clear lack of foresight as to what harm could be wrought on the environment if the rate of carbon omissions were allowed to grow to their current levels. As we work collectively to try and mitigate the harm that this lack of foresight has brought about, we must learn our lesson from that folly and strive not repeat it in other largely consequential endeavours such as the planned integration of advanced artificial intelligence systems into our working lives. Whatever is the level of consciousness from which these systems are created, the problems to emerge from that consciousness will be magnified exponentially by those powerful systems, so we better be sure that the voice of our individual and collective wisdom is also being engaged to have its say on how these systems will be built and deployed, not to detract from the flourishing of human life, but to work alongside us in enhancing it on a greater scale.

As the biblical corpus makes clear to us, without vision we are destined to create our own road to ruin. To avoid the suffering that comes when we take that road, we must slow down the pace of our existence to see clearly where we are headed, and give ourselves the time to course correct when we find ourselves making unanticipated detours. With everything on our journey appearing as a blur as we speed through life at the ego's instruction, it is only when we take our foot off the accelerator pedal that we can gain clarity on how our current movements are serving to meet the guiding aim of what our spirit has called us to do, individually and as a collective.

Providing us with the perspective that we need to properly orient ourselves in the world, it also presents us with the valuable opportunity to look out of the window of our experience to appreciate what is beautiful along our journey. Even for leaders, the ability to perceive and appreciate beauty has a renewing effect on their being that bolsters their stamina in being able to deal with the daily challenges that confront them. Being literally a breath of inspiration that grounds them more solidly in their spirit, it is but one of many gifts that presence enables when we draw forth the patience to practice it.

Even presence itself mitigates the need for patience to be exercised as one realises that there is nothing other than what the present moment holds that is worth waiting for. With the future consisting of a multiplicity of present moments that will play out in their own time, it doesn't make sense for us to render our precious peace and autonomy casualties of the undisciplined desire to control these future present moments with our attention. To hold the space that nourishes life, we must preserve the gift that keeps open the door of consciousness for our spirit to do its work in the world. That is the present, so aptly named for the richness that it delivers to those who remember to centre their being in it. While I was originally going to end this section here, I wanted to include a pearl of a quote from leading actor Matthew McConaughey that I serendipitously came across on the day that I was to begin writing the next section on clarity. In his book, *Greenlights*, McConaughey describes how he experienced a moment of awe during a spiritual journey to the Amazon River in South America, which was accompanied by the inspired thought that *"all I want is what I can see, all I can see is in front of me."* I couldn't have said it better myself!

Clarity

When we align with our spirit, we come to see and understand things about ourselves and the world that in our previous moments of unconsciousness, we never had the perspicacity to observe with any quality or depth. Through these revelatory encounters with Truth, what we may come to see is the dysfunction that we have contributed to our most significant relationships, or the causal role that our ego has had in sabotaging our efforts to create a more meaningful life. As these insights relate to our calling, they may reveal to us the internal barriers that we have erected to progressing on our path, or the next steps that we need take to encounter an opportunity that could change the trajectory of our vocational journey.

Typically, when we function from ordinary consciousness, all that we are capable of perceiving is the surface level of reality that is represented by the objects of form and their activity. While this helps to explain the workings of the world on a practical level, at the deeper metaphysical level there are other dimensions to life that seek our conscious attention so that they can be recognised as being foundational to its unfoldment and thus incarnated into form through us. These include the latent potentiality and virtuous inclinations that are reflective of our true nature, beyond the confines of the ego that serves as our earth guide. The gifts of wisdom and intuitive learnings can also become available to us as we make ourselves receptive to the insights that emerge from this higher realm of awareness.

As we partake in the process of exploring this new terrain in ourselves and the world, we engage in a style of transformational leadership that bridges what we are with who we could be. Like the famous explorers of history expanded the horizons of possibility by their discoveries, so can we play a part in charting a clearer and more conscious course for humanity when what we unearth from our spiritual exploration comes to inform our life, and the workings of the broader social domains that we move in. Just as the protagonist on the hero's journey who returns home with an awareness of the naivety and limited self-concept that they embodied when they first set out on their adventure, this gift of transformational seeing is what we have to offer to the world so that through our presence it may come to know itself more intimately.

Unfortunately at this moment in history, there is a great lack of clarity around who we are and where we should be headed because individually and collectively we have become so over-identified with the various categorisations that our ego defines itself by. Gender, race, nationality, political affiliation, religious denomination, working titles, value sets. Seeming themselves to want to rival the metaphysical quality of life and know no limits, these superficial classifications have a considerable distorting effect on our eyes and perceptual ability to acknowledge the animating presence of spirit within all worldly forms. While our spiritual foundation is not altered by our unconsciousness because it cannot be, what becomes scaled over as a result of this unconsciousness is the vision of our third eye that can discern the spiritual meta-story of life from the ego's crafted narratives that are filtered through the categorical representations that it most identifies with in a particular person.

When we see politicians, for example, who are so polarised in their position on certain matters that they can't entertain the policies of other parties, even when their implementation would prove beneficial for the interests of their constituency in the long run, we know that their vision has been compromised and they have lost the ability to see the forest for the trees. Similarly in a religious context, when we encounter leaders who preach that the only path to the divine runs through a particular prophet or faith tradition, we can recognise their limitations as ideologues who can't see beyond the dogmas that they have been conditioned to believe are embodiments of the truth. Being acutely aware of these impediments and blind spots, conscious leaders hold loosely these surface level categorisations that others want to define them by, but which they themselves do not take as being representative of who they are in absolute terms. By standing above these limiting concepts, they find themselves capable of seeing further in the direction that their spirit calls them towards. Where others allow themselves to be shrouded in a cloak of fog as they make meaning of the world, these leaders are more critical of their perceptual biases and assumptions, questioning not just what they look upon, but how they have come to see those things as they do.

In recent times, much emphasis has been given to the phenomenon of unconscious bias, which all human beings, regardless of their particular identity characteristics, are susceptible to being contaminated by. Each and every one of us has a unique history of interfacing with the world that informs what we look upon, and these perceptions are also shaped by many features that are specific to our being, like our socio-economic standing, cultural conditioning, race or gender. When we occupy a state of unconsciousness or blindly identify with these more superficial features of our being, we are ignorant to how these influences distort our perception and drive a wedge between reality as it is and how we make meaning of the world through the lens of our experience. Leading to a lack of clarity in how we comprehend the goings on of the world, the attendant problems that this can produce include among other things, discrimination, denial and defensiveness when one is challenged on how they are being reflexively driven by their pre-judgements.

With each of these things poisoning the relational well that leaders need to draw from for their organisations to operate at their optimal level, these individuals play a pivotal role as arbiters of truth and falsehood in their respective domains. But before they can serve in this capacity, they must have undertaken the challenging internal work of examining their ego and its self-serving way of interpreting the world. To just have them undertake a form of unconscious bias training or testing, will not serve this end, especially if their participation in these programs is compelled. While this training may play a useful role in drawing their awareness to these blind spots, it is not the antidote that will ultimately deliver lasting change or progress. The only remedy for unconsciousness is the voluntary embodiment of spiritual consciousness which, as I make the case for throughout the book, fundamentally transforms our relationship to reality and our knowing of what it consists.

For respondents who were living their calling, the theme of clarity was prevalent in how they oriented themselves in the world (*have a clear identity and know what their calling/purpose is, know their limits and work to their strengths*), demonstrated leadership for others (*being clear in their communication, being clear with their expectations, know how/what they need to do in a particular situation, provide a clear direction/vision*), and advised others about living their calling (*be clear about what you want in life and what you stand for, know why and how you want to make a difference in the world, know who you will need to bring along with you on the journey*). In outlining the potential barriers to an individual living their calling, respondents raised a lack of clarity concerning the nature of that calling as being a prominent reason why a person would fail to live it. Similarly, it was their view that not having a clear set of principles to guide their path in the world could lead an individual to deny their calling and become susceptible to the ego's influence in their life. On these points, I concur with the observations made. When one separates themselves from that which essentially grounds their existence, they will inevitably lose insight into who they are, and what they have been given life to affect, which will lead to much tumultuousness in their lives and the surrounding environment where that chaos can't help but be externalised through their behaviour.

To allow these ego directed individuals to rise into leadership positions of power is to magnify the dysfunction that they are capable of producing, and disorient the collective mission that their people must work towards. The successful accomplishment of any organisational objective requires those responsible for leading its achievement being clear in what needs to be done, and how others are required to contribute to the effort. Only once that target has been set and seen by those members can they work together to hit it with accuracy. In the absence of this clarity concerning the destination and the means by which it should be reached, the system within which that work takes place can easily become corrupted as the criteria of collective accountability remains vague, and the motivation to act out of self-interest is stoked into existence. Much of the greed, unethical behaviour and myopic decision making that have been rife in the corporate and political domains in recent times stem from this lack of transparency and the operation of misaligned incentives that work at cross purposes with the orienting goals that should reflect the higher purpose of these organisations.

The blessing of leaders who are grounded in spirit and clear on both their personal calling and the vision to emerge from it, is that they can help illumine the same in others and stimulate insights that can give them clarity on whether they are on the right path or not. Mentors who have walked their own path of knowing what they have been put on this earth for, serve this role exceptionally well because the guidance that they offer is legitimised by their lived experience. While they can't walk that path for those who they seek to help, or compensate for their ignorance of the spiritual dimension to their life, they can invite them to deepen their relationship with all that they are, which is an important first step in allowing the recognition of a calling to come forth, and avoiding the pitfalls that are part and parcel of the unconscious life.

Inspiration

When we're in-spirit, we're inspired…and when we're inspired, it's because we're back in-spirit, fully awake to the spirit within us ~ Wayne Dyer.

As is conveyed in the quotation above, the feeling of being inspired in our life indicates that our being has come into alignment with the spiritual energy of the universe that is representative of the God force.[44] By our allowing of this congruous movement in the present moments of our life, the felt depth and intensity of their experience is magnified noticeably, and once we have had a taste of that elevated state of being, we will become very reluctant to entangle ourselves with anyone or anything that compromises our ability to stay in tune with our spirit. This is why when we occupy an uplifted space in our life, our natural inclination is to want to surround ourselves with positive people and circumstances that enliven us with energy.

Unlike the finite nature of form material in the world that diminishes in proportion to how much of it is given away, the quality of inspiration is abundant, and the more that we come to embody it, the more effusive its presence becomes in the wider world we inhabit. When we are inspired, our being itself is inspiring to others, and what we naturally radiate in terms of the energy that others interact with will have an uplifting effect on the level of consciousness that they embody, particularly if their being is open to our presence. While the inspired energy derived from those interactions won't sustain them for a prolonged period of time, it will serve to invite them into a deeper relationship with spirit that they themselves can cultivate in their life. I have found in my own life that when I have encountered individuals who are vocationally on purpose and who demonstrate a clear lack of ego, their example has proved very influential in me becoming less self-centred and more intentional in the desire to be generous with my deepest gifts.

My PhD supervisor Alma Whiteley, is one such person who leads by this quality. Through her willingness to generously share of her knowledge and wisdom as she patiently guided me through the project, she left a lasting mark on the way in which I relate to and mentor my own students. With her tireless enthusiasm and faithfulness to her own vocation, she presented a wonderful example of the leadership that is espoused by this book, which in many ways her spirit strongly infuses. Being also one of the most charismatic people that I have ever met, it was by her understated embodiment of this

---

[44] The word 'inspiration' was originally understood to mean 'immediate influence of God or a god'.

quality that I came to understand what charisma really is, and the relationship that it bears to inspiration.

Etymologically, the word 'charisma' was associated with the expression of the divine force or grace within, or the utilisation of one's spiritual gifts. Therefore, in its truest form charisma describes the state of flow that one embodies when they are inspired. By this construction, it entails more than merely acting with charm or putting on a shiny facade, which are shallow behaviours that people mistakenly ascribe the word to because they are ignorant to its original meaning, and don't have the spiritual connectedness within themselves to properly discern what form it takes in others. Many a 'charismatic' personality, particularly in the world of celebrity or social media influencing, have been revealed as hollow men or women when the stylish veneer that they have projected to the public has been pulled back to reveal a lack of substance, or the incongruous character to suggest that if they were living their calling at one point in time, then they diverted from that authentic path somewhere along the journey.

When we see others who are truly charismatic, living in flow and on purpose, there is a mesmerising quality to their being that we are naturally drawn to emulate in our own life. Even if what they are engaged in is not a primary interest of ours, we almost can't help but get swept up by their passionate enthusiasm and absorption in doing that which they clearly love. Being its own potent form of leadership that influences others without them necessarily realising it, this was the effect that the late 'Crocodile Hunter' Steve Irwin had on his audiences. Through his uninhibited enactment of his calling to care for wildlife, he made us care about conservation in a way that we probably would not have otherwise. For me, well known British chefs Jamie Oliver and Heston Blumenthal also present very powerful examples of leading by inspiration, but in quite different ways. In the case of Jamie, it is through his infectious energy and relatable personality that we are drawn into the kitchen to cook as he does. Heston, on the other hand, has tapped into levels of inquisitiveness and creativity for his craft that are simply awe inspiring. Bedazzling his dinner guests and viewers alike by his culinary concoctions, he leaves no doubt for those who observe his exploits that he is immersed in doing the very thing that he was put on earth to do.

In describing the state of flow that is symptomatic of us having become a conduit of our calling, Mihaly Csikszentmihalyi characterises the experience as:
"Being completely involved in an activity for its own sake. The ego falls away. Time flies. Every action, movement, and thought follows inevitably from the previous one, like playing jazz. Your whole being is involved, and you're using your skills to the utmost."

Notable in this definition of flow is the ego falling away to allow the whole being of the individual to be completely involved/engaged in the activity, which expresses a similar sentiment to that conveyed by a number of respondents when they identified ego interference as being a principal barrier to aligning with our spirit to live out our calling. By the mask we wear, the spirit's breath is suffocated, and labouring under this inability to breathe in to life, we know not the inspiration that describes this most fundamental requirement for survival. Preventing similarly our exhalation of the spirit's life giving energy into the world, we will be rendered a futile source of inspiration for others. Denied of this magnetic leadership energy, we will offer nothing for them to breathe in, and have aroused their impetus to follow us on a shared journey.

When respondents were asked about the most prized qualities of leadership, and the leadership style that they practiced, leading by inspiration emerged as a dominant theme:
"It's about the inspiring and bringing back everybody to their calling, everybody to the common purpose and vision. // Leadership is to, you know, be able to inspire, enthuse and encourage others to find their path and their calling and to do and be. // So it just goes to show that I had that leadership model confirmed through seven or eight years of working on the streets with people from all over the world, and that is the model of leadership that I try and operate here, and that is the kind of good model of leadership that I think is important. It is not an authority, but to lead by inspiration."

I would contend that leading by inspiration is the ultimate authority as it does not rely on the artificial means of title or rank for legitimacy. This informal style of leadership embodied by respondents was also practiced by prominent world leaders such as Vaclav Havel, Aung San Suu Kyi, and perhaps most notably, Martin Luther King, in the wake of his famous 'I have a dream' speech. Not everyone who listened to that aspirational speech and was moved to advocate for racial equality and civil rights as a consequence, shared King's religious views as a Baptist minister or affiliation to the church. What bound them to his message was an inherent recognition of the spiritual Truth which King communicated that all people are created equal in the eyes of God. Evoking their support and willingness to follow him towards the realisation of this vision, he would not have been able to influence them that way if he was not receptive to his spirit and its calling for his life to lead the civil rights movement through that pivotal phase of progress.

When we lead from inspiration, our followers become those whose innate purpose naturally resonates with our own, and who draw their own inspiration and leadership from the connectedness that they have to their spiritual calling. Serving as a filtering process where we can identify those who will be the right people to take the journey with us, this helps us to avoid the pitfall that many leaders and managers fall into in having to continually motivate those on their teams to do work that their heart is not really in. Being out of alignment within themselves, if these people are to perform at all, they will need to be prodded by the rewards and punishments that make up the carrot and stick approach to motivation that is both limited in its effectiveness and draining on those who must resort to using them. With our individual and collective purposes requiring the full amount of our energy to be expended towards their accomplishment, we don't have the energy to fritter away on those who ultimately don't want to walk the path that we are on. Such a fracturing of our focus also diminishes our openness to the spiritual impulse that seeks to create through us, as we ourselves were created by it. This virtue of openness, and its leading forth of the creative potential that is enacted through the living of our calling, requires our presence for its demonstration as we will come to see in the following section.

Openness

Before we can live in alignment with spirit, we must be open to its presence in our life and the world around us. As we demonstrate this quality, we share its characteristic of being that is not bounded by the materiality of the physical world which it inhabits. While we can clearly create from the space of inspiration and localise the presence of spirit in that which is created, we know that the totality of its presence stretches far beyond any attempted reduction of its being into form. The same can be said of the physical bodies we inhabit which for the time that we are alive house the eternal spirit that was before, and will forever be, after our worldly existence has come to an end. While the ego may attempt to have us conceive of ourselves as a closed circuit that functions independently of the system of life, the reality is that the connection which we share with each other, to nature, and all other living forms that carry within them this spark of the divine, is all-pervading and immutable.

Drawing us into an ever deepening relationship with the infinite dimension of our being, it is as we live our calling that the constraints of the ego identity recede to lead us towards the expanse of potentiality in which we can unfurl the reality of that which we are destined to become. In referring back to Patanjali, he described well this enlarging movement when he exhorted that when we are inspired by some great purpose (a calling) all our thoughts break their bonds, our mind transcends limitations, and our consciousness expands in every direction to transform the world that we inhabit. Among the respondent group, I had a number of participants communicate a similar sentiment to this when they explained that as they got on the path to live their calling, things began to open up for them and come their way. By making themselves available and receptive not only to their spirit's internal guidance, but also to its embodied movements in the world around them, they were able to participate in this greater unfolding, and attract to themselves the people, resources and opportunities that would allow them to more fully live into their purpose.

The serendipitous events that so often accompany this aligning, prompt us to see beyond the apparent chaos that surrounds us to the higher order that our inspired efforts contribute to concretising in form. Cutting through the closedness of our unconscious state of being, these meaningful occurrences of co-creating with spirit serve to remind us of our innate propensity to materialise this higher order as we honour the call of our vocational nature. Here, a distinction must be made between what we create when we evoke the ego, and what we birth when we invoke the spirit within ourselves. What we bring forth from the realm of ego is self-serving, malevolent in its utility and thus destructive (e.g. Hitler and the Nazi regime instigating the genocide of millions of Jews, and Bernie Madoff, who through the vehicle of a Ponzi scheme, greedily defrauded investors of billions of dollars). Contrast this with what we are capable of creating in union with our highest spiritual self. When we create in the spirit's company, what takes form is endowed with the qualities of benevolence, service and collective enrichment (e.g. Mother Teresa's Missionaries of Charity, who work to improve the living standards of the world's poorest people, and the Dalai Lama, who has tirelessly advocated for peace and the upholding of fundamental human rights).

Summing up wonderfully the creative nature of spirit that it wills us to enact was one of the respondents to the study who expressed that, *"I think spirit wishes to be creative because the basic impulse of the universe is to create something new. To blow its own socks off that it didn't even know…I think human society - our work is to do that, to really knock our socks off with creative things that are beautiful, buildings, groups of people in hospitals working together to heal people. Imagine if we could manifest through our own selves that spirit in the way we work together."* This basic impulse can be observed across the spectrum of our lives. We reproduce to create a family. Our work contributes to building, growing and developing the institutions that create value for a variety of stakeholders, not only in the economy but within our communities as well. Our relationships hold the potential for fruitful collaboration and transformational growth, and if we are living from our spirit, we strive to make a difference by leaving the domains in which we have moved in a better condition than when we came to them.

The beauty that this respondent refers to in their quote is an expression of virtue that we make manifest as we do the work of living our calling, whether through art, child-rearing, volunteering, tending a garden, whatever that might be. Not so coincidently, these acts of creating the space for the beautification of the world also require the demonstration of leadership. Without a parent, the child has no one to follow into adulthood. In the absence of a volunteer, service cannot be rendered to those who need it most. If art does not take form, there will be few places where those seeking inspiration can direct their gaze. A leader is recognised as someone whose role it is to move things forward and affect change that will capitalise on the opportunities presented by the external world that by its nature is continually changing. This necessitates the creation of a new path to enable this progress. For innovation to occur, that which previously existed must die, or be dissolved, to allow something new to come into existence. Economist Joseph Schumpeter described this process in his theory of creative destruction which he believed was the basis of innovation in a capitalist society. With this type of destruction, it isn't motivated by the nihilistic impulse of the ego to wreak harm on society and its institutions. Quite the contrary. That which is rendered obsolete by this process is replaced by something better that drives innovation in the market, and enhances the quality of output produced across industries over time.

Resembling an actualising movement in the economic sphere, it is conscious leaders who are best positioned to drive this evolution. Embodying these spiritual qualities of openness and creativity were the respondents to my study who demonstrated this mode of leadership as they lived their calling. Some of the ways that they demonstrated the trait of openness was through being open-minded and having a flexible worldview, active listening, being vulnerable with their people, being receptive to the input and feedback of others, having an 'open door policy', advocating for open source access with their offerings, making oneself and others receptive to the broader possibilities for their life, being inclusive and accepting of others, being adaptable to change and welcoming the opportunity to learn and do things differently, facilitating open dialogue and shaping a transparent culture in which people can be honest and hold each other to account. On this last manifestation of openness which is critical in establishing the key quality of trust in an organisation, Austrian philosopher Karl Popper observed that *"If you want openness in an institution, you need a spirit of openness in those manning it."* In this respect, leaders set the tone for the cohesive establishment of their teams and the integrity that their organisation will embody in relationship with its stakeholders. By exemplifying this openness, leaders can stop the erosion of employee loyalty and restore consumer trust in brands, products, and business in general. In a different context, openness and transparency in religious organisations are vital to maintaining credibility and responsibility in the eyes of the public. Here, respondents highlighted the problems with the Catholic

Church in covering up sexual abuse claims, and the subsequent erosion of trust and credibility in both the institution and its leadership that has resulted.

As for the creative dimension of behaviour that was demonstrated by these respondents, some of the ways this took form was through the creating of novel products and systems that improved their workplace and the services that they were able to deliver to clients, creating a positive working culture that enabled others to derive meaning and purpose from their work, generating flow and synergy in their teams or organisation, finding innovative solutions to difficult problems, and creating opportunities for others to grow into their calling. In a related finding from the study, a lack of creativity and openness were identified by respondents as being defining features of individuals who were not living their calling. When we live in denial of our calling, we live stultified lives that are bereft of the initiative that drives creative effort in the development of the self and the realisation of our spiritual gifts. Instead of stepping out to make this creative contribution, we, as a shadow behaviour, withdraw to consume those things which others have created with courage. Over the years I have known such individuals who by their disconnection from their spirit and vocational prompting have grown very little, and as a consequence seem to live the same stifled existence year after year. These individuals, and others like them, who are steeped in the unconsciousness of the ego also exhibit a multiplicity of behaviours that are antithetical to the quality of openness. A sample of these behaviours that were articulated by respondents included not being receptive to feedback or criticism, being close-minded, isolating themselves from others (often in a leadership context - think the 'Ivory tower syndrome'), getting caught up in busyness/distractions/the rat race, and being otherwise unreceptive to how life is unfolding in the present moment. As we move on to discuss the final virtue of gratitude, it should come as no surprise why individuals such as this are blind to the abundance of blessings in their life. Being a pre-condition for the experiencing of this virtue, it is presence that opens the door for its stirring in our heart.

Gratitude

To commence this section, I want to teach you a transformative gratitude exercise that you can use at any time to start feeling more centred and fulfilled in your life. Take a break from what you are doing, and be in presence with me for a minute. Let go from your mind your worries, preoccupations and the ego's harried messaging. Focus on the breath and use it as the foundational reference point for what you have to be thankful for in each and every moment of your life. With every inhalation, or in-spiration, you are breathing in the life force that is animating your body, and presenting you with the opportunity to live into your calling and make a meaningful contribution to the world. As you bathe deeply in this realisation, you would be forgiven for thinking that all you have time for in life is to repeatedly offer thanks for the incarnation of spirit that your being represents in the here and now. But you could not justly dedicate yourself to that task without being ignorant to the multiplicity of blessings that lay over this principal gift of life. What of the people closest to you who animate the most meaningful interactions in your life, or the food and drink that you have consumed today which have helped to sustain the physical vessel that you inhabit? Being but two examples of an assortment of blessings that you have enjoyed today, their presence in the realm of your experience only serves to further highlight the abundance of blessings that surround us if we only care to relate to life with a conscious mind.

Positing that *"the single dynamic that helps people be most aware of God and most experiencing the fruit of the Spirit is gratitude"*, John Ortberg highlights the invitational nature of gratitude that draws us into a deeper relationship with this higher dimension of our being. When we feel gratitude for the people/things in our life, we are at the same time acknowledging them as gifts from the universal source of life. Taking this further and practicing gratitude in the same way that we might practice meditation or prayer, we strengthen our spiritual life and hold open the door for its presence to touch and enrich our life with further blessings. I have experienced this personally over the past five or so years since I incorporated a daily gratitude routine into my life. Every night before I go to bed, I literally repeat the phrase 'thank you' silently to myself fifty or so times while rapidly bringing to mind the range of things from the day that I have to be grateful for. No matter how large or trivial these things are that I recall, they all share the characteristic of having enriched my life in a unique way, and I have not once to date run out of things to express gratitude for.

Having these thoughts of thankfulness being the last thing that my mind and heart hold before I go to sleep has transformed me to the point where I can honestly say that there is no one in the world whose life I would want to live other than my own. Regardless of whatever status or wealth they may have attained, or the honing of their talents that they have managed to achieve, I would not take any of that above the life that I have been given to unfold and find myself in. One of the most beautiful things that I have ever heard said, came from American comedian Marlon Wayans when he pronounced that *"I don't want what anyone else has; I just want what God gives me."* What an incredible expression of gratitude for what we find, and what comes our way, when we orient ourselves towards the path of our calling!

157

The fact that each of us has been endowed with a calling is something that we should feel immense gratitude for. To have an aim that we can attain through the application of our best efforts, and by so doing make the world a more hospitable place for the flourishing of the human spirit. This opportunity is not something that we should allow our ego to take for granted. To refuse to appreciate this opportunity, and understand the profound meaning that a vocational pursuit gives to our life is to be blinded by the arrogance that has us falsely believe that we can chart a more satisfying path of our own accord. Why live a calling, and bear the responsibility for its long term unfoldment when one can choose a more expedient path that brings to them what they want or attach value to in the short term? This question, posed by the recalcitrant ego in response to the moral injunction to heed this transcendent summons, is one that signals the immaturity and short-sightedness that are characteristic of our modern age of entitlement.

Why give when you can just take, or why wait when you can just have what you covet now? For the ego, it perceives no value in sacrificing what can be gained in the present for what could be created in the future. Only the former is a sure bet, and to be deprived of its rewards for more than a minute is experienced as a loss, or insult to its sense of 'specialness' that must be indulged at all times. But what type of significant or meaningful life can be built with this perspective? Nothing close to what is actually worth living for. While some may be surprised when the lives of individuals who adopt this outlook collapse on them in the form of say depression or nihilism, I see it as entirely predictable that they would set themselves up for a catastrophic fall if their life was marked by self-centredness and ingratitude. In the absence of substance, or a base of meaning that we have abdicated the responsibility for cultivating inside of ourselves, it would appear natural to me for that hollowness to taint our perception of what we look upon in the outside world. People, for example, aren't looked upon as those who would be the beneficiaries of our gifts, but as instruments to serve our agenda and have our needs met. The same can be said for systems that are exploited by agents who fundamentally have no appreciation of the essential purpose that they serve in society. Becoming myopically reduced to a means of serving the ego's superficial desire for material enrichment, the corruption that this leads to has a hollowing out effect that renders the system as a futile mechanism for achieving that purpose.

Egocentric leaders are guilty, not only on these two fronts, but also more generally of taking for granted the privileges that their position affords them. Having come to see themselves as the central planet around which everything in their universe revolves, there is very little in their environment that they don't feel themselves as having a claim too. While of course there are gradations to this, a subtle example of this mindset in action can be seen in the use of the phrase 'my staff', which can evidence the unconscious belief of the leader that they exercise some sort of proprietary control over those who work under them. Being a belief which assumes that these subordinates should act in a way that the leader expects, or is at least concordant with the existing power dynamic, its manifestation in the context of these relationships can easily have a corrosive effect and breed ingratitude for what these valuable team members bring to their work.

Should this eventuate, the flow on effect for the organisation can be disastrous, as we know that people who don't feel valued in their work will put forth a sub-optimal effort in servicing customers and making them feel appreciated for their custom. Without themselves also feeling valued by the organisation, these customers will be strongly inclined to switch their loyalties to a competitor that, with all other things being equal, engages people who genuinely embody this virtue of gratitude.

Inevitably, we treat differently those people or things that we are grateful for, and by extension this transforms the relationship that we have with them for the better. Respondents who are living their calling and demonstrating conscious leadership in the process expressed gratitude for the journey they have taken and the people who have positively impacted them along the way. In terms of the people who they work with currently, they make it a habit of thanking them for what they do, often publicly so that these people receive the recognition they deserve. Not taking for granted those who they serve by their efforts either, customers aren't left with any doubt about the value they hold as the lifeblood of the organisation. By their generous offering of thanks in a broader context, these individuals also evidenced an ability to elicit gratitude and appreciation from others, which is an understated leadership quality that over the long term builds influence, respect and loyalty with followers and other stakeholders alike.

From the harnessing of our presence and vision comes the opportunity, or more accurately, the obligation, to recognise the blessings in our life, and put them to use in making the world a more habitable place for flourishing to occur. With our cup running over, what more noble activity can we partake in than sharing of this abundance of blessings that we have at our disposal? Being an investment in the future that will nurture and enrich the ever expanding circle of self, family, community, culture and civilisation, it is the spirit that pays this forward with a level of interest that our material concepts of value and wealth cannot adequately return to the world.

SECTION THREE: OTHER FACETS OF THE VOCATIONAL JOURNEY TO LEADERSHIP

CHAPTER 9: Enablers and Barriers to a Lived Calling

In the course of every person's life, there are people, events and challenging circumstances that they will encounter which hold the potential to facilitate an integral alignment between the call of their spirit and how they orient themselves in the world. Being what I refer to as enablers in this chapter, these pavers of the way to our fullest embodiment of this spiritual self can take forms that are both internal (within the person) and external (in their environment). How these enablers manifest in the context of an individual's life will of course be shaped by the unique journey that they have taken to reach that point in their life, but despite these idiosyncrasies, there were many enablers that were commonly identified and recognised by the re- spondent group as being of significant import if individuals were to live their calling successfully. Of these enablers that were highlighted, I will dedicate the most energy to addressing the ones that were prevalent in the data, and it is my hope that in their coverage you may come to see how they have impacted your calling journey to date. If you have not encountered or devel- oped them yet, then by them being fleshed out here, you will learn of their character which can help to illuminate your path forward.

The most prominently identified enabler to a lived calling was embracing opportunities and making the most of them. As one respondent put it, *"If somebody offers me the opportunity to do something I will say yes, rather than no."* Such a perspective in the context of a lived calling is reflective of a growth orien- tation in which one is willing to overcome inertia and move beyond their comfort zone to experience something new that enlivens their calling and allows them to more fully manifest it. Not only does this require a high level of courage, but enormous trust in our calling (and its source) given that there are no guarantees of what this change in circumstances will bring. With peo- ple being creatures of habit, who for the most part are adverse to change and its effects, it is the rare human being who is willing to break from the status quo to make the steep ascent towards an actualised life. Taking this road less travelled is the essence of what it means to live one's calling, as demonstrated by the respondents who took risks when it felt right to them, and sacrificed much of what was comfortable and familiar along the journey to create a life that has meaning and purpose for them.

Other dimensions of making the most of opportunities that were also raised by respondents were being alert to opportunities, and skilled at identifying them when they presented themselves. Such an ability could be a by-product of the internal clarity that one gains from knowing what their calling is and where it is leading them. Being able to envision a path ahead, or at the very least having a strong idea of the next steps to giving a fuller expression to their calling, it would be relatively easy to identify and embrace opportunities that align with who we are and where our calling would have us go. In contrast to this, if a person does not know what their calling is and what an authentic path forward looks like for them, they will be prone to confusion and indecisiveness when an opportunity descends upon them. Lacking this clarity, they will likely not even see the opportunity for what it is, and instead perceive it as a threat to the status quo which regulates how they live their life.

Having this closed mind that dulls their perspicacity and prevents them from seeing opportunities in their environment, these people do not exhibit the quality of open-mindedness. When we have an open mind, we are more receptive to life, and prove more capable of taking an active stance in responding to the cues of our environment. Preparing ourselves in this respect to be alerted to opportunities which come along, one thing leads to another in a way that we may not always be able to make sense of at the time that it is happening. Such was the description of many a lived calling journey which was validated by the research data.

The other most prominently identified enabler was having the support of family, friends and other people, who believe enough in who we are and what we are doing that they want to assist in facilitating our progress in the direction of our calling. This suggests that our interdependence is a crucial aspect of our individual and collective flourishing, and that if we attempt to assert our independence on this lived calling journey, we might actually be holding ourselves back. Such a finding challenges one of the basic tenets of rugged individualism, being that we are entirely responsible for our own successes in life. Injecting a measure of humility into the consideration of the broader factors that have paved the way for success to occur, we can come to properly acknowledge the key role that others have to play in this process. Much has been written about the interconnectedness of all forms of life at the metaphysical level and how this should alter our understanding of what it means to live in community with one another. In genuine community, we have a responsibility to nurture and support others in a way that extends beyond just taking care of ourselves. This community mindedness was found to be a strong trait amongst respondents who were living their calling. Seeing themselves as part of a greater ecosystem, they prioritised helping and supporting others in their organisations to grow personally and professionally. Their demonstration of this behaviour was in many instances rooted in reciprocity because they had previously received such help and support from others along their journey. Having experienced these enabling affects firsthand appeared to engender them with the impetus to pass that support on to those who they worked with.

Having this support in the workplace, being the domain outside of the home and the parenting role where a calling is usually most strongly felt, was also raised by respondents as being an enabling factor in their lived calling journey. For the vast majority of people who seek to express their calling in their work, this must find life in an organisational context where they are required to work together with others. With the organisation being an ecosystem of its own, the success or failure in progressing along the path of a lived calling is to varying extents dependent on our ability to bring others with us. If those with whom we work do not want us to progress along this path, their proximal relationship in that environment can allow them to stifle that progress and present a barrier to our lived calling. This was confirmed by many respondents who had experienced such interference or sabotage in the workplace. To capture these recurring instances in the data, *crabs in a bucket* was used as a code label to equate this ego-driven human tendency to the behaviour that crabs exhibit when they are placed in a bucket (when you have more than one crab in a bucket and one of the crabs tries to escape by climbing to the top, one or more of other crabs will grab hold of the escaping crab and drag it back down into the bucket).

Perhaps having experienced this harmful phenomenon in the workplace made the affected respondents more sensitive to, and appreciative of, bosses and colleagues who have supported and uplifted them to higher levels of personal growth and professional competence. Other enabling factors related to this theme were working with great people, having a good work environment, and the work engaged in being in alignment with a calling. Presenting us with valuable information that can be used to pave the way for organisational dynamics and synergy to be improved, it will be as a consequence of the integration of these factors into our evolving systems of work that these systems will become more conducive to the actualisation of lived callings in the workplace.

Being invaluable providers of this guidance and support are mentors, who respondents experienced as having enabled them to live their callings more fully. With these mentors acting as a bridge between the different stages of the developmental journey, it is often the case that an apprenticeship under their tutelage precedes a leap to higher levels of competence and responsibility. Whatever the domain that our calling finds life in, there will always be others moving within that field, or in other industries, who are further along the path of mastery in their demonstration of skill or character than we are, and having reverence for who they are, or the journey that they have taken (which may resonate with us at a personal level), we may seek their advice or insight in order to emulate the successful results that they have produced along their own journey.

This may especially be the case when we are new to something that we are passionate about and yearn to excel at. Rather than subjecting ourselves to the making of novice mistakes that could hinder our upward trajectory, we become willing to subjugate our ego in order to learn from these people what we did not know that we needed to know. While there are no shortcuts and getting around the diligent effort that got these people to where they are, our ability to harvest their knowledge, experience and earned wisdom can nonetheless make the path to actualising our potential much straighter than it otherwise might have been if we made the decision to stumble forward on our own.

Coming to mimic their habits and behaviour as we integrate their advice, the time will inevitably arrive however when we have to originate and make a unique contribution that differentiates our calling from theirs. By failing to take this crucial individuating step, we will be reducing ourselves to being cheap copies of great masters, and as a consequence of this, the unfurling of our spiritual purpose and giftings will remain suppressed. Being only given the liberty to emerge as we allow our authentic voice to speak to us through the work that we have been called to do, the shadow side of this enabler is to become so enmeshed with who our mentors are and their teachings that we become divorced from the orienting presence of our true self that instructs us through our instincts and moral intuition.

Having the self-confidence and belief in oneself was cited by respondents as the most valuable inner resource that enables a lived calling. As a few of the respondents noted during their interviews, living one's calling is hard work that challenges us both internally and in our external dealings with the world. Having to face these many forms of obstruction, we cannot hope to overcome the obstacles to living our calling if we don't have a strong sense of not only who we are in relation to our calling, but also what we are capable of accomplishing if we stay true to its path.

Requiring also the demonstration of courage to instigate this process despite the trepidation that we might be feeling, for every act of courage that we partake in, we strengthen our confidence to navigate our lived calling journey successfully. Such is the intimate relationship between courage and confidence that has its origins in the human spirit. When one quality finds strength in expression, so does the other, and in individuals who are well on the path to actualising their potential, we see a high level of both courage and confidence being embodied.

To understand the veracity of this assertion, it also helps to look at how an absence of courage and wavering confidence feed off each other. When we live for comfort and convenience, and don't push back the boundaries of what we are capable of being, we lose the confidence in our ability to handle the inevitable challenges that life will send our way, and this has a cascading effect where our lack of confidence leads us to act less courageously when we are presented with opportunities to expand our horizons. Much of the timidity that we see in the world stems from this happening. Yes, people are short of the confidence that they need to move in the direction of their heart's desire, but their plight is exacerbated by their refusal to take bold steps to even get on that authentic path. In this respect, our courage and confidence are like a complementary set of muscles that we need to work out on a consistent basis if we are to increase our spiritual strength and endurance along the journey.

During the process of articulating their lived calling journeys, respondents highlighted numerous instances of taking on new challenges and moving to greater levels of responsibility and competence because they believed in themselves, and were confident in their ability to successfully make that transition, despite the risks that they faced by venturing into the unknown. Had they lacked the internal clarity about who they were in the light of their calling, and doubted their ability to manifest it, they would not have acted so boldly, and would have rather timidly retreated to where they felt comfortable and excused of the responsibility to move to the next level of growth as human beings. In attempting to characterise individuals they had encountered who have not lived their calling or betrayed it in some way, one of the most emphasised traits that respondents communicated was this lack of self-confidence and belief in oneself, which is a major internal barrier that must be overcome before a lived calling can be manifested.

In describing the characteristics that they demonstrated as they lived out their calling, and noticed in other examples of a lived calling that they were able to identify in the external world, respondents recognised having a conviction as being an important quality that drives a lived calling. Using examples such as Nelson Mandela, Mother Teresa, Martin Luther King Jr. and Mahatma Gandhi, whose life work was backed by what can be described as a spiritual knowing that their calling was in the process of being actualised, respondents talked about feeling a similar way towards what they have been called to do with their life, as evidenced by the following quotes:

I certainly didn't hear a voice out of the clouds but had within me a deep sense that this is what was opening up for me. This is what I wanted to do with my life. This is what felt the right thing and in fact came to the point where it felt as though it was the only thing. The best thing. That there might be many other things I could do but what I was meant to do is ministry. // I'd say it's my soul's journey. It's like once again it's a knowing inside…It's just that I don't look on what I do as a job. It's a knowing that this is what I know I'm here to do.

On the surface of our understanding, it is easy to confuse confidence with conviction, and think that because one might believe in themselves, this translates into them possessing an unwavering recognition of what their true purpose is, and the resources that are present within themselves to ensure its fulfilment. When we drill a little deeper into what these two concepts mean however, it becomes apparent that they are not of the same character. Confidence is built on the belief that one has in their self-concept, or who they believe themselves to be, which may be deficient in failing to acknowledge the spiritual dimension of their identity. Conviction, on the other hand, is born of a knowing that a person has about who they essentially are, and what they have been put on this earth to become.

With their calling being enlivened as a part of this knowing, this is what endows the agent with the power of clarity concerning its vision for their life. While the journey to its unfolding may not always be easily observable, this doesn't present a formidable barrier when one comes to trust in their innate capacity to forge that path successfully. Unlike confidence, which can be flimsy and oscillate because of its susceptibility to the requirement that things fall our way, our conviction is not dependent on the world bending to our will, or placating our constructed identity from the outside in. Where our bruised confidence can cause us to lash out at the world in an attempt to save face or reclaim a lost sense of power, our conviction isn't subject to the same fragility. But in order to continue to have it serve the fulfilment of our highest purpose, its promptings must remain exposed to the light of our conscious awareness.

Here, it needs to be noted that the findings of my study suggest that a lived calling produces virtuous outcomes, both for the individual manifesting it, and for the world that is enriched by their faithful service. Therefore, the use of the word 'conviction' in the preceding paragraphs cannot be said to encompass the blind adoption of an ego-based ideology, or its dissemination as propaganda e.g. Hitler's actions in terrorising the Jewish population and invading to dominate other countries in Europe were driven by a delusional and maniacal ego-based belief that he was destined to create this reality, not by a spiritual knowing of what his true calling would have been.

Having the opportunity to self-actualise is an enabler to living our calling that can easily be taken for granted by those of us who live in social conditions that are conducive to human flourishing. As Maslow posited in his theory of self-actualisation, before we are able to meet our self-fulfilment needs at the top of his pyramid, we will need to have our psychological and basic needs taken care of first. Without these lower-order needs being satisfied, we will experience what are tantamount to evolutionary barriers that keep our attention preoccupied with the preservation of our physical, psychological and social security. Our psychological needs include our need to be loved, to feel a sense of acceptance and belonging, and having a healthy self-esteem, while our basic needs are for the things that are necessary for the continued existence of our species, such as food, hydration, shelter and sex.

If we were to live in a war zone as opposed to a civil, stable and peaceful society, then there would be many factors that work against us in being able to live our calling. In these dire circumstances, food may be in short supply, or the threat of violence so great that it wouldn't be safe for a person to leave their house. With these concerns understandably exhausting the physical and psychic energy of those who must navigate this catastrophe in order to ensure their survival, there would be little of this energy left in reserve to dedicate towards thriving in the direction of one's calling, or assisting others to actualise theirs.

Thankfully, the conditions of war are less prevalent now that they were in the past, and as a species this has allowed us to enjoy a level of prosperity and opportunity that is conducive to the fulfilment of our higher order needs. The explosion of creative output in recent times is a testament to this fact. When individuals within a society have the ability and available resources to engage in artistic endeavour such as music, drama or literature, this is a pretty good indicator that the basic and intermediate needs of their being have been satisfied to such a level that the expression of their spiritual yearnings are possible, and even supported by forces in their environment.

Challenges still exist however, and collectively we have further to travel before the conditions are created for all people to actualise their callings. Gross levels of wealth inequality, for example, is a scourge that will continue to impede us on the path to human progress, and for as long as we have societies that consist of the haves and the have nots, there will be a shortfall in the realisation of potential. No community can holistically thrive if some of its members are going without because these individuals will be hamstrung in their ability to effectively contribute to the advancement of the collective.

When we are fixated on meeting our individual needs, we become blind to the need that our community has for our presence and participation, and the need that we have for connection to it. Mired in this separation and subsequent dearth of belonging, we won't be able to entertain that this larger unit of society might care about our circumstances and endeavour to support us through our challenges. Leading us to lose heart and become susceptible to states of intense negativity that compromise our health and wellbeing, we will inevitably enact this suffering in the very places that we feel have denied us our dignity. The correlation between poverty and poor health and community outcomes has been well established[45], and there is more that we could do (for example, through the provision of a universal basic income) to alleviate this source of misery that suffocates so much of the life and potential that is inherent in the human spirit. While there is some conjecture about how such a scheme of universal basic income would work and what its consequential effects could be, I believe that if instituted under the right framework, it could go some way towards promoting a more equitable foundation that has positive flow on effects for our societal systems. Rates of petty crime, for example, like theft, should theoretically decrease if those in need are not made to scrounge around for the essential means of their provision. Individuals suffer a great indignity when they cannot provide for their own basic needs, and in an ideal world they would have full access to opportunities that would enable them to do that. Unfortunately at present, these opportunities for self-sufficiency are not available to everyone, everywhere, and where this deficit of opportunity exists I believe that we have a fundamental human responsibility to assist in laying a foundation from which individuals can draw hope and encounter opportunities to better their station in life.

As the findings instruct, having an education/educational opportunities plays an important role in being able to live a calling. For numerous professions e.g. law, medicine, architecture and engineering, having a relevant university degree is a pre-requisite to being able to enter those industries, and not having achieved those qualifications, or being in a position to pursue them, presents a significant barrier to living a calling in one of those professions. Even for less skilled industries, like hospitality and fitness, the completion of a shorter form of study must be demonstrated before relevant employers will give legitimate consideration to a work application.

---

[45] Haan, M., Kaplan, G. A., & Camacho, T. (1986) *Poverty and health: Prospective evidence from the Alameda County study*, American Journal of Epidemiology, 185(11), 1161-1170.; Wagstaff, A. (2000) *Research on equity, poverty and health outcomes: Lessons for the developing world*, Health, Nutrition and Population (HNP) Discussion Paper, The World Bank, 1-57.

At a systemic level, this barrier for entry into these professional industries will be exceedingly difficult to change, considering that for the most part it exists with good reason (to ensure that people entering those industries have a base level of knowledge to operate with competence in the field, and to preserve the reputation of those industries from a regulatory perspective). The better course, it would seem, is to work to create a broader range of educational opportunities for people who would ordinarily not have access to them. The advent of open universities which offer courses of study that have no first-year entry requirements have made good headway in this re-spect, as have other online educational platforms that utilise a diverse range of emerging technologies to facilitate learning. The primary limitations asso-ciated with these forms of education are that they require an internet con-nection, which not everyone, depending on their geographic location, has reliable access to; and they still require a rather significant financial outlay, which may be challenging for people in low income positions, who are most in need of an education to advance their socio-economic standing, to come up with.

Having this financial security/available resources to live a calling was also a prevalent enabler that was identified by respondents. Money, like other forms of resources that we have at our disposal, present us with choices about how they can be used to create different forms of opportunity that can propel us forward on our lived calling journey. Without having these resources to draw upon, our options in terms of living our calling will be limited, and we will likely have to make decisions on the basis of necessity, not on what we genuinely want to pursue that is purposeful and aligned with our deep interests. In terms of work, this might see us take on a job that pays the mortgage and bills, but provides us with little else in terms of meaning or intrinsic fulfilment. In this type of scenario, if we decide to give a voice to our calling at all, it would be relegated to a side venture that one partakes in as a hobby in their spare time. Being engaged in to this limited extent, the calling will struggle to grow, as we will spiritually, having such a stifled rela-tionship with this fundamental aspect of our being.

Ultimately, we cannot come to know and embody integrity when we are sup-pressing parts of our being by not living our calling. Journeying towards our vocational unfoldment requires a willingness to risk, self-exploration and faith (in God, or whatever other name one wants to give to the creative source of life or universal energy). Without faith in the one who calls, there is no impetus to be receptive to our calling. Respondents credited their faith relationship with the source of their calling as being a pivotal enabler to living it. Having such a relationship gave them clarity around how they should live and imbued them with resilience when the challenges to progress further along their path were inevitably encountered.

In the absence of this faith relationship, it is easy to disconnect from our divine purpose, or subjugate what we understand it to be, and give the ego free reign to dictate what we should do and how we should do it. Functioning from this indulgent dimension of self, we will prioritise the meeting of our own needs first, and neglect the higher order needs of the world that our calling would have us redress. With no legitimate guiding force to subordinate ourselves to, false idols take its place. Commonly taking the forms of material possessions that our society values so highly, or substances that take us out of ourselves which we come to crave, our efforts to bring to ourselves these hollow substitutes dissipate our will to strive beyond these temporary satisfactions to a life of meaningful contribution that is possible through our calling.

One of the most potent examples of an unlived calling given by a sub-set of respondents who work in the drug treatment field, were their clients whose lives have been ravaged by addiction, and the self-consuming nature of that behaviour that doesn't allow for a higher purpose to be enacted through their being.[46] As one of these respondent's so insightfully pointed out:
"With clients, the difference there is a failure to recognise their own calling and who they are as a person…to use in such a way and cause such pain to themselves and others is an example of when we actually don't value who we are…For the rest of the community, the rest of the community needs their unique skills and gifts and characteristics to actually contribute to the community as a whole, we forget that but we're missing out by them actually not contributing; we miss out, we can't fully function until all of the community functions".

When we misplace our faith in these false idols, the emptiness that we experience will erode our base of strength and stability. As a consequence, it will become much easier to feel burdened and overwhelmed by our life circumstances, with the likely effect that we will experience anxiety, stress, and even depression, which we may seek to alleviate by abusing substances like those previously mentioned, or by other harmful means. Feeling the need to hold the weight of these circumstances entirely on our shoulders, we can easily become resentful for our lot and stripped of the hope that things will get

---

[46] Amongst respondents, the most frequently cited example of a person who has denied their calling was fallen Australian football star Ben Cousins. Around the time that the research interviews were being conducted, Cousins was receiving a significant amount of media attention for violations of the law that stemmed in part from his substance addiction.

better or easier with time, which can prompt us to ask ourselves the questions, *'what am I doing all this for, and it is even worth it?'* Having faith inoculates us, not to the experience of life's challenges, but to the chaotic depths that some of these challenges can threaten to take us. Reinforced by the relationship that we share with our creator or spirit, we find ourselves becoming more robust, resilient, and capable of responding in life giving ways to the adversities of life. For many respondents to this study, they recalled the experience of significant life events e.g. death of children/loved ones, relationship breakdowns, financial hardship, that they felt they would not have been able to confront and move through in the absence of faith. Having the potential to lead them off the path of their lived calling, they were able to resist this deviation and grow personally and spiritually from those experiences. By allowing their wounds to imbue them with wisdom that they could use to help heal and alleviate the suffering of others, these events in their own mysterious ways worked to draw those contributions forth for the greater benefit of the world.

Three other enablers that were highlighted by respondents, which relate to the overcoming of life's obstacles, were determination, persistence and clarity of purpose. When we are connected to our calling and on the path to living it in our daily life, our determination to manifest it intensifies because we know that our efforts are leading to something worthwhile. Experiencing joy and fulfilment from the meaning that we find in that path, we naturally want to actualise those feelings more fully as we move further along the journey. This drive, born of our spirit, is what sustains us when times get tough, and where others might give up facing these same challenges along a less resonant path, we know that on this right path for our soul we don't have this luxury. Being fully invested in making manifest what we can be, we dig in even harder, not because we are recalcitrant or stubborn in an egotistical sense, but because of the clarity of purpose that burns brightly within us, and the conviction that if we persist, what we are called to be and do will become a reality.

Related to these findings was the quality of respondents which demonstrated a positive attitude towards their calling, and life in general. Being as one respondent called it, 'a glass half full kind of perspective', these examples of a lived calling sought to see the best in their experience, even when some of those experiences were what most people would consider as negative. Some of these respondents even went so far as to characterise adverse circumstances, such as having dyslexia, as an enabler to their lived calling. Without having a positive attitude to process these adverse circumstances and integrate their lessons into a productive way forward, these happenings would have been characterised in negative and limiting terms; serving as a barrier to progress towards a self-directed goal, rather than as an enabling influence. Systems of affirming beliefs or guiding life philosophies often accompanied these positive perspectives to shed further light on how progress towards their calling was attained.

Presenting as a frequently cited enabler was 'luck', which is an interesting concept to explore. Commonly accepted definitions of luck revolve around the random experience of good fortune, or chance, which brings about favourable circumstances in one's life. Such an understanding was reflected in the respondents' perceptions of their lived experience, for example, *"My husband got a job here, so I called up and luckily they were looking for somebody, so I came here."* Given that the force of luck is experienced as originating beyond the self and its control, and is thus comprehended at some remove, I believe that there are deficiencies with this common understanding of the concept that upon closer inspection may reveal it to be an explanatory failure. While it is exceedingly difficult to identify definitive causal factors in the complex system where our life takes form, I think that in many instances, if we are willing to look deep enough into the sum total of occurrences that led the events of our lives to unfold, we will be able to pinpoint decisive factors that preceded the arrival of 'luck' in a particular context. Take for example the educational background that one spends many years bolstering through study, which can be easily overlooked as a reason why a work opportunity arises, seemingly out of the blue.

The phenomenon of synchronicity was also raised by respondents as a significant enabler to their lived calling. In describing the workings of this aligning energy, Jaworski explains that *"If we have truly committed to follow our dream, there exists beyond ourselves and our conscious will a powerful force that helps us along the way and nurtures our growth and transformation. Our journey is guided by invisible hands with infinitely greater accuracy than is possible through our unaided conscious will".* In articulating the synchronous unfoldings in his own life, Jaworski may as well be describing the phenomenon of luck, as it is commonly understood. The difference between these two perspectives however is that Jaworski's experience of this intervention is informed by an awareness and appreciation of a higher power at work, whereas the alternate view does not ascribe the experience of luck to anything beyond randomness, or assimilate the workings of a higher power into the process of understanding what luck might mean. While it is not my intention to determine the true nature of these interceding forces here, I would challenge the shallow crediting of these enabling events to luck.

On a more interior level, the ability to be self-aware was raised by respondents as being an important inner resource that enables a lived calling. Having this understanding of who we are, and how we respond or react to what we experience in the world, empowers us to act in life enhancing ways that serve and benefit not only ourselves, but others with whom we interact in the daily course of our lives. In my capacity as an academic, I am often approached by students asking my advice to find an authentic path for their life. Sharing with them my own lived calling journey in the hope that it may assist them in discerning a next step forward that resonates for them, my efforts at stimulating this reflection are sometimes met with the searching question, *'what would you do if you were in my position?'* Being really an impossible question for me to answer with the limited understanding that I have of the nuances and complexities of their life, what I don't want to offer them is a projected solution that is similar to the one that many of their parents give to them in the hope of directing their career path. Luckily, or perhaps serendipitously, for my students, I have enough self-awareness to choose a different mode of responding which better assists them in making sense of the next step that is right *for them.*

Another aspect of self-awareness in terms of living our calling is being able to understand what our strengths and weaknesses are. Armed with this important insight about ourselves, we can align our efforts with these areas of strength, and elicit the help of others in our areas of weakness. Orienting our activity in this way is what it means to leverage ourselves effectively and partner with others whose strengths naturally complement our own. As Simon Sinek muses on this point, *"If we were good at everything, we would have no need for each other."* Respondents reported engaging in this leveraging behaviour and strategic collaboration (particularly in the business or entrepreneurial context), and some even cited them as being enabling factors to their lived calling.

A number of enablers identified by respondents centred upon the notion of experience. Primarily, it was identified in terms of having experience in the chosen work context which equipped them with expertise and other skills which facilitated the journey towards a lived calling, but experience was also raised to describe how for some respondents, their diverse life, work and travel experiences served to bring them more fully into alignment with their calling.

The enabling feature of these diverse life, work and travel experiences centres around their capacity to facilitate growth. When we are exposed to different things in life, we are presented not only with the opportunity to understand it from a range of perspectives, but also to understand ourselves more fully in relationship to the new facets that we have been exposed to. For example, when we travel to a foreign country, there are differences in cultural and behavioural norms that serve to challenge how we live and view the world. If we allow ourselves to experience this new environment with an open spirit, our being will expand on a multitude of levels to integrate the lessons that these novel circumstances present. At the societal level, we might come to appreciate how stronger social bonds in the community can make its members more resilient and other-oriented. At the personal level, we can come to see how even though others in a foreign country may act differently than we do, they are still driven by the same fundamental needs for acceptance, belonging and security that we are. Such a realisation is potent in its ability to connect us at the base level of our humanity, from which we can better understand each other, express empathy and work together on initiatives that promise to improve the collective quality of life on this planet. At the spiritual level, perhaps the most profound breakthrough that we can obtain through this deepening of the relationship that we have to the world is being able to discern our calling with greater clarity. When we see abject poverty or the suffering of persecuted groups at the hands of a corrupt system, this stirs our heart to enact its most meaningful form of contribution to either allay those problems, or others that are equally significant but resonate more strongly with our natural talents and interests.

An important point to make here is that just because these diverse experiences present us with the opportunity for growth, it does not mean that we will necessarily make the most of that opportunity. We may choose to remain ignorant and not recognise the potential for learning that is inherent in these experiences, or we may incorporate only as much as we feel comfortable in digesting, so as not to disrupt the perceived security of our fixed world view, regardless of how limiting that may be to our lives. Mitigating against this proclivity to remain static and closed off from the new lessons that life seeks to impart for our evolution was the growth orientation which respondents to this study characterised themselves, and others who are living their calling, as having. Taken together with their opportunistic nature, which was chronicled earlier in this chapter, it was no surprise that these respondents perceived these novel experiences to be enablers of their lived calling.

On a physical level, a foundational enabler to a lived calling that a number of respondents pointed to was having good health and a high level of energy to do the work which our vocation requires. If we don't enjoy good health and vitality, that limitation will negatively impact the amount of effort that we can put forward, and the energy that would otherwise be put towards enacting our calling will be dissipated, with a large proportion of it having to be expended in healing the malady that we are experiencing. As Augusten Burroughs insightfully remarked on this enabler and barrier, *"When you have your health, you have everything. When you do not have your health, nothing else matters at all."*

To cultivate a high level of mental, physical and spiritual energy, we must actively look after ourselves, and engage in practices that nurture and fortify these key dimensions of our being. As one respondent stated about this stewardship imperative, *"You have to have self-care, and you have to have it as a regular practice."* Amongst this group of respondents, the self-care practices that they employed included exercise, meditation, journaling, engaging in activities that they enjoy, taking time out to relax and rejuvenate, and living a balanced life that doesn't revolve around work. One respondent in particular, talked at length about his conscious habit of managing his mind, on the one hand, to feed it positive, growthful and inspiring content, and on the other, to guard against toxic influences and negative states of being like fearfulness or depression before they have the chance to infiltrate our present moment experience of life.

Another feature of respondents who were living their calling was that they eschewed busyness and sought to avoid distractions which interfered with their calling. Being sensitive to the chaotic and overbearing nature of modern life, they actively took steps to simplify their lives and focus their time and energy on their most important priorities. By doing this, they were able to create a lifestyle that was more harmoniously aligned with their lived calling. The important lesson to take from this is that we must value ourselves highly enough to habitually engage in self-care practices that feel good to us and nurture our calling in the process. The day will never come when the world will make the time for us to do this. We alone must make this a priority. By having this internal locus of control, we present ourselves with the best opportunity to live our calling, and as we take ultimate responsibility for this journey that we are on by doing what we ought and trusting what may be, that is when the invisible hands that Jaworski writes about will help us along that path, and nurture our development and transformation in the process.

During the course of my interviews, patience was not something that was overtly raised by respondents, but the presence of this virtue could be seen to be an implicit part of their journeys to living their calling. In the fast paced world that we live in, where things are constantly being demanded of us, and we feel the need to accede to those demands in order to get ahead, it can appear rational to not want to sacrifice this moment for something that won't provide an immediate benefit for the ego that we strongly believe ourselves to be. Yet, if we are to build a meaningful life, and a legacy that has any form of longevity, that is exactly what we must do. From what has been foregone today, will the progress of tomorrow be made, and as we extend the fruit of these sacrifices further out into the future, we will find a greatly enlarged capacity to build things of significance that can stand the test of time. Had the proverbial Rome been built in a day, it surely wouldn't have become an empire that was worthy of being remembered. What sets that which endures apart is the foundation on which it rests, and when our character becomes the basis on which we construct a life, we invest heavily in the process of its development, which of course takes time, practice and patience. By the demonstration of this virtue, do the other virtues find their formation and embodiment in us, who have more to live for than the unrestrained hedonistic pleasure seeking of the moment that has seduced many a man and woman into living an inferior form of life that was not worthy of the calling instilled in them.

The barriers that I have detailed above and will describe further in bringing this chapter to an end are akin to kinks in a hose that have the effect of blocking the flow of spiritual energy which animates our lived calling. What I have often found when encountering individuals who are not vocationally aligned is that their mode of being is much suppressed, and the energy that they give off reflects this. Being not engaged in the workings of their life to any significant degree, how they progress in the world is like a car that is travelling at half speed with its handbrake on. While they may yearn to live a life of greater significance and prosperity, this will not be possible if the barriers that are holding them back are not first identified and then removed. These barriers, which are both internal to our being and located outside of us in the world, are of a different nature in many unique respects which makes their overcoming more difficult in some circumstances than in others. A serious physical malady for example will prove much more challenging to overcome than the shedding of acquaintances who don't have our best interests at heart. With the former, we may have to live with that hindrance over a prolonged timeframe and do our best to push on with our vocational aspirations despite the clear obstruction that it presents.

While some of the encumbrances that respondents faced were not as serious as a terminal illness, I was struck to hear some of them report that they didn't perceive themselves as having being inhibited by any barriers on the path to living their calling. Despite some of the details of their personal stories exhibiting circumstances that could objectively be described as limiting factors, they clearly didn't see those happenings in the same light. Being so determined, focused and empowered by their feeling an internal locus of control over their lives, they wouldn't concede that these challenges which they had encountered had played any role in stifling the enactment of their calling. Similarly, with the personal and professional failures that they had experienced, they were willing to own those, and not make excuses for their happening or play the victim. By taking this high level of responsibility over their lives, it appears that this played a significant role in allowing them to preserve the spirit's guidance along their vocational path to its successful unfoldment. As I have highlighted throughout this book, it is when we permit the ego to orient our thoughts, perceptions and actions that we run into trouble and experience an inner divide that sets us in opposition to the spiritual dimension of our being. Of the multitude of barriers that were raised by respondents in the study, the barrier that was most cited was the one that reflected this Truth: *ego interference*. While I don't have the room here to lay out the full range of quotations from the data which reflect this theme, I have included a select group of them below that frame some of the respondents thinking about the ego and why it is such a formidable barrier to being able to live our calling and lead with consciousness as we traverse that journey:

If you're in it for yourself or if it is some ego stuff then, if it is just ego, it will not grow, it will not develop. It will burn in your lifetime. // I think my first job - It's mostly on the hooking the other stuff that limits my being, the dropping of the ego. We have a challenge here in the organisation and I have a different view from others. But I have to stand away from my ego. What I'm trying to protect and once I drop that away - so it's a lot of making sure my mind is clear, my ego isn't involved...Our calling gets covered over with a crust or mud. Everybody has it. But through our conditioning, our society, our anxieties and our fears, our ego overlays and crusts up this. // The ego issue is actually very difficult for people who need to polish their ego a bit...Throw out the ego, it never did anyone any good. // There's an internal guide and that's different to ego. That it's different to self-aggrandisement. That is different to being successful...The way I work is not to introduce a sense of the self and the ego to the point where it becomes egocentric and self – it's more about myself rather than about the organisation....Are you here just to meet your own need to be in front of something or to be able to say I'm a leader or whatever, and if that's what it's about it's an ego thing that's going to not work very well... So it's to what extent we are able to believe that that's important I think and then to allow ourselves to reflect enough that with certain things we're going to see as important as much as we may once have considered them important. Or that we don't buy into the rhetoric of success and the rhetoric of individuality, of ego and you believe that's where it's at. Well to me it's not where it's at, that's not what leadership is and I think that the old movement towards leadership I think - and there's a lot of books on it - is trying to discover how to be a human being. // If you had an ego, you found it difficult because you couldn't conform and work in with the group the way you needed to. And the suffering, the challenge was there to break that down and then to bring the boy in communion with that responsibility, that wholeness that community requires. // You can get very attached to the leadership role because of the status and the deference that comes with that. So I think you also need to just keep on checking in that you're not letting your ego get a little carried away with what that all means because I think it easily happens. // That was the other thing, using - not being ego driven but try and get the best out of things and not having to do it all yourself...I don't have a big ego but I know that I get my greatest achievements when I get a whole lot of people aligned and doing those things and people get a lot out of that. I think I always have to give back to the community and the more you give back the more you get. / / I'm not one of those leaders that like to be high profile and out there. I don't do it for ego. I do it the opposite of ego, whatever and that is the calling that you're talking about. / / I guess to me someone who's denying their calling who's been maybe focused – who's not listening to their calling, who's focused on egocentric aspects, whether it be finances, whether it be reputation, whether it be the way that other people view them - people who are unhappy in the work that they do, that are focused on the money and the status as opposed to what they really want to do - I think that's an incredible waste.

Fear in its many forms was highlighted by respondents as being a significant factor that can lead individuals to shy away from living their calling. When we are infected by fear, we become timid in the face of life's challenges that when confronted and dealt with courageously prompt us to learn and grow into our fullness. Fear thus makes us much less than we are capable of being, and in this diminished state, our susceptibility to being controlled by the ego's narrative of what our place in the world is becomes heightened. 'Who in the world are you to be living your calling?', we might ask ourselves, as if we don't deserve to live with such significance or purpose. Believing ourselves to also be without the power to really determine the direction of our life leads our doubts to intensify, and any confidence that we may have come to personify will rest on shaky ground. Such outcomes are a natural consequence of allowing this shadow emotion to fragment our connection with spirit.

If love is the light that leads us back to Truth and an awareness of the presence of God within, fear is the darkness that obscures our vision and mangles our relationship to that which is real in absolute terms. The acronym 'False Evidence Appearing Real' conveys this sentiment well. Why this vice is so antithetical to leadership is because when we are overcome with fear, we don't see clearly, and as we retreat into our shell, we can't effectively be there for others or hold the line for the collective journey to be taken. As difficult as it is to embody fearlessness across time, I believe that one's ability to do this marks them out as a truly evolved person whose potentiality in the physical world is effectively limitless. While you or I may never evolve to that level, what we can hold on to and be guided by is the presence of spirit in the moment that with its characteristic virtues of courage, strength and persistence affords us the best opportunity to grow in that direction.

Often being grounded in fear is the perfectionism that by its exacting toll on how we must live our life moves us out of alignment with the call of our spirit. Creating an unrealistic standard that is impossible to attain, what motivates this futile striving is the ego that is always seeking to exert control over the unpredictability of the world, and wanting to compensate for its own deficits that are revealed in vulnerable moments of perceived 'imperfection'. Not wanting that veil of illusory imperviousness and infallibility lifted, it has us madly busy ourselves in the task of getting things right. Being what we come to believe will gain us the admiration and approval of others, we sacrifice true engagement in the journey of bringing our best self forward for this end driven need to prove to the world that we have no discernible weaknesses.

How else are we going to establish our worthiness or superiority except by doing something that others can't, or should not be expected to attain? After all, they are not the people that we are, so let them evidence their inferiority in relation to how we live our life. The insinuation here emerges from the ego's fundamental belief that more should be expected of us because we are better than those people who we are measuring our progress against. But this game brings us no peace or joy to our heart. Setting us up for a frustrating and uninspired existence, we cannot truly thrive if what preoccupies our attention is our abject failure to live up to this corrupted ideal, and the unwillingness of the world to conform to its dictates. While we can no doubt bring forth our best efforts in any situation, we must be prepared to accept that this doesn't guarantee a 'perfect' outcome or that things will go 'to plan' for us.

Life just is, as it unfolds, and so much of what determines the form that our experience takes is beyond our sole ability to influence. As much as we might like to believe that we can make life bend to our whim, especially during times of stasis, there are limits to this capacity that our arrogance often blinds us to. By being willing to look at how our perfectionist mental models of the world break down when stress tested, we can break through these misapprehensions and connect with the deeper Truth that we are perfect with our imperfections, not in spite of them.

This paradoxical proposition applies just as equally to the state of the world that we encounter in our daily lives. If all that we can see when we look out at society is the dysfunction that is fodder for the media, cynics and doomsday prophets, we will be convinced that the world with all of its imperfections is irredeemable. But what of the evolving consciousness that gains traction through this suboptimal state of affairs? In the midst of this important work that needs to be undertaken are you and I with our vocational fuses lit, willing to bring to bear on these problems the full force of our animating purpose and giftedness. Having been given life in the time and place where we have been called to alleviate this chaos and suffering, there is perfection in us being made available to meet that challenge and render a contribution that is worthy of the spirit's investment in us.

Bringing us to the verge of our calling path or guiding us further along it are the pivotal moments of our lives that orient us in meaningful ways towards the making of this contribution. While we may not always understand or appreciate the value that these experiences have as they occur in real time, my hope is that retrospectively, or by your new found awareness of what life's unfolding is revealing, your recognition of their presence and attendant lessons will serve as a reminder of what you have been given life to know, but cannot ever truly forget.

CHAPTER 10: Pivotal Moments along the Path and what they have to Teach Us

Along every life journey, an individual will encounter a series of moments that are significant in their ability to orient that person towards their calling path, or if they are already on it, to move them towards its next stage of unfolding. How these moments are experienced by the protagonist will vary depending on their unique life circumstances, and how their spirit chooses to speak to them through the people, places and events they encounter. In some instances, these moments can have a sudden and forceful impact like the biblical story of Saint Paul's conversion on the road to Damascus, and in others the transformational nature of the experience will be more intricate and subtle. Often, it is the case that the passing of time and reflection reveals the presence of grace in a past moment that was not seen or appreciated at the time that we lived it out. Even if what was to be gleaned was an important lesson that would have utility at a future time when we would become open to receiving it, the seed of that learning often needs to be sown beforehand so that when we became receptive to it, it would already be there waiting for us like a patient teacher.

For so many of the respondents to the study, these pivotal experiences were like sliding doors moments where if they had made different choices in the circumstances that they were confronted with, they would have arrived at a very different destination from where they ended up. I think that in any person's life, there are a handful of significant decisions that they can point to and say that they either enabled or hindered their ability to live into their calling. Maybe it was marrying the right person or being unwilling to leave a safe and secure line of employment to pursue an opportunity that was more in alignment with where they wanted to take their life. The purpose of this chapter is to explore these pivotal moments and extract from them the prevailing reasons of why they are of significant import to the process of vocational aligning. I will start with perhaps the most transformative experience that a person can have outside of death, and that is the birth of a child.

With this, you might be wondering, well if a person doesn't experience parenting as a higher call from God then why does it have a broader vocational significance for our lives? Before I answer this question, it should be noted that just because a person may not see their role as a parent in the same vocational terms by which they may characterise their work role outside of the home, this doesn't detract from the fact that upon their child entering the world they will invariably come to the realisation that the task of raising that child to the best of their ability automatically becomes a central priority, or purpose, of their life. Being one of the defining features of a calling, this deep animating sense of purpose and meaning will inevitably draw forth many of the virtues that I have discussed in the second part of this book as a natural consequence of one having subordinated themselves to become a creative channel for the spark of the divine to enter the world in human form.

No matter how much love we think that we will feel for our children when they are born, this pales in comparison to the boundless love that overcomes us when they do actually enter the world. Surpassing even the love that we have had for ourselves up until that point, what we experience in almost an instant is a broad expansion of the reaches to where our love and sense of duty to this new life flows. One of the first things that I remember thinking when my first child, Eloise, was born was that I was no longer the sun around which my attention would revolve. While my circle of concern had already started to expand when I formed a relationship with her mother and we got married, when we took that further and decided to have a family I couldn't even fathom at the time how much that experience would force me to grow and see far beyond the narrow confines of my ego that was really the chief controller of my life up until that point. The types of questions this provoked for me were both profound and life-enhancing: *what actions am I taking to ensure that the state of the world which they occupy will be better than the world I have lived in? What example am I setting them, not only in terms of being a person of high character, but also by my willingness to courageously follow the path of my vocation?* As I pondered these questions, I couldn't help but also notice how desirous I was for all other children who they will share the world with to be cherished and taken care of so that individually and collectively they would have the best possible opportunity to actualise their potential, and make their own contributions to enriching the quality of life on the planet for generations to come.

By this process of growing into the world, the purpose that I understood my life as having also deepened in its significance. No longer was I tasked with tending to only a minor plot of land that was limited in its ability to bear fruit and nurture the environment that surrounded it. Now my impact would be magnified through the children I would raise and the destinies that they would forge under my stewardship. With this added responsibility, I felt initially overawed by the challenge it presented to fill that role properly, but in time I would find it to be invigorating for my soul's work that would touch the world in ways it hadn't previously when my motivation was purely self-focused. Even with my writing, which is a core part of my calling, I have observed that since I have had children, it has come to reveal a more integral understanding of the nature of life and my relationship to it. Being such a precious gift that I don't know how I would have come by otherwise, I can only express gratitude for being broken open in that way so that the confines of who I understood myself to be were not left in place to bound my way forward.

The encountering of adversity can also expose the limits of the ego's understanding of what we experience. So shallow is the ego's perceptual ability that the learning it engenders doesn't facilitate our growth in any meaningful sense by providing insight into the deeper workings of the world. This is especially the case in times of stasis where we become firmly entrenched in its constructed worldview. Having a toxic effect on the direction in which we will take our life, this will lead us to meet with different forms of suffering that can break apart our shallow and disordered thinking, and orient us towards a true path of purpose.

I say 'can' because whether we actualise the curative or corrective potential that is inherent in these adverse circumstances will be determined by how we choose to respond to them. As much as our ego may be served by playing the victim of circumstances that have brought us harm, we are not destined to play that role. The respondents from my study taught me this as they recounted a range of tragedies and abuses that they had endured to grow beyond the people that they were at the time they had experienced them. Having been reconstituted by the learnings that they derived from those hardships, these insights would also come to strongly inform how they understood their vocation as unfolding. Presenting in some cases a new avenue of service that was aligned with a dormant or emerging meaning for their life, they ironically might never have awakened to that purpose if the particular experience of adversity that they had encountered was not present on their path. Harry Potter novelist J.K. Rowling experienced this in a profound way which was reflected in her musing that *"rock bottom became the solid foundation on which I rebuilt my life."*

While we may never have consciously invited these circumstances to befall us, there they nevertheless appear, almost as a gift, to return us back to a position where we can bring into matter that which matters in absolute terms. If the ego's objectives are illusory, then when we are pursuing these goals, in a very real sense we are perpetuating a myth that doesn't materialise anything of value in the world. Is it any wonder then why we experience these pursuits as empty? As painful as adversity can be, principally for the ego by the dissolving effect that suffering has on it, it can present the antidote to our existential uncertainty. Exposure to the marginalisation experienced by the disadvantaged in society, for example, can steel our resolve to becoming a solution to that problem. The same can be said of those with the unique skills and talents to tackle some of the world's most pressing problems like environmental degradation and disease control. In non-profit, or for-purpose, organisations as I have otherwise heard them referred to, this is why we tend to see a larger concentration of individuals living their calling because those organisations have been set up specifically to make a difference to the lives of those suffering significant hardships. One respondent who comes to mind with this was the CEO of an organisation that was focused on providing meaningful work opportunities for people with disabilities. Having grown up in a family where a number of its extended members suffered from disabilities, this was cited as an animating force for her calling that initially drew her to work for the organisation at its lower levels before moving up the ranks to its highest office.

The experience of other respondents in terms of their upbringing were also pivotal in moving them in the direction of their calling. Being such a formative period for our development and understanding of the world, it is the people with whom we interacted and learnt from, the places where we were raised, their culture, and the exposure that these catalytic elements provided us with that can be so influential in crystallising our identity and vocational path. While these aspects of our life are not of themselves the source of the calling that we have, it's unfolding is facilitated through their functioning, either as a cause of resistance or as a nurturing force for our instincts or deep seated passions. We can see this particularly in relationship to our parents and other influential figures who enter our life at just the right moment to help steer us down a particular path. Even if we had overbearing parents who were intent on determining the career path that we would pursue, that can have a clarifying effect on what we want to commit ourselves to. Being faced with that imposition which doesn't feel natural can really challenge us and evoke our primal yearning for purpose in an area that is aligned with who our soul tells us that we are.

Other individuals can also serve this liberating role in our life, and many respondents recounted experiences of serendipitously meeting perceptive strangers who acted as a proxy for their spirit and gave them the encouragement or permission to swim against the tide of convention and give expression to their vocational essence. These emissaries of grace can also open up doors to alternate realities that expand the limits of what we believe we are capable of achieving. With these people having often walked their own authentic path to spiritually defined success, they represent shining examples that we can tangibly point to and say 'if they can do it, then so can I!' On multiple occasions along my own path, I have encountered people who embodied the qualities that I would need to develop in order to evolve into the next stage of my calling journey. While in my ignorance or resistance, I may not have wanted to confront my deficiencies through those people, the universe knew better than my ego what I needed to be exposed to in order to learn these transformative lessons.

This breaking down of the ego through experiences that may not involve adversity have their own potency that can be strongly felt once we open ourselves to them. A natural wonder of the world; a breathtaking artistic creation; a group endeavour that produces something which no one of its members could have hoped to achieve alone. Being in the presence of these marvels can evoke such awe and wonder that the bounds of our being literally expand in response to them. Summonsing the limitless nature of our spirit as we take them in, we glimpse in those moments past the ego self that holds our potentiality and relationship to the infinite in bondage. For many years now, my family have spent New Year's eve taking in the sunset at a picturesque Perth beach near where we live, and every year the beach is packed full of people who have decided to turn over the chapter of the past year in that setting. Beyond there normally being splendid weather at that time of year to spend with cherished family and friends, I believe that at a deeper level what is drawing these people to be in the presence of that vast and open horizon is the possibility of who they can become in the next year and beyond, and their past conceptions of who they have been not having to confine them in that imagining.

Often it is the case that we gravitate to nature for reasons that we don't consciously understand. While on the face of it we may get swept up by the scenic quality of its being, at a more fundamental level what it returns us to is the essentiality of life that underlies the layers of complexity that we have added to our existence. Even by its revelation of beauty does it orient us towards what is worth observing in the world. Being universally regarded as a virtue in its creation and embodiment, it is beauty that can inspire us to replicate its quality in the work that we do. We see this effect in the domain of art where those who are called to the craft base their creations on the landscapes that have moved them enough to want to recreate them in a form that is more permanent than the original condition which they took.

No matter the guise that our muse takes, at its core is the spirit that is continually seeking to attract our attention and rouse our soul to meaningful action. This is does by leading us towards people, experiences and opportunities that excite us and move us into our element. For many respondents, their first exposure to these aligning forces was remembered as being pivotal to their vocational unfolding. Being where their curiosity was stoked and the seeds of love for what they would come to do were planted, these moments are not easily forgotten, for what subsequently flows from them are often turning points which see us become more fully ourselves in a way that we haven't experienced before.

At the start of the book, I recounted the story of being stirred from my slumber in the early hours of the morning to write what would become my first manuscript. With that exposure to the work being a precursor to the daily engagement that I have with it now, I never would have gotten to a position where I could have written this book if on that morning in 2008 I had ignored that spiritual prompting and gone back to sleep. By honouring my deepest instinct in that moment, I seized the opportunity in a way that I otherwise wouldn't have been able to when I was not possessed of the spirit. Maybe the next time that I received the call to write, it would have been easier to dismiss by my not having attended to it with due seriousness the first time. While I am merely speculating here, what makes me not have to regret this counterfactual scenario is that I didn't let that call to Truth for my life go unheard. Being at a crossroads on my life journey where I could have stayed in my career in the law or given myself to a path that was emerging from within me to take, my ability to be guided towards the road I did journey down came from my openness and inquisitive asking of life for clarity on who I was in relation to the work that I was destined to pursue.

I can't overstate the importance of being willing to ask this question of life because if we fail to ask it, the dead end road that we travelled down yesterday will be the same road that we travel down today and into the future. One of my favourite sayings, which has been proved right time and time again in my life is *"when the student is ready, the teacher will appear."* Part of putting ourselves in the role of student is having the humility to ask questions and being receptive to the answers that come to us, even from the unlikeliest sources. Together with this, we must have an awareness of our deficits in understanding who we are and what purpose we are to serve in the world. To not know what we don't know about where we yearn to go will only doom us to take wrong turns as we move forward on our journey of life. Had I allowed myself to blindly accept the ego's rationalisation that a career in the law was the apex of what I aspired to do, I would not have felt the urge to search my soul for something that was more meaningful and fulfilling.

It was only by knowing myself that I was able to feel the discontent from my disconnect and use that as a spur to find what I was really looking for at that stage of my life. As the wisdom of the Bible explains on this point, *"For everyone who asks receives; the one who seeks finds; and to the one who knocks, the door will be opened."* At the start of this chapter, I referred to pivotal moments being like sliding doors that can open us to a richer form of life in which our individual and collective potentialities can be realised. But our opening of these doors is a reciprocal act and not a passive one. Requiring our willingness to embrace where they lead us, we will also have to trust what we come to learn down those paths of revelation. Being called a faith journey for a reason, we can't experience the march of progress without allowing the transformation of ourselves in the process.

In order for us to evolve towards the highest expression of our human potential, the parts of us that are antithetical to that unfolding must be cast aside or allowed to die. Our ancient ancestors knew this well, which is why they instituted rites of passage for would be leaders of their communities. With these rituals serving to break down the ego of these individuals and have them grow beyond their ignorance and conceit, the deficit of our modern culture is that we haven't substituted these rituals with other means that serve the same end. Yes, we have ceremonies such as bar mitzvahs and confirmation, but these formalities work more towards indoctrinating their subjects into their respective religious traditions rather than genuinely initiating them into the spiritual life. Without a significant sacrifice being made by the one who would be initiated, their crutches will inevitably remain in place as they move forward in life.

The coddling nature of our culture that seeks to protect the superficial and constructed aspects of our identity at all costs also does us no favours with this. Playing into egocentric notions such as the belief that we can have it all, we find our impetus being to gain, not grow; to level up, not sacrificially give up. Yet, it is precisely by this giving up that we create the space for something that is richer than what we already have to enter our lives. Before renewal must come loss, and less is often more in our ability to affect this. When we come to a point in our life where we realise that our baggage is not an asset but an unnecessary load to be shed, then we will experience much more psychological and spiritual freedom to explore the essential aspects of our nature. Breakdowns of various types can be tipping points for this transformation because they drop the complexities of our life onto the floor, and give us the opportunity to look down at them with some remove to determine what is worth reclaiming as we put ourselves back together. Unfortunately, for many people, it is only at this ebb that they are able to see just how much deadweight that they have been loading up their lives with to placate the ego and the external expectations that others have sought to impose upon them. You will notice here that I didn't state the weight of these expectations have been placed on our shoulders because ultimately it is we who decide to pick them up and bear that burden.

When we achieve this self-understanding of how we have encumbered ourselves and impeded our own receptivity to the spirit's call for our life, we empower ourselves to simplify our existence and lead from that core dimension of being which can now speak through the clutter that once silenced it. I experienced this revivification when I made the decision to get off social media, which I felt was really disrupting my focus in pursuing what was important in my life. With its incentivising of self-aggrandising and sensationalist behaviour to generate clicks and likes from 'followers', which I never cared too much to partake in, I had also become unsettled by the feeling that I was like a leaf blowing in the wind on these platforms, and too much at the mercy of shallow trends, biased news, and other people's fickle opinions. Having an adverse effect on my mental and spiritual health, I knew that I could no longer be a complicit pawn in that perverse world. After making the decision to be an active participant in my own rescue, the weight of fruitless concern that my involvement in these platforms had evoked, regressed to reveal a newfound clarity around what behaviours would support my intention to evolve in the direction of my calling.

I think that regardless of the form that these illuminating experiences take, when we connect to that deeper Truth of who we are, we will desire to excise the surface layers of identity that prevent us from more permanently embodying our quintessential nature. In my social media example above, that would be the persona who wants to put on the perfect front, or be contentious with their comments to draw attention to themselves and create drama for the ego to feed off. When we are in touch with who we are spiritually, we won't feel the need to prove ourselves to others because we realise that the part of our identity that is demanding to be seen and acknowledged by the world isn't who we are anyway. Bringing us a renewed energy to enjoy a more peaceful and centred existence, our life will become as Sophie Swetchine discerned, richer for these illusions that we have abandoned.

Whether we come to experience a firsthand taste of our soul's Truth through a dark night that is not of our own making, or through a more proactively explorative process, what is most important is that we make that contact which allows us to become conscious in our life. Only when we are awake can we turn a corner towards a destination that we aspire to reach, and be guided by our spiritual GPS in that process. Speaking to us through our conscience and intuition, we will come to trust this inbuilt system the more that we tune in to its voice and turn up the volume of its promptings. The spiritual practices that allow us to do this are pivotal in their repetitious engagement, despite not appearing so when looked at in isolation. No one session of meditation, prayer or gratitude offering will make a discernible difference to the quality of our life or connectedness to the divine aspect of our being, but when these behaviours are ritualised then their transformative potential is unlocked and the world we see and relate to will change because we ourselves have changed to become more integral actors in it.

To honour this principle is not to take for granted our participation in these routines. I can tell you from my experience with meditation that the amount of overall clarity that I have found in different moments of my life has been commensurate with the dedication that I have given to the practice. In hindsight, as I look back on a period of hedonistic and purposeless drifting, I can see how that coincided with my abandonment of the practice for reasons of 'busyness' and hubris in thinking that I could create my own happiness. Having also a humbling effect through the subordination and restraint that we must demonstrate through this practice, we become less protective of and attached to our ego, which opens up our mind to receiving the heart's wisdom and insight. Typically, when we experience flow or revelatory 'aha' moments that are deeply meaningful, what we find is that the ground has been laid beforehand through the disciplined practice of spiritual engagement. Leading to the culmination of that union which we experience as transformational, it cannot be forgotten that it was always an iterative journey that required our investment in doing the continuous work of becoming more attuned to our spirit.

Regardless of where we have ended up in our life, in our wake lies a multiplicity of decisions in which we have either made this investment or not. If we have failed to sacrifice for fear of missing out on what would provide the ego with a stimulus, then our circumstances will be devoid of the fruits that come from having stretched to build a life of greater significance. I love the saying which I came across recently that *"the grass isn't greener on the other side. It's greener where you water it."* So often, we become fixated on attaining what is external to us that we desire, that we fail to realise we can have something that is much better if we give ourselves to the task of creating or nurturing it. The belief that the grass is greener on the other side is so alluring primarily because it is a fantasy that presents as a quick fix to the dissatisfaction that we might feel in the moment. Caught up in its throes, the last thing that we want to contemplate is the effort that we could expend towards reversing our fortunes, to the extent that those things are within our power. To improve those conditions in the short term requires so much more from us than indulging the illusion that the solution to our problems lies outside of us and is dependent on our circumstances changing for the better.

Whatever are the centring routines that we adopt in our life, their power lies in their ability to reintegrate us with the Truth that we co-create our experience of life from moment to moment. Even if through our unconsciousness we have been co-creating our circumstances with the ego, through the awareness that these insightful practices produce, we can spot and stop this dysfunctional pattern of relating to the world before it is expressed in our present moment behaviour. Armed with that capacity to invoke the spirit in an instant, we can transform the quality of not just our own experience, but the experience of others who come into contact with us as we consciously lead ourselves forward. Changing their world in this process, we also change the world in a broader sense as that mark which we leave will be what they take forward with them as they influence the lives of others in their respective domains.

Having experienced this for many years as a higher educator, I can think of very few things that are as life affirming from a vocational standpoint as having a student tell you that you have inspired them, awakened them to their purpose, or given them the belief or hope that a challenging period in their life can be overcome. Along any vocational path, we will experience lulls where our work doesn't feel as vital as it once did, and because of this we may start to doubt our direction and want to change course from where our spirit calls us to be. Being a point of tension that can have serious consequences for the life of our calling, the things that keep us in tune with our purpose and thus engaged are significant, even if we don't identify them as being of crucial importance at the time we encountered them. For me, how I weathered these barren periods was by becoming attuned to the impact that I was making in the classroom and through my daily interactions with my students. Even if through most of those interactions I wasn't changing their lives in a profound way, what I was doing at the very least was presenting them with an earnest example of how a calling could be lived. This shouldn't be looked past because in any setting that we move in, there will always be people who are struggling to find that spark of life to embody, and if they can see that semblance of fire in us as we go about our daily lives, then that can present a lifeline for them as they search forward on their own path of discovery.

By staying connected at the coal face with those who we serve by our efforts, we keep that fire alive in us. Being where we make our direct and most meaningful impact, we shouldn't take for granted the time that we spend there, for as we move up an organisational hierarchy, we will typically become more distant from these interfacing roles. What I have often seen in organisational life is individuals who have lost their passion for the work because by their career progression they have become too far removed from the core facets of the work that drew them to it in the first place. In the academic field that I work in, this disconnect takes the form of lecturers or researchers being elevated to faculty directorships or other executive level positions which keep them so busy with administrative work that they no longer have the time for the teaching or theorising that they once revelled in. If we find ourselves facing this prospect, we will need to evaluate what the benefits and detriments are to making this progression so that we can be sure that the decision we make doesn't get us crosswise with our animating purpose as we experience it at the time. What makes decisions such as these difficult is that we are likely to still have the opportunity to give effect to our calling in these higher positions, but in a different form than what we are used to. So in my example concerning academia, while our experience of our calling may have centred around the practice of teaching in years prior, in the new executive role that we have been promoted to, we may have greater scope to implement innovative pedagogical approaches across a whole department or faculty, which in their administration would lead us to make a broader impact on the student cohort than we would have otherwise made in implementing those approaches solely in our classroom.

The emotions that we experience in response to these transitions will often speak volumes about whether we have moved further into alignment with our calling, or out of step with it. Feelings of excitement, a positive anticipation of the opportunity to grow and make a difference, and a sense of belonging in the new situation, can strongly indicate that we are living into the next stage of our calling journey. If what consumes us however are feelings of meaninglessness, apathy, disconnection from the work and colleagues, and a longing for what we used to be involved in, our being is likely to be telling us that we have moved out of vocational alignment. Of course, with any new work role that takes us outside of our comfort zone, we are bound to experience pangs of uncertainty and trepidation, but the arising of these emotions should not automatically be taken as a sign that we have ventured down the wrong path. I think that the key to navigating these periods successfully is to ensure that we are strongly attuned to ourselves, and aware of the ploys that our ego might use to direct us towards a situation that elevates its priorities above what our soul needs to experience meaning in our work. By having this connectedness and insight, we won't become as vulnerable to the ego's misrepresentations which confound, for example, the climbing of the corporate ladder for a consequential form of progress. In addition, the destabilising emotions that the ego evokes to sabotage the enactment of our higher aim will be able to be seen with greater clarity and challenged by the veracity of the spirit's exhortations concerning our capacity to realise our potential.

The recognition of fear as a deterrent to the enactment of our calling constitutes a significant breakthrough, particularly when it has unconsciously determined our course in getting to a place where we no longer want to be.

By bringing that fear to light, we can begin to dispel the harmful myths of who we thought we were, and reconcile those lessons with the reality that we are currently facing. With less of our shadow dimming our engagement in the process of becoming, we can see how courageous we really are in confronting the demons that call for our surrender. Like the Tibetan master Milarepa who opened himself to what the demons who consumed his cave had to teach him, it is when we cease resisting these neglected aspects of our being that they become integrated with our light and an added source of power.

The great tragedy with fear that remains unreconciled is that it keeps us stuck and at war with ourselves. Being the handbrake that holds us back from the change that we desire to make, its corollary is to stifle the experiencing of these pivotal moments. While he wasn't referring to the effect of fear frustrating our attempts at transformation, Einstein captured this sentiment when he remarked that *"nothing happens until something moves."* If we choose to stay mired in fear, it is guaranteed that what we have experienced in its company will be what we continue to manifest as we attempt to move forward in our life. I say 'attempt' because we cannot act effectually towards that end if our being is divided, and thus uncommitted to making progress. In order for genuine transformation to occur, there must be a death of the old parts of ourselves to allow the new dimensions of our being to emerge, but fear interferes with this process by keeping death before our eyes. Making us reactive to what we encounter in the world, this leaves too little room in the realm of our perception for a shift in consciousness to be affected.

Think about the last time that an intense feeling of fear overcame your body. Having the effect of shutting you down and making you protective of the ego self that felt threatened by the prospect of loss or harm occurring in that situation, no part of your conscious attention was present to enable a thoughtful understanding of what was taking place. Even scientific studies have established the adverse effect that stressors such as fear have on our learning and memory retention.[47] By this narrowing of our perspicacity, our innate wisdom is also prevented from coming forth to inform the transformative experience that our spirit is seeking to deliver us. Without availability, there can be no insight, and in the absence of this light being allowed to illuminate our inner life, we are doomed to stay confined in dark places of our own making. Even if the fear that we wrestle with is not a figment of

---

[47] Arnsten, A. F. (2009) *Stress signalling pathways that impair prefrontal cortex structure and function*, Nature Reviews Neuroscience, 10(6), 410-422.; Vogel, S. & Schwabe, L. (2016) *Learning and memory under stress: Implications for the classroom*, npj Science of Learning, 1(16011), 1-10.

our imagination, we still bear the responsibility for confronting it with courage so that it doesn't sabotage our best efforts to evolve by leading to avoidance and the unconscious repetition of patterns that are destructive to the life of our vocation.

Breaking this cycle to derive meaningful lessons from these experiences requires the exercise of self-leadership which anybody is capable of exemplifying. For many individuals who have not learnt or been told about their inherent leadership capacity, they doubt their ability to assume that role in their personal and professional lives. Leadership, they assert, is for others who were born with the gift, but not me! Even if with some of their life decisions or habits they have demonstrated this leadership quality, they will be reluctant to recognise or own their ability to practice it because of their lack of awareness and limiting self-assessment. This form of denial benefits no-one, especially the person who has relegated themselves to being the marionette rather than the orchestrator of their own life story.

Coming to the point of recognising that we can be more than just a follower is one of the most significant breakthroughs that we can achieve in our life. Whether we come to that point by being promoted at work with a new level of responsibility for building a team, starting a project that requires the co-operation of others, or by becoming involved in extracurricular activities that benefit the community, these things serve as an initiation of sorts that bring us in touch with our ability to move beyond ourselves and produce generative action in the world. In each of these circumstances, a purpose much larger than our own personal concerns and desires is being sought to be affected. So we venture forth, despite the reservations born of our fears and insecurities to participate in that greater unfolding. As we do this, we come to experience what it feels like to be ourselves in a true spiritual sense.

So often, when we are racked with an emotion or immersed in an identification, we can't see ourselves as anything other than those things, which is a misperception because we are more than our fears when we are scared, and we are more powerful than we think we are when we identify as just a follower. Coming into this power is what I refer to as authority which requires that we have distanced ourselves from these limiting emotions and identifications. In that spaciousness where we can connect with our spiritual solidity, our leadership story begins to be written. While we may begin to grow in that direction through our practical learning of leadership principles, running parallel to that at the core of our being, the real transformation that enables conscious leadership to be embodied is taking place. While we can get into role by playing the leader in any of the examples that I mentioned in the preceding paragraph, we will only come to lead consciously in serving their ends if vocationally they are resonant with who we are. If we start a project that requires the cooperation of others, but are motivated in this endeavour by personal gain or taking credit for what eventuates then our lack of authority will be exposed. Being just a follower of our ego in those circumstances, this is what we will signal most strongly to those who at best will begrudgingly provide their cooperation in exchange for whatever material benefit that they are deriving from their work with us.

This transformation that enables conscious leadership to be embodied is a moment by moment process that can't be shortcut. With every moment of spiritual alignment weaving together a tighter bond with the integral work that has preceded it, this is how the fabric of our character is built over time. As tedious as this work can be, it is necessary if we are to form a robust enough constitution that can withstand the adversity we will encounter as we progress on our leadership journey. Even if what we have developed through our learning seems to over-qualify us for the circumstances that we currently find ourselves in, we need to remind ourselves that we are investing in our future, and will require those surplus competencies to address the bigger challenges that await us down the line. With the responsibility of leadership being so onerous, it is much better to be well equipped with what we need before we need it, than it is to be ill equipped and found wanting in a future moment of crisis or opportunity. Being its own form of leverage that can be continually built upon as we progress along our path, we must be willing to make our sacrifices in the present moment to imbue them with an enhanced significance down the line.

You would be forgiven for thinking that this presents a contradiction in terms of not properly honouring the present moments of our lives by dedicating them towards some future end that may never eventuate. In one sense, this is true if each moment is looked at as an independent unit of time that serves its own end, but in reality, one unit of time by this measure bears an infinite relationship to the present moments that have preceded and followed it. In much the same way that human beings, while appearing independent of each other by their physical separateness, are interdependently connected to all other human beings, how we inhabit the space of the now will shape the form that tomorrow takes. If our present moments are animated by conscious thought and action, then the future will see the virtues of the spirit become the expected norm of behaviour. While our moral sensibilities may hold that the time for this mode of living should have already come, the groundwork for this evolution hasn't yet been laid in enough hearts, with the pasts of these individuals having been forfeited to the ego's unconscious agenda.

But even as I write this, I must acknowledge that the world is slowly waking up, which I have sensed in recent times, particularly since the start of the millennium. During that time we have collectively learnt that we cannot live from the mind alone, or through the veil of personality with its emotional effects and expect to manifest consciousness in our lives. For all of our focus on emotional intelligence, or one's intellectual quotient as the prime determinant of value that they have to offer the world, there still remains a lack of understanding about matters of the heart that living from the spirit is the only cure for. We can be the smartest person in the world with an IQ score that puts us in the realm of genius, but unless we have a heart that is informing how that intellect is put to use, our actions won't fulfil their transformative potential. To live in such a way is to lay waste to the opportunity that the present moment presents to transcend the limits of our current condition.

If, for example, we are trying to influence others to live more congruent and complete lives, we can't just appeal to their rational mind with reasoned logic for why they should change their behaviour. Instead, we will need to bring them in touch with their own deep, and often unacknowledged, desire to evolve. Encompassing more of them than any limiting identification that they have with the mind alone, this spiritual recognition and longing for what is has to offer to their life is what will stir them to inspired action that will positively alter the trajectory of their life. It is in this spirit that the next chapter is offered. Being an amalgam of the advice concerning the living of one's calling that my respondents put forward during the course of our interviews, what I offer in addition to their ponderings are my own thoughts about their advice and how it could be interpreted through a broader lens. While much of what is contained in the preceding chapters could be considered as advice in its own right, the substance of Chapter eleven will be more pointed and useful as a guide for discerning the path to true north in the context of your life.

CHAPTER 11: An Amalgam of Advice Concerning the Living of One's Calling

While I believe that there is some wisdom in the saying that *"sometimes the best advice is not to offer any advice at all"*, particularly when that advice is given with a view to imposing it on another person 'for their benefit', I do think that it would be irresponsible and neglectful for those who are living their calling to not offer the fruits of their learning to those who are open to receiving them. Whether that advice is heeded or not is up to the individual receiving it, for only they can really know how it may apply in the context of their journey to get them where they yearn to go. The journey to living one's calling is difficult enough to traverse without guidance, so if some can be offered to better enable a person to navigate that path, then I think it should be shared for when it might be needed. This reminds me of the Hasidic tale of the rabbi who always told his people that if they studied the Torah, it would put Scripture on their hearts. When one of his followers asked, *"Why on our hearts, and not in them?"*, the rabbi answered, *"Only God can put Scripture inside. But reading sacred text can put it on your heart, and then when your heart breaks, the holy words will fall inside."* As I have articulated throughout this work, heartbreak and the associated suffering of unconsciousness are inevitable features of the calling journey and coming into the light of the spirit's presence. While you may reside in darkness or confusion in the present moment, what follows can lay upon your heart until the time is right for it to fall inside and animate your consciousness.

Understand why you are doing the work - Unless you know yourself and the realm of consciousness that you live from, you will be unclear about your motivations for doing what you do. This applies to your everyday actions and of course your vocational direction. Is your 'why' to enhance your ego and bring to yourself what strengthens it, or is it more pure and grounded in spirit? Only your spiritual purpose is a worthy 'why' to be animated by in your life. For greater insight on whether you are being driven by ego or inspired by the purpose that is your calling, it can help to utilise the five why's technique[48] that gets to the core of what within you is driving your behaviour. The first couple of times that you ask yourself the question in relation

---

[48] In relation to any behaviour that you engage in or anything that you want to attain, this technique requires you to ask five successive 'why' questions which dig deeper into the core motivations that are driving the behaviour or striving. An example of this striving may be wanting to get a promotion to a particular role at work. The first answer to the 'why' question may be 'because I want a greater challenge.' Asking yourself for a second time 'why' you want a greater challenge, the answer may be 'because I find my current work role boring and uninspiring.' Flowing on from this

to a certain objective, only surface level explanations will be yielded, but persist with the exercise to the end and that which emerges will prove to be revelatory.

Know when to put an end to things - Where you start will not be where you finish, so along the journey you need to be discerning of when one road is coming to an end so that you can effectively take the next road that will lead you closer to your desired destination. This knowing when to call time is not always easy, especially when we feel comfort and a sense of safety with our situation. If we are surrounded by dysfunction that may be a good sign that a change is needed to disrupt the negative effect of those circumstances. In making this call, you can consult others who have valuable input to offer on your situation, but you can't abdicate responsibility for your ultimate decision that undoubtedly rests with you. As you come to that decision, don't forget to engage your intuition, as that is amongst your most powerful allies in navigating a way forward. Also, remember that quitters do prosper when what they were involved in doesn't resonate with the spiritual dimension of their being that is the source of their calling.

Good things come when you're in a good place - When we are living in alignment with our spirit, we will attract to ourselves that which resonates with its virtuous nature. With our goodness being a reflection of the presence of God within, it is as we live from that source energy that we draw forth good from the world in the form of people and circumstances that nourish our soul and keep us connected to life. Conversely, when we are in a state of internal discord, the people and circumstances that we bring to ourselves will exacerbate our discontent. Misery loves company, or so the saying goes, and when that becomes our point of attraction, we spiral down into the pit of believing that our life is deficient or that the world is depriving us of something that we feel entitled to. But nothing positive comes from this pessimistic glass half empty perspective because it is rooted in the ego's lack, which is the antithesis of the gratitude that should be inspired by the recognition that we are blessed beyond measure to be able to revel in the prosperous life of the spirit.

---

is the third question of why you find your current work role boring and uninspiring. The answer to this may be because it doesn't allow you to work on projects that make a difference to a particular group of people who you want to play a role in serving. Getting you closer to a deeper understanding of your desire for this transition, the answers to the last two 'why' questions will likely speak to you of your vocational longing at that time. Note though that it may not always take you until the fifth 'why' question to get to the heart of what is driving you, but if you do, then what should become abundantly clear is whether you are being animated by the presence of spirit or ego.

Do your due diligence - If you desire to live your calling then it is wise to be strategic about it. Nobody is telling you to quit your job on a whim and abandon your dependents to pursue a fantastical dream that you have discovered. To do this would be to sacrifice altogether too much that is sustaining you in the present moment. Even if you dislike the job you are currently in, its currency is the time that it buys you to properly prepare for a transition that is sustainable and more likely to succeed in the long term. What support or buy in do you have from your loved ones regarding your plans? Do you need to earn a qualification to progress on your chosen path or otherwise upskill to have new doors open for you? Who will be those people who can assist in opening those doors for you? Are they already in your network, or will you have to reach out and make new connections with mentors or others who are further along the journey than you are? Planning is what makes execution possible, and while you can't plan all of the details ahead of time, taking calculated steps at the outset will position you closer to where you want to be further down the road.

Don't sweat the small stuff - Remember that you are playing the long game here so don't dissipate your precious energy worrying about things that matter very little in the grand scheme of things. Living your calling will require you to become a bigger person whose circle of concern transcends the pettiness and self-consumption of the ego. If you notice closely, this is what those who are mired in ego consciousness prioritise in their life. They ask what others think of their appearance, social media posts or awards, and if they don't feel that others are giving these things the attention they deserve then they feel diminished or upset. This is ludicrous if you have you sights set on making a broader social impact. Naturally, when we are resonant with the presence of the spirit that animates all things, our perspective will enlarge because we will have a more holistic appreciation of everything that we are connected to, and what we have the ability to influence by our embodiment of consciousness. Armed with this power, it makes even less sense to forgo it for the trivial aspects of life, which wisdom teaches should be assiduously avoided by those whose intention is to remain on the path of purpose.

Get your priorities right - Getting to a space where we are giving our all to the things that truly matter in our life is a difficult task, especially when one considers the options that we have before us, and the corrupting power that the ego has to pull us in the direction of what it values for its indulgence. In the absence of having clarity around what is most important in our life, we will give our energy to inconsequential things that are devoid of meaning and vocational significance. Leading us also to experience a loss of balance, we will suffer the consequences of having subordinated the things that are an authentic representation of who we are for what the ego has convinced us ultimately defines our identity. This is why people so easily fall into the trap of overworking and leave in their wake a broken relationship or marriage. Because their ego was so completely identified with who they were in their work role, this crowded out the space that was needed to give the relationship the energy it required to develop. In your cylinder of concentration, lay the big rocks down first so that the pebbles which follow can be suitably accommodated.

Don't expect things to be easy - As I once heard NBA basketball coach Monty Williams communicate to his players during a championship run, *"everything that you want is on the other side of hard."* When we know the amount of effort that will be required to arrive at the destination that we are called to reach, our resolve is strengthened to put one foot in front of the other in doing the necessary work that will allow for the journey to be successfully traversed. No matter what our calling is, there will be an array of challenges that we will encounter along our path that will present themselves across a long range of time. In this, it is not a matter of overcoming a few initial hurdles and then we will experience clear sailing from there. Each of these challenges serves to refine both our character and capabilities, along with testing how faithful we ultimately are to our purpose. But to have that effect, they must be faced with the right spirit, the only spirit, as we take those steps forward incrementally and consistently. Remember, hard gets harder if a task is seen as an unbroken whole that must be tackled all in one go.

Believe that you can make a difference - Out of a tiny acorn grows a giant oak tree, but as we look upon the form that the acorn takes, we may doubt the potentiality which exists in that fruit. So it is with ourselves, and our capacity to actualise our latent abilities. With whatever it is that our vocational instincts orient us towards, we will look at the challenges that are present in that domain and say to ourselves, *'how can I as one person make any real difference in that area?'* It almost seems so overwhelming that we are discouraged from even trying to affect that change. Yet, taking those initial steps to make manifest our contribution is what we must do, to among other things grow our confidence. Like many other of the innate qualities that we seek to cultivate, our belief in ourselves and our ability to move things forward is iterative and proportional to the risks that we find ourselves capable of taking. The more familiar that we become with the terrain, the less we have to fear what remains of its unknown elements. Courage begets confidence which in turn fortifies our willingness to move beyond our comfort zone and partake in legacy work where this difference to the lives of others is made.

Slow build; Long burn - Just like the growth of that giant oak tree, your authentic contribution will take a long time to manifest itself. Brace yourself therefore for the journey ahead. Your ego, upon hearing this, will resist against the making of this commitment and the necessary sacrifices that this will entail, so be prepared for that attempt at vocational sabotage. So tempting it is to play the short game and squeeze from our immediate experience of life all of the pleasures and material accruements that our lust for gratification allows. But where will this lead, except down the path of artificial self-definition and hedonistic destruction where the experience of true meaning and fulfilment eludes us. If we are to live our calling faithfully, we must come to accept that every moment challenges us to live into it more fully, with an admixture of both passion and patience for what is to come. No matter what we did yesterday, today calls out for us to do what we ought in making ourselves worthy to enjoy the fruits of our labour, not just now, but into the future, where our legacy of service will be both earned and cemented in the hearts of those whose lives our efforts have impacted.

Make the best of where you are - Not every stop along the road to our vocational fulfilment will be a desirable destination, or what our ego would have envisioned as the 'right' place for us. The jobs in particular that we partake in may on the surface be perceived as being beneath us, which can lead us to take them for granted and forego the tremendous opportunities that they present to develop ourselves and our latent capacities. No matter where we find ourselves, we control our ability to give the best of who we are and what we have to the work we are tasked with doing. Only as we do this do we maximise our growth potential and the value that others will derive by our efforts. Think of this standard as the precondition to attracting more fertile opportunities in the future, and to give any less of ourselves to that work would be to in effect disqualify ourselves from advancing to bigger and better things. What we demonstrate to others that we can handle today will tell them what we can take on tomorrow, and if we can't find it within ourselves to summon our best efforts in doing the basic aspects of our work, we won't have the discipline or humility to learn what is necessary to effectively undertake the more complex challenges that come with greater responsibility.

Never ever give up - This may sound paradoxical in light of what I stated earlier about quitting sometimes being the best thing you can do in a situation, but if you are on the path to living your calling and there is no doubt that you are where you are supposed to be, you should resolve to yourself never to give up on that journey. Though the worst may go before you and that during those times you could be stretched to your absolute limits, it is imperative that you stay committed to moving forward and making the contribution that only you can give to the world. In this, think of yourself as a great bastion of hope that those who you serve by your efforts have to hold on to. Were it not for you and the fire that you have for what animates you, who would step in to fill that void with any sense of justice for the passion and purpose that you have for the work? With this provision of unique value not being able to be replicated or replaced, it is thus incumbent on you to stay the course and become the person you are capable of becoming in service to that cause. Nothing that you would sacrifice this path for is more worthy of your investment of time and dogged energy.

Involve yourself in bigger things - Often, when we are stuck suffering within ourselves, the focus of our life has become too myopic and insular. Having given ourselves in service of the ego, what our actions will incline us towards are the self-indulgence or aggrandisement that builds the ego's artificial strength. By seeking to quell the lack of authentic power that we perceive ourselves as being deficient in, the last place that we think to direct our energy towards is the outside world and the myriad problems within it that are begging for our attention to be solved. Thinking that by directing our energy outwards in service of this end, we will be drained of what we need to assuage our discontent, the opposite is actually true, and it is by giving ourselves to something that is much larger than us that we fill that inner void and infuse our experience of life with meaning and significance. Even the mental health establishment prompts us to act, belong and commit to preserve our wellbeing which is intricately related to our community and vocational connectedness. To act is to involve yourself. To belong is to join in the larger purpose that calls to you. To commit is to sustain your participation in this higher order of things.

Expect for yourself what you give to others - This pearl of wisdom finds its foundation in the golden rule which centres of the principal of reciprocity: *Do unto others as you would have them do unto you.* The first part of this positive injunction focuses on what we bring to others by our service. What we give to others however isn't just defined by our vocational offering, but also by our quality of being as we make that contribution. With this state of presence being determinative of what treatment we can expect to receive from these people in turn, we shouldn't be unduly righteous in believing that they owe us something which we haven't earned by our irreverent treatment of them. If we aren't aware of what quality of consciousness we are actually bringing to these interactions, it is easy to slip into a mentality of entitlement that is duplicitous in the sense that it expects a certain type of behaviour to be demonstrated by others towards us, without us acting to meet the same standard in how we deal with them. To lead in these interactions and set a positive tone for how we are going to relate to these people, we must first take responsibility for our role in teaching them how to treat us.

Think about your calling and reflect on it along the way - As preoccupied as we can often be with reaching the endpoints along our journey, the quest to living our calling with greater integrity never ends. Keeping us honest, humble and introspective on this path, what it means for our growth is that there is always going to be more work for us to do in giving consistent expression to our vocational longings. In any moment that the spirit calls out to us, we need to be receptive to that messaging and give due attention to understanding what it means for our life. To do this effectively, we require presence and the space that it provides to listen, learn and discern a path forward that is life giving for both ourselves and the world. With our busy and distracted mode of modern living, it is so easy to lose awareness and get thrown off course as a consequence. If we find ourselves in this situation and want to regain our bearings, we need to reflect on the important questions of our lives, and where we will find meaning relative to both who and where we are. Even if we are well and truly on the right path in this moment, we can also benefit from proactively exploring these existential uncertainties as they arise. With this, we don't have to be lost to find ourselves, and we can find ourselves anew in a moment that calls out to us with a renewed sense of clarity and purpose.

Continually reinforce the reasons why you are doing it - Once we come to understand why we do what we do, and how that gives expression to our true self, we must routinely affirm these animating ideals so that we can continue to build the momentum that we have gained by walking down this authentic path. At numerous stages along the journey, which resemble valleys that we will often have to travel down alone, it is easy to lose hope, along with our zeal and sense of purpose. Leading us to waver in our relationship with spirit, the impetus will be on us to stoke that inner fire to stave of the darkness that threatens to consume us. But how do we do this? By staying attuned to what inspires us and being receptive to what the world has to convey about these impacts. In this, the people who we have served or mentored can express to us how we have shaped them and this can act as fuel for when we feel our tank running dry. Alternately, we may have a meaningful and centring silent mantra that we repeat to ourselves during busy periods of work. Despite the unceasing nature of what we encounter, we are reminded by these touch points of how worthwhile the work of our vocation is to our heart, and why we must get out of bed in the morning to face another day.

Try to monetise your calling, but not being able to should not be a barrier to being involved in it - There are many contexts in which a calling can be lived; some paid, others unpaid, with some variability in how much autonomy and creative control we can exercise over what we produce. Depending on what our calling is, there may already be existing outlets or institutions that can smooth our way to getting paid for doing what we love. These, we should take advantage of, along with less conventional opportunities to get before an audience who is interested in meeting our custom. If you are able to monetise your calling, that will be greatly beneficial in ensuring the viability of your offering. The blessing for you with this is that the emergence of new technological platforms and the 'gig' economy has provided pathways to monetisation that simply didn't exist before. While I am not generally a big admirer of social media, it does present avenues of connecting directly with people who may want what we have to offer, or to follow us as we engage with our passion. If none of this appeals to us and we are content to live our calling without the pressure of having to monetise it, then of course we have that option also. This may be a wise course if we find the imperative to monetise stifling our creative energy or the enjoyment of engaging with it for the simple pleasure that it brings us.

Always remember who you are leading and what you are leading them to (a leadership lesson) - A conscious leader, who is just as much attuned to their outer circumstances as they are their interior life, prioritises their people and the animating purpose that underpins their collaborative effort. Having clarity around the destination that is sought to be reached, and what their team members have to contribute to the journey of getting there, they can affect an alignment that allows the group to work in synchronicity to achieve that higher end. Because they have subjugated their ego to be in service of these priorities, this doesn't present a barrier that distorts how they see their people (they are not perceived as human capital that only carry value as a means to a financially driven end) and purpose (this is not limited to a small self-serving objective or vision). By preserving their consciousness as they go about the work of leading, they can keep central to the task the collective calling that brought them together in the first place. Being the heart that the tributaries of the individual members' callings flow into, this is what accounts for the meaningful engagement, loyalty and passionate enthusiasm that sustains the rare magic of what a team like this is capable of achieving.

Have a support system and associate with good/positive people - Whatever it is that our calling involves, we won't be able to properly fulfil it without the help of other people, and the quality of the relationships that we have with these individuals will ultimately determine how effective we are in contributing to the advancement of the common good in our relevant sphere. Any worthwhile endeavour in life requires a group or team to come together and generously bring the best of who they are individually to the collective effort. If we can't offer our support to others in serving this objective, or be receptive to others willingness to do the same for us, we will be greatly diminished in our ability to experience the meaning that comes from being connected to others as a shared purpose is being accomplished. Having been created to inhabit a cooperative social system, we risk suffering in isolation when we withdraw in this way, and becoming removed from the good people and other blessings that occupy our life. In the void this creates, we will come to appreciate how significant the presence of uplifting people are to the life that we seek to build. Being like rare jewels that elevate us by the sight of their unacknowledged beauty, so are these people who radiate the essence of what the providential spirit represents in human form.

Success is self-respect - Success can be defined in many different ways. While a number of these definitions are grounded superficially in the external dimensions of life, others that hold greater substance find their foundation in the cultivation of character and a rich interior life. Falling into the latter category is the respect that we have for ourselves as a consequence of having taken a vocational path that is true to who we are spiritually. Having preserved our integrity as we have gone about the process of creating a meaningful life, we can look in the mirror without suffering the pangs of loathing or regret over having been inauthentic and neglectful of who our spirit has called us to be. When we make success about the things that indulge the ego, it is inevitable that we will feel like a failure or an imposter in our own skin. Being spiritually mandated to honour Truth in the expression of our calling, we won't be able to respect ourselves if by our example we have perpetuated the lie that what characterises the ego is who we are. Only with dignity can we lead and exert influence, and our followers can't make up for any shortfall in this quality if we aren't our own wellspring of what they should respect about us.

Before you can lead others, you must first be able to lead yourself (a leadership lesson) - All too often, individuals get carried away by the ambition to step into a leader's shoes. So to realise this desire, they develop the requisite practical competencies and experience associated with the role, and learn to play the political games that can elevate them to the top. While this path of progression may serve to mould their character in important ways, it can also leave a deficit of what really matters in terms of being able to lead oneself from the realm of spirit within. In this void of consciousness, the ego will remain the orienting force for their life and effectively lead them in the process of leading others. They therefore may be said to demonstrate leadership, without wholly embodying it, for how could they, not having aligned themselves with their inner source of authority. This explains the hollowness of many individuals who occupy positions of power. In effect, they need the position to compensate for their powerlessness, but this can't help shining through and delegitimising their attempts at exercising influence over their people. Fake it till you make it is never a sound leadership strategy, and will not suffice as a transformative vehicle to the conscious mode of leadership which I advocate for in this work.

Look after yourself along the journey - To maximise the contribution that your spirit calls you to make in the world, you will need to nurture and preserve that energy of life within you, for without exercising this self-care, you won't last the journey and will exhaust yourself in the process of 'making things happen'. This is why it is so important that we run our own race of being faithful to our purpose because if we keep our eyes on how much progress we are making relative to others, we can always justify to ourselves the rationalisation to push harder in the present no matter what it costs us in the future. But such a competitive and self-compromising perspective lacks the broader understanding of what we have accomplished over time to reflect a more well-rounded character and capacity for service. Instead of succumbing to the feeling that we are falling behind in our ambitions, we can cut ourselves some slack by acknowledging the strides that we have made in these areas. Being its own form of self-love, this extending of grace towards ourselves complements a regimen of taking time out to recharge our batteries through restorative practices.

Harness what angers you with the world - If we really pay attention to the things that intensely rouse our negative emotions, often they can be indicative of where our vocation lies. When we really care about something and want to excel at it, that is when the fear of failing at the endeavour can come to contaminate our thought processes. When we fall short in accomplishing something that we are naturally good at, that can deepen our feeling of disappointment in our performance. When we encounter a particular social problem that is not getting the attention that we feel it deserves, our primary reaction will likely be an invocation of anger towards those who we feel are responsible and have neglected to solve it. The raw but concentrated indignation that we feel towards this injustice or ineptitude is something valuable that we must channel and use productively to play a part in remedying the harm that the malady wreaks on others lives. Left unharnessed and unconscious, this powerful energy can have a destructive influence on our lives, and lead to among other things the abuse of substances such as drugs and alcohol, or lashing out at the world in vengeful fits of rage. As powerful as the emotion of anger inevitably is, at all times we can determine its outlet.

Channelling this anger productively also has the added benefit of bolstering our discipline and accompanying self-respect.

Allow your curiosity to lead you forward (a leadership lesson) - That which naturally stirs our curiosity can be a powerful guide to finding our vocation. When we feel a sense of curiosity towards some thing or activity, it indicates that our spirit has been roused and is desirous for us to engage with that thing or activity at a deeper level. Rooted at the centre of this is the need to understand the essence of that thing, and where we stand in relationship to it. Not coincidentally, the things that we are most curious about align with our passions, for how could we be moved to know them more intimately if at the foundational level we didn't feel pangs of love for what they represent. Reinforcing this are the multiplicity of things that we don't know at the most basic level, which we couldn't care less about exploring in greater depth. Not being inspired to uncover the core presence of spirit in those things, the beauty of this absent interest is that it provides a peripheral clarity around what we don't have a heart for. By deducing from these insights, we can form a stronger picture of what we are meant to be doing with our life. Pay attention to the things in life that draw you in. In a very real sense, that is their calling out to you. Maybe it is a lesson they have to impart, or something more profound. You won't know until you follow your instinct to find out.

Challenge the status quo - Whatever it is that your calling involves, the natural consequence of your movement to enact it will be to progress that field forward. Make peace therefore with the fact that this will rub against the grain of what is currently accepted in your industry, and the expectations that others have of you as a cog in that system. 'Don't upset the apple cart', others will warn you, as if that is your whimsical desire, just to affect change for the sake of doing something different. But your calling has moulded you to be more intentional than that. Inspiring you to be forthrightly committed to manifesting the unique quality of your contribution to the world, this is what will lead you to 'make a difference' by adding something valuable to what already exists in that field. This may not necessarily involve a technical innovation, but may concern improving client care or streamlining services that produce greater efficiencies in how the system operates. There are a multitude of ways that we can push back the boundaries of what is possible in our respective spheres. Each of the crazy ones and misfits that were immortalised in Apple's iconic commercial embodied this quality, as did Steve Jobs himself. What drove them was not the involvement in a job or career, but something more transcendent and compelling than the conventional thinking of their time could define or was ready for. The outcome: they made a dent in the universe!

Develop routines that support your calling - If you are to live your calling on a consistent basis, what will be the things that ground your receptiveness to spirit? With the spirit as the source of energy that animates your being as you enact your purpose, you must be intentional in staying connected to that life force if you are to remain inspired and committed to your vocation. Serving this objective are the routines that we practice in the course of our daily lives. Whether they involve the training of our mind, body or spirit, their effect is to strengthen our discipline from which we will holistically derive benefits across all three dimensions of our being. In my own life, I write, pray, meditate, read and exercise every day, and each of these practices invigorates what I am able to bring of myself to the other aspects of my life. Meditation, for example, has a calming and clarifying effect on my mind, so when I proceed to engage in writing, the words flow through me with greater ease and coherency. The converse also points to the efficacy of cultivating these habits. When I didn't have these anchoring rituals in my life, that was when I felt the drag of being pulled in many different directions, and not coincidentally, in this state of misalignment, the progress that I had hoped to make in realising my calling would stall. Getting on the path is one thing. Doing the things that allow you to *stay* on the path is another.

Don't define yourself by what it is that you oppose - As tempting as this may be for your ego, don't define yourself by what you are against. Our opposition towards something is predominantly fuelled by hate or disgust, and when we are animated by these negative emotions, we are not acting in alignment with our spiritual source of being. Our abiding purpose as human beings is not to hate, but to love; not to incite conflict, but to be in a state of union. This is why when we are living our calling, we naturally gravitate towards something that we care deeply about, which also rouses our deepest passions. Loving others from the depths of our being also induces a peak state of existence that is undeniable in its Truth and potency. Oppositional movements are therefore not natural to our spirit. Producing polarities that bring about fractured states of being, we can't truly serve our spiritual function as a mediator of harmony if we make our life about delegitimising others and making them wrong so that our fragile, constructed ego based identity can be validated in the eyes of the world. Such a validation does not enhance our ultimate authority, only the pseudo form of narcissistic power that strengthens our resolve to cut others down so that we can build ourselves up. Our ultimate authority and identity emerge as a consequence of knowing who we are in the light of our spirit. By returning to that centre, we can quell these parasitic urges to fight others in order to find ourselves.

Conceive of yourself as blessed, not lucky - Whenever good things happen to you in life, give thanks for their arrival. As the children of life, we are worthy of these blessings. When we come to recognise our connectedness to life, and how what we give to it from our spiritual nature is reciprocated in turn, we won't be so dismissive of these enablers to our continued unfolding. All too often, we put the success that we have achieved down to luck, or forces beyond ourselves that bear no relationship to our past actions or other causative effects. I see this tendency being frequently demonstrated by high profile leaders when they describe their rise to prominence in their vocational field. While they are obviously trying to appear humble in the eyes of others, I think that the narrative they are presenting with this is materially misleading in its denial of the predictive factors that have supported their advancement. When you dig beneath the surface of these backstories, they reveal a history of hard work, continual sacrifices being made, the intentional nurturing of relationships, and opportunities that were first recognised before being taken advantage of. Each of these factors in the context of their lives has much more explanatory power than just luck. In the wake of our lived experience is a patchwork of decisions that we have individually and collectively made to shape the fabric of our interlaced existence. The synchronicity that emerges from this is therefore not an accident but a natural outcome of this conscious order. True humility would have us open our eyes to this reality, so that we can better participate in its creation through our lived calling.

Value your time and use it wisely - How you use your time will determine what path you will travel down in life, and how far you will make it down that path towards a worthy aim. Therefore, it is important that you give your time the respect it deserves and not fritter it away on things that are meaningless. Being the most valuable non-renewable resource that we have, it would behove us to stand in the right relationship to time, so that our use of it may enable our progress rather than hindering it. In this sense, we should view as an investment, the present moments that we dedicate towards developing ourselves to do the work of our calling that will lead us to have a significant future impact on the world. While we could no doubt be spending that time indulging in hedonistic pursuits, that would only limit the utility of our application of time towards a worthwhile end, and we would feel that acutely. Leading us to suffer under the implicit recognition that we are wasting our life, this existential tension can also act as a powerful prompt to adjust course and engage in something that will outlive us in some meaningful sense. It is also important to note here that play and recreation, with their rejuvenating impacts, have their place in a balanced and conscious life, so don't allow the screams of busyness to have you forget them.

Choose how you organise your life - This is about sitting at the centre of your life and consciously choosing what you will allow to consume your time and energy. If we are not present and intentional about this process, our life can so easily get away from us and come under the control of external forces that will scramble our bearings or use us to serve their own agendas. With work for example, if we have very little in our lives outside of that domain to provide some balance and perspective, it can become all-consuming and a master of us, rather than us being a master of it. This is how a number of people wind up becoming workaholics, addicted to social media or entangled in toxic relationships because they have not prioritised coming to know who they are relative to the decisions they are making to determine the course of their life. As the saying goes, nature abhors a vacuum, so the unfilled spaces in our lives will find themselves occupied by the ego's compulsions if the volitional nature of our spirit is suppressed. Who we truly are knows how to express itself, and give precedence to what is ultimately important in the context of our life. Part of our calling in this respect is to trust in this sovereign capacity to bring order to the chaos of who we mistakenly thought that we were in the world.

Live so as to not have regrets - To have regrets in our life is proof that we are not rooted in the presence that we are called to embody. With this, the precondition to having the regret is to be thinking about the past and what we should have done differently in it. But how useful is this, when we can't change how we acted in a previous moment? Yes, our decision making across the span of our life will not have always been sound, and yet despite these 'errors', they in part have led us to where we are today with a better understanding of ourselves and how we need to be in the world to bring about better outcomes for our life. Living with consciousness is a crucial part of avoiding this fate of having to wrestle with regret. If you really think about it, the things in our past that we wish we could take back are born of unconsciousness. The acts of deceit, disrespect, jealousy, anger, or even violence were all conceived by our false identification with the ego. If we look back to how we acted then and know that we wouldn't act in that way now, then that is a marker of growth that has seen some of these scales of illusion fall from our eyes. With our nature being to evolve and progress, so should we act differently now than we have in the past. If the alternative is to stay stuck and mired in the folly of unconsciousness, then there is nothing about the process of having matured that we need to regret.

Change your heart to change the world - This piece of advice echoes the wisdom of Russian writer Leo Tolstoy when he said that, *"everyone thinks of changing the world, but no one thinks of changing himself."* However connected or disconnected that we individually and collectively are to our spiritual essence will influence the conditions of life that we create with our actions. In this respect, circumstances will reflect the consciousness of the actors who have brought them about. In the most hellish places on earth are those who rule through intimidation, exploitation and corruption, amongst other vices, but despite the best intentioned interventions to alleviate suffering in these places, these interventions fail because those responsible for creating those oppressive conditions won't change what they perceive as working to further their own selfish interests. The only hope in this situation is for the ego identity that is instigating this tyranny to break down or be overcome by instruments of the good that can move things in a positive direction. Whether by force (revolution) or the volitional embodiment of the ways of the human heart (evolution), the end result is a transformation of the physical reality that we find ourselves in. Led by the spiritual fundament of our being, this evolutionary shift holds the most promise for our continued progress, as is evidenced by the legacies of our enlightened forebears who stand taller today than they did in their time.

Be open to possibilities and opportunities - Hold less tightly to where your ego desires for you to be, and become more attuned to how life may be opening up to you. By our willingness to be guided by this emergent quality of the spirit, we will travel much further towards our calling, and enjoy a richer adventure of life than when our wilfulness to control the direction of our life takes hold of our mind. When our ego and its goals are orienting our path forward, its predetermined aims or anticipated rewards are primarily what is occupying our attention and energy to bring about. Coming at the cost of this myopic focus is our responsiveness to reality, or life as life is. With our map in mind and the unwillingness to deviate from the path to 'X' that will mark our perceived success, the territory, rather paradoxically, cannot be successfully navigated because by its changing nature, our awareness and dexterity is found wanting in being able to effectively adapt to the challenge it presents. Just like rock formations over time have their shape altered, the obstacle for us if we are to scale their surfaces is to find new footholds of possibility. Presenting paths to advancement that we never would have countenanced while adhering to the old map, the opportunity here lies in taking the leap of faith that providence would have us trust as we put one foot in front of the other on this ascent.

Being a good human being comes first - I think that if people could listen to their own eulogy once they have passed on from this life, what they would most want to be said about them is that they were a good person who sought to do, and did, good things in the world. While all of the more particular details around the life that we were able to create are nice for others to remember, I don't believe that they mean as much as possessing that solid base of character which was our locus in how we related to the world. When we live from the ego, it is so easy to get side-tracked by the reputational considerations that appear to matter more in the eyes of the world than who we are at the most essential level. Perhaps this is because we get recognised and praised more for what we accomplish in public view, than for who we are and how we act when nobody else is looking. The problem with allowing this surface dressing to define our success as a person is that it creates an immense internal discord and void, especially if we have compromised our character along the way by stepping over others to elevate ourselves, or forgone our calling for an unfulfilling venture that brought to us some material benefits, but very little else of substance. Neither of these two betrayals, or other abuses like them, are any basis to build a legacy on that we can be at peace with as we move forward to write the final chapters of our life story.

Make your relationship to spirit the most important relationship in your life - Not all relationships in our life are on the same level, and for our relationships in the physical world to thrive, they must be anchored by us having a strong relationship with our spirit. Why this is the primary relationship in our life is because its nurturance or neglect will orient how we position ourselves relative to others and relate to them. If we don't have a strong connection to our spirit, we will harbour a deep confusion, not only about ourselves, but also concerning the purpose of our life and the role that our relationships are to play in it. As a consequence of this, our mode of relating to others through the facade of ego will be marked by superficiality, dependence and the misunderstanding that will inevitably lead to conflict. Before we can truly connect with others at the deepest level, we must be tethered to our own soul and its capacity to hold these unions in a broader expanse that is beyond being merely self-serving. This allows us to be a conduit of these virtues of the spirit and give them to others in a way that enhances both our individual and collective existence. To love, accept and appreciate them in their fullness, we must not diminish ourselves in this light. The spirit is the mirror that allows us to see this light in ourselves and in those who we are bound to in its company.

Create an environment where people want to go where you need them to go (a leadership lesson) - One of the great challenges of leadership is getting a group of people to become a team and pull together in the same direction when incentives are present from them to pull away and pursue their own self-interest. To create this cohesiveness, the leader/s as the primary culture setters for the collective endeavour must be animated by a vocational purpose that they are congruent in enacting, and those followers who would co-create this vision with them must be possessed of the same calling. When this occurs, everyone involved in the venture is inspired of their own accord, by the vision and what the members of the group are giving to each other and the cause by their involvement, regardless of their position or rank within the group. The leaders by title in this scenario, don't have to waste their energy trying to motivate their people to do something that their heart is not really in, and instead their task here is to channel the flow of passionate energy towards the ends that this fervent application of talent and expertise needs to be put. Having such a synergistic culture is so valuable precisely because it is so rare in the modern economy where the presence of ego consciousness tends to predominate the workings of organisations in that system.

Listen to your inner voice/intuition - When you are faced with making difficult decisions in your life, know that within you is a wise and insightful presence that can help you find the way to clarity while facilitating your life learning. Our task in relation to this guiding force, is to be open and receptive to its promptings, for it is only when we do this that we will be able to draw on its counsel. If we close our ear to this inner voice, and instead give the ego the attention it so craves, this is typically when we will venture off the path of our vocation to make choices that do not serve to nurture our spiritual health and wellbeing. In taking this action, we effectively fracture our integrity by disassociating from the source of Truth in our life. The blessing for us in being able to remedy this denial is that every moment represents an opportunity for reconciling who we essentially are with what we are being taught about the workings of the world. With the spirit's commitment to our developmental flourishing being unceasing, the onus rests on us to allow it to inform our understanding of how we should move forward to give effect to our calling as a human being and be a protagonist in the story of the world's awakening.

Don't make money the primary motivation for what you do - While money is no doubt important in being able to live a prosperous life and help others, it should not be our main orienting force for what we do in life. I know a number of people who have eschewed their calling to pursue something that allowed them to be 'materially successful', but what they found as they ventured down that road was just how empty the rewards along it were in the absence of an intrinsic experience of meaning and purpose for what they were moving towards. With their misplaced focus having hollowed them out of the knowing of what is truly worth pursuing, what was left to occupy that space were the vacuous desires of the ego that can never meet the deep longing that we have to contribute to the world as we were uniquely created to. For the ego, money is how we keep score of our value in the world. Being nothing more than an end to prop up its fragile conception of self in this respect, the ego would not have us hesitate to sacrifice the vocational means of our fulfilment in order to acquire it. But we need not acquiesce to this undignified demand. When we put our calling first and work diligently and enthusiastically to unfurl our innate talents for a purpose that holds a high social utility, that money will come in exchange for our excellent provision of service and leadership, in amounts which very likely will exceed what we would have earned in a job or career that made the subjugation of our soul a prerequisite for monetary attainment.

Be independent of the opinions and judgments of others - Regardless of what path you take, others will have their own opinions and judgments about it. Learn to make peace with this and don't become bitter and resentful at them for not supporting you in the way that you would like. Your ego expects this validation and when it doesn't receive it, it wants to oppose the source of that resistance. Resist partaking in this reactive tension, as it will only dilute your focus and receptiveness to your calling. Your vocation can't grip you if you are not present to its presence. If your calling is to leadership, this advice is especially critical. To effectively deal with a problem, a leader must bring everything of their wisdom, knowledge and insight to bear on that challenge, and they can't be dependent on whether others will approve of their decisions or not. Some will, naturally, as others won't, or they may think that they could have done it better themselves. Detach and let them think what they want. If you want to lead the orchestra, you have to turn your back to the audience, says comedian Ricky Gervais. He should know with his sense of humour that his style will not be to everyone's taste, but this does not stop him from being one of the funniest human beings on the planet. As this pertains to the substance of your creative outputs, also bear in mind that you can't be beholden to the whims of your customer base. Their tastes come and go, but the ultimate source of your inspiration doesn't, so you need to hold true to that. Some of the more fickle members of this base may move on, but trust that others will sense your originality and eagerly take their place. We can't be original without honouring the origin of our being, which as I have said throughout the pages of this book is our spirit.

Know yourself so that you may know others - Your brother or sister is not as much of a stranger as you may think. While undoubtedly having their own disposition, quirks and idiosyncrasies, at their heart is the same force of life that animates yours. Being driven by the familiar base needs and aspirations for a good life that you hold, they are no different from you in this longing. If we can't see this in them because we have failed to discern the spiritual basis of our own existence, then it is inevitable that we will misjudge their nature and motives for acting as they do. Absent of the understanding that is facilitated by relating to them through the connective tissue of our shared humanness, our separation from them will be complete, and marked by the suspicion and distrust that we harbour towards ourselves as we live from the false self. None of this we can perceive of course when we don't know ourselves intimately, and our proclivity to judge our neighbour harshly should be our first clue that our relationship with our self is not on solid ground. Whatever faults or deficits that we see in this other can be forgiven if we accept their vulnerabilities as our very own. To open up to ourselves in this way allows the transformation of these relationships through empathy, compassion and the other virtues of the spirit that symbolise them having become a part of our larger calling to heal the divide between our heart and theirs.

CONCLUSION

As I look out at the shifts that have taken place in the world since I started writing this book four years ago, I am more convinced than ever of the importance of conscious leadership and the promise that it holds for effectively dealing with the raft of complex challenges that we now face, and will continue to confront as we move into the future. While technical competence, the ability to analyse systems and the utilisation of machine learning will no doubt become central to the operation of the evolving digital economy, these skills by themselves won't be able to stand in the place of wise decision making that is grounded in character and reflective of an enduring commitment to serve the common good. No matter how far our technologies or culture develops, leadership will always centre around caring for, working with and inspiring people to reach their highest potential. The so called 'soft skills' will never grow old in this endeavour, and will only become more vital to the task of building thriving teams that are capable of applying their collective knowledge and insight to solving society's most pressing problems. But we can't continue to diminish their primacy if we are to succeed in moving humanity forward, as not doing the deep inner work that enables us to authentically embody them only serves to prolong the processual dominance of the ego that leads us to reproduce outcomes that are destructive in their consequence.

As I posit this, I fear that we are not learning our lessons from our past challenges. All too often, we settle for band aid solutions that only tinker at the edges of the real causes of the problems that we face. With our short term imperatives to get results and appease those who rely on us to deliver benefits to them, we shuffle forward with a weakened resolve to do the necessary reformative work to these systems that would fortify their long term health and sustainability. In this, we see the work required as too hard to undertake, and deal with that challenge by delay or denial, sweeping under the rug that which would impede the progress on which our individual work security or institutional share price depend. However, by cutting corners in this way, we greatly undermine the resilience of our organisations and the cultural elements of commitment, trust and solidarity that hold them together. When one considers the endemic levels of disengagement and feelings of purposelessness that are experienced in these organisations, I think that this failure to act with courage and do the meaningful work of reshaping these organisations contributes a lot to these problems persisting as they do. People smell the rot under the floorboards and know how insidious and counterproductive it is to excellent work being performed, but their leaders don't want to acknowledge the extent of the dysfunction because by and large they don't feel competent to rectify it, and are adverse to risking failure by attempting to do so. So instead they institute achievable but marginal changes that in their ability to be affected, make them look competent in the eyes of their people. Or so their ego has them think.

Individuals working under leaders like this lose respect for their authority, and doubt the substance of the character that animates their actions. If these leaders are not willing to confront the reality of what needs doing, then what else are they hiding from or refusing to acknowledge? Another cause of cynicism in the 'woke' culture that we operate in is the reactionary and performative virtue signalling that leaders engage in to not alienate their stakeholders. Wanting to be seen to be doing good, rather than genuinely caring about doing good, this divide is revealed by their incongruous claims and self-serving actions that cloak the desire for increased profitability with a social purpose shingle that a growing conscious consumer base would be willing to buy into (otherwise known as 'woke-washing').

In recent times I have observed the bastardisation and exploitation of the central tenets of books such as this one by companies who hypocritically don't walk their talk about conscious business, or who just spout ideological axioms in their place to curry favour with popular public or political sentiment. The recent scandals involving Volkswagen, Gillette and Anheuser-Busch, along with the greenwashing controversies that have ensnared a number of high profile fast fashion brands, provide evidence of this disconnect. While I don't doubt the difficulty in genuinely pursuing a stakeholder orientation that requires a recurrent reconciling of the divergent interests of these parties, my sense is that in a number of instances this approach is being used as a smokescreen to avoid accountability to a broader constituency. After all, if it is not entirely clear to whom one owes specific obligations and to what degree, this can provide a grey area for manipulation by unconscionable actors within these organisations. Quite clearly, old habits die hard, and during this time when a significant transition is being made from a purely profit centred business focus to operations that are more purpose centred, some are being opportunistic in testing how they can game the new model and use it to serve the familiar end of maximising profits, I say 'familiar' here because in the profit centred model of doing business, these individuals have been conditioned to think and incentivised to act in ways that further their self-interest. To them, unless you (personally and organisationally) are getting ahead, you are falling behind, and with this zero sum way of looking at the world, another's gain will logically be seen as their loss. This is not to excuse their unwillingness to evolve and open themselves to the philosophy behind the new model, just to say that I understand where their resistance is coming from. Being rooted largely in fear, this is such a powerful driver of behaviour when we are functioning from ego consciousness because the changing circumstances will feel like a death to the part of ourselves that was so heavily invested in the old system, and receiving of the benefits that it offered as security and a means of strengthening the currency that our identity would hold as a participant in that order.

Try as one might to have the best of both worlds and come out looking golden on all sides, they won't be able to effectively pull this off because their integrity will be seen to have been compromised by their incongruous statements or behaviour. This is especially the case in the social media age where the full spectrum of recording technologies are being utilised to produce and disseminate content that never would have seen the light of day before the turn of the millennium. Many a leader in the realms of politics, business, sport and entertainment have been called to task for contradictory or derisive statements that they have made in the past (on platforms such as Twitter) which don't accord with what they say they stand for in the present day. While I am not a proponent of censorship or cancel culture that would seek to have these 'offenders' de-platformed or banished to the fringes of society, I must say that I am not adverse to the impetus that this phenomenon places on individuals to become more conscious of what they are choosing to express, and the effect that this may have on other people. Here, I don't want individuals to experience fear or paranoia, but just a healthy level of awareness about what they are conveying and where it is coming from within themselves. Whereas before, we may have just been functioning on autopilot and allowing our ego to speak its piece regardless of the consequences, now we should be thinking about the real utility of what we have to say and whether that is genuinely reflective of who we are at the core of our humanity.

Of course, none of this matters if we are living from our spirit and relating to the world from this essential Truth because we will not be projecting dissonance into the world to stimulate others questioning of our character and motives. Saving us also the energy of having to justify and defend our ideologically constructed identity to our neighbours, we can just focus on living with integrity (that I have defined principally as a state of wholeness) and enacting our calling in a way that is both personally meaningful and life enhancing for the world. I cannot begin to adequately describe here the depths of freedom and contentment that one experiences in treading this path, and as I have conveyed throughout this book, I can speak to that personally because that is the journey I have taken (and am still taking) in my own life. Had I not explored my own ego's dysfunctionality and bonded with my spirit in the task of allowing it to lead my way forward, I wouldn't have been able to elucidate on the workings of these dual forces that shape our course in radically different ways (the spirit moving us towards greater consciousness and the ego miring us in unconsciousness).

As is the case for many an author who writes books of this type, the feeling or drive in wanting to convey this information to others is that they know without a shadow of a doubt how transformative these lessons can be for those who are struggling to find their way in life. Yearning to make this path smoother for those who will follow them down it, this is the interest that they want to repay to their forebears for clearing the way to their found clarity. With their leadership having preserved the lineage of the perennial philosophy across time, it is the same spirit in them that animates us now when we honour the call to make this difference in others' lives. By doing so with the particularity that draws forth the best of our unique characteristics to serve their specific need, we make universal this restorative impact in an unbounded context. When the reverberations of our manifested calling exceed our wildest expectations, this is what is taking place. How far can this embodiment of consciousness extend? Only God knows. Actually, let me correct myself. Only the God *in you* knows! To answer this question, we must answer our spirit's call, to Truth, to adventure, to leadership, to heroism, to the virtuous unfolding, of first ourselves and then the world, by extension of our offerings.

By having the advice chapter as the last of the book, my intention was for it to act as a bridge to the practical implementation of the central tenets of the work. This book would be impotent if all it inspired was naval gazing of a type that has no effect on improving the condition of the world. Similarly, I don't want it to be used as a vehicle for spiritually bypassing the work that is essential for each of us to do if we are to move to a higher place in our lives. As I said in the introduction of the book, *'you can't have the gold without the road'*. Here, I am reminded of the seminal quote from T.S. Eliot, *"We shall not cease from exploration, and the end of all our exploring will be to arrive where we started and know the place for the first time."* The spiritual journey of living our calling to enact the highest virtues of humanity leads us, not just to the manifestation of leadership in the world, but also to the foundational understanding of who we are and what we were created for in the first place.

Without the exploration that Eliot identifies as being central to this process, there cannot be this circular recognition, and while the necessity for exploration never ceases, as we journey forward with that spiritual connectedness, we can deepen our relationship to Truth and our appreciation of the world's intricate complexities. As we grow and enlarge our capacity for integrity through this aligning, we become freed from having to be hemmed in by the categorisations that serve only to strengthen the ego by their identification, and can embrace the tension between what is and ought to be in the context of our lives and the wider world. We can, for example, perceive the blessings in our lives and be grateful for their presence, while recognising what is not optimal and the opportunity that presents for improving their condition.

Instead of needing to label this suboptimal state of affairs as 'broken' or 'oppressive', for example, which tilts us towards nihilistic inaction or hubristic rebellion, we can preserve our perspective and power to act on those circumstances in ways that engender meaning, hope and ultimately progress for humanity. As I have shown throughout the pages of this book, the most direct path to leading the world towards that end is by the individual and collective living of our vocational purposes to manifest spirit, and its virtues, into form. Producing infinite win-win-win outcomes for us to mutually benefit from, it also presents us with the only utopian vision that is worth holding in our hearts.

ACKNOWLEDGEMENTS

It would be remiss of me to begin the acknowledgements for this book about vocation without honouring the animating force of life who called me to write it. To God, you placed this work in my heart a very long time ago, and I hope that I have done this calling justice. With your grace may I stay aligned with the spirit's path for my life, and continue to walk that journey with a clear mind and open heart.

To the respondents who selflessly gave of their time and energy to provide me with the research data, and enrich my understanding of this topic, I am eternally grateful and I hope that you will be similarly nourished by what I have to offer you in these pages. For her guidance on the research front, I would like to express my undying gratitude to Professor Alma Whiteley. Her vision for the project, inspirational leadership and generous provision of knowledge and support greatly assisted in bringing it into fruition. Your genuine care and depth of presence were palpable at every stage of this process and there was no one better to take that journey with.

To my publisher, Central West Publishing. Thank you for believing in the work and me by extension. For the wonderful cover design that perfectly conveys the central message of the book, thanks to Tess McCabe for her professionalism and dedication to the process of creating it.

On a more personal note, I would like to thank my family and friends for their love, encouragement and the stimulating discussions that invigorated me along the journey. Chief among them was Aunty Mela (known to others as Associate Professor Carmela Briguglio) whose wise counsel on the use of language and ever present willingness to read over and edit drafts was greatly appreciated. Mum, your example of how to remain open to spirit in how you have dealt with the challenges of life has inspired me beyond words and I am immensely grateful for all of the assistance you have provided along my vocational journey. To Elizabeth, and my two beautiful children, Eloise and Bastien, you have each enriched my life immeasurably and taught me what it means to be a better human being. Also, to my late father, Clive Duperouzel. Without you and the learnings that I have gleaned in the 32 years since your passing, I wouldn't be the person I am today who is capable of writing this, so thank you.

Lastly, to my students who I have the privilege of being able to shape through my teaching, I hope that this work can act as a compass and impetus for you to bring the fullness of who you are into fruition, not only for your own personal fulfilment, but for the greater thriving of the world. Be the tie that binds consciousness to the present, and hope to the future.

BIBLIOGRAPHY

Afremow, Jim. *The Champion's Mind: How Great Athletes Think, Train, and Thrive.* New York: Harmony/Rodale, 2018.

Batz, Paul and Hillen, Paul. *How Goodness Pays: Why good leaders THRIVE in a transparent business world.* Edina: Good Leadership Press, 2018.

Brown, Brene. *Dare to Lead: Brave Work. Tough Conversations. Whole Hearts.* London: Vermilion, 2018.

Campbell, Joseph. *The Hero With A Thousand Faces.* Novato: New World Library, 2012.

Coelho, Paulo. *The Alchemist.* New York: HarperCollins, 2006.

Covey, Stephen R. *7 Habits Of Highly Effective People.* New York: Simon & Schuster, 2004.

Csikszentmihalyi, Mihaly. *Flow: The Psychology of Optimal Experience.* New York: HarperCollins, 2011.

Dweck, Carol S. *Mindset: The New Psychology of Success.* New York: Ballantine Books, 2007.

Dyer, Wayne W. *Inspiration: Your Ultimate Calling.* Carlsbad: Hay House, 2002.

Dyer, Wayne W. *The Power of Intention: Learning to Co-create Your World Your Way.* Carlsbad: Hay House, 2004.

Frankl, Viktor E. *Man's Search for Meaning.* London: Rider Books, 2006.

Gibran, Khalil. *The Prophet.* New York: Vintage Books, 2015.

Greene, Robert. *The Laws of Human Nature.* London: Profile Books, 2018.

Greenleaf, Robert K. *Servant Leadership: A Journey into the Nature of Legitimate Power and Greatness.* Mahwah: Paulist Press, 2002.

Hansen, Morton T. *Great at Work: How Top Performers Work Less and Achieve More.* New York: Simon & Schuster, 2018.

Hari, Johann. *Lost Connections: Why You're Depressed and How to Find Hope.* London: Bloomsbury Publishing, 2019.

Hersey, Paul and Blanchard, Kenneth. *Management of Organizational Behavior (Tenth Edition).* London: Pearson, 2012.

Hill, Napoleon. *Think and Grow Rich.* Mankato: Capstone, 2010.

Holiday, Ryan. *Ego Is the Enemy.* London: Profile Books, 2016.

Jaworski, Joseph. *Synchronicity: The Inner Path of Leadership.* San Francisco: Berrett-Koehler, 2011.

King James Bible. Nashville: Thomas Nelson, 2017.

Knight, Phil. *Shoe Dog: A Memoir by the Creator of NIKE.* London: Simon & Schuster, 2018.

Kofman, Fred. *Conscious Business: How to Build Value through Values.* Boulder: Sounds True, 2013.

Lencioni, Patrick M. *The Five Dysfunctions of a Team: A Leadership Fable.* San Francisco: Jossey-Bass, 2002.

Mackey, John and Sisodia, Raj. *Conscious Capitalism: Liberating the Heroic Spirit of Business*. Boston: Harvard Business Review Press, 2013.

Mackey, John; McIntosh, Steve & Phipps, Carter. *Conscious Leadership: Elevating Humanity Through Business*. New York: Portfolio/Penguin, 2020.

Mandela, Nelson. *Long Walk to Freedom*. London: Abacus, 1994.

Maslow, Abraham H. *A Theory of Human Motivation*. Eastford: Martino Publishing, 2013.

Maxwell, John C. *The 21 Irrefutable Laws of Leadership: Follow Them and People Will Follow You*. Nashville: HarperCollins Leadership, 2008.

McChrystal, Stanley. *Leaders: Myth and Reality*. New York: Penguin, 2018.

McConaughey, Matthew. *Greenlights*. New York: Crown Publishing, 2020.

Mycoskie, Blake. *Start Something That Matters*. New York: Random House, 2012.

Nair, Keshavan. *A Higher Standard of Leadership: Lessons from the Life of Gandhi*. Oakland: Berrett-Koehler, 2018.

Newport, Cal. *Digital Minimalism: Choosing a Focused Life in a Noisy World*. London: Penguin, 2020.

Palmer, Parker J. *A Hidden Wholeness: The Journey Toward an Undivided Life*. San Francisco: Jossey-Bass, 2009.

Parks, Rosa. *Rosa Parks: My Story*. Logan: Perfection Learning, 1999.

Peck, M. Scott. *The Road Less Travelled*. London: Penguin, 1990.

Peterson, Jordan B. *12 Rules for Life: An Antidote to Chaos*. London: Allen Lane, 2018.

Pink, Daniel H. *Drive: The Surprising Truth about what Motivates us*. London: Penguin Putnam, 2011.

Pinker, Steven. *The Better Angels of our Nature: Why Violence has Declined*. New York: Viking, 2011.

Ponder, Catherine. *The Dynamic Laws of Prosperity*. Floyd: Wilder Publications, 2011.

Pressfield, Steven. *The War of Art: Break Through the Blocks and Win Your Inner Creative Battles*. Scotts Valley: CreateSpace, 2012.

Rohr, Richard. *The Universal Christ: How a Forgotten Reality Can Change Everything We See, Hope For, and Believe*. New York: Crown Publishing, 2019.

Rosling, Hans. *Factfulness: Ten Reasons We're Wrong About the World - and Why Things Are Better Than You Think*. London: Hodder & Stoughton, 2018.

Schucman, Helen and Thetford, William. *A Course in Miracles*. Mill Valley: Foundation for Inner Peace, 1976.

Selye, Hans. *The Stress of Life (Second Edition)*. New York: McGraw-Hill Education, 1978.

Sharma, Robin. *The Leader Who Had No Title: A Modern Fable on Real Success in Business and in Life*. New York: Free Press, 2010.

Sinek, Simon. *The Infinite Game*. New York: Portfolio, 2019.

The Holy Qur'an. Ware: Wordsworth Editions, 2001.

Thoreau, Henry David. *Walden or Life in the Woods.* Sweden: Wisehouse Classics, 2016.

Tolle, Eckhart. *A New Earth: Awakening to Your Life's Purpose.* New York: Penguin Books, 2008.

Tzu, Lao. *Tao Te Ching.* London: Penguin Books, 2000.

Tzu, Sun. *The Art of War.* London: Penguin Books, 2008.

Ware, Bronnie. *The Top Five Regrets of the Dying: A Life Transformed by the Dearly Departing.* Carlsbad: Hay House, 2019.

Index

Dr. Christian Duperouzel is a Lecturer at the Curtin Law School and a Conscious Leadership consultant. In 2016, he completed his PhD which explored the topic of the Role of a Lived Calling in Driving Virtuous Leadership Behaviour. In addition to this work, he has also published in national and international academic journals. He lives in Perth, Western Australia and regularly contributes to his blog at https://drlchristianduperouzel.wordpress.com/.

www.ingramcontent.com/pod-product-compliance
Lightning Source LLC
Chambersburg PA
CBHW052111030426
42335CB00025B/2932